INTERNATIONAL STUDIES

The second Baldwin government and the
United States, 1924–1929

INTERNATIONAL STUDIES

The Centre for International Studies at the London School of Economics and Political Science was established in 1967 with the aid of a grant from the Ford Foundation. Its aim is to promote research and advanced training on a multi-disciplinary basis in the general field of international studies.

To this end the Centre sponsors research projects and seminars and endeavours to secure the publication of manuscripts arising out of them.

Whilst the Editorial Board accepts responsibility for recommending the inclusion of a volume in the series, the author is alone responsible for views and opinions expressed.

THE SECOND BALDWIN GOVERNMENT AND THE UNITED STATES, 1924–1929

Attitudes and diplomacy

B. J. C. McKERCHER
Department of History, University of Alberta

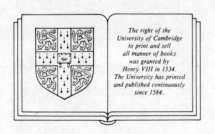

The right of the
University of Cambridge
to print and sell
all manner of books
was granted by
Henry VIII in 1534.
The University has printed
and published continuously
since 1584.

CAMBRIDGE UNIVERSITY PRESS

Cambridge
London   New York   New Rochelle
Melbourne   Sydney

Published by the Press Syndicate of the University of Cambridge
The Pitt Building, Trumpington Street, Cambridge CB2 1RP
32 East 57th Street, New York, NY 10022, USA
10 Stamford Road, Oakleigh, Melbourne 3166, Australia

First published 1984

Printed in Great Britain at the University Press, Cambridge

Library of Congress catalogue card number: 84–3168

British Library Cataloguing in Publication Data

McKercher, B.J.C.
The second Baldwin government and the United
States 1924–1929.—(International studies)
1. Great Britain—Foreign relations—United
States   2. United States—Foreign relations
—Great Britain   3. Great Britain—Foreign
relations—1910–1936   4. United States—
Foreign relations—1923–1929
I. Title   II. Series
327.41073   E183.8.G7

ISBN 0 521 25802 2

For
PAUL HURST

CONTENTS

vii

ACKNOWLEDGEMENTS

I wish to thank the following for permission to make use of archival materials under their jurisdiction: the University Library, the University of Birmingham (the papers of Sir Austen Chamberlain); the British Library, the British Museum (the papers of the first Earl Balfour, Viscount Cecil of Chelwood, Viscount D'Abernon of Esher, Sir Charles Scott, and Sir Evelyn Wrench); the University Library, Cambridge University (the papers of the first Earl Baldwin of Bewdley); the Master, Fellows, and Scholars of Churchill College, Cambridge (the papers of the first Baron Hankey); the present Lord Howard of Penrith (the papers of the first Baron Howard of Penrith); the present Lord Keyes (the papers of Admiral of the Fleet, Lord Keyes); the National Maritime Museum, Greenwich (the papers of Admiral Sir Barry Domvile and Admiral Sir Howard Kelly); the Controller of H.M. Stationery Office (the archives of the Admiralty, the Cabinet, and the Foreign Office, as well as the papers of Sir Austen Chamberlain, the first Baron Cushendun, and J. Ramsay MacDonald); Mr A. J. P. Taylor and the Beaverbrook Foundation, London, along with the Clerk of the Records, House of Lords Records Office (the papers of the first Baron Beaverbrook and the first Earl Lloyd-George of Dwyfor); and The Times Newspaper Limited (the papers of Wilmot Lewis).

For their help and assistance at various stages, I would like to thank the staffs of the above-mentioned archives, as well as those of: the Government Publications Reading Room, the University of Alberta, Edmonton; the Roskill Archives, Churchill College, Cambridge; the Cumbria County Record Office, Carlisle; the Public Record Office, London; and *The Times* Archives, London.

A reference must always be made to those who provide funding for research projects. I would like to thank my parents for their generosity in this respect; without their unreserved support I could not have studied abroad for three years. I would also like to thank the Isobel Thornley Bequest for its generosity.

A number of scholars kindly discussed aspects of this study with me. I would like to mention Professor James Barrington, Dr Kathleen Burk, Professor Grant Davy, Dr Michael Dockrill, Professor Douglas Johnson, the late Captain Stephen Roskill, and Dr Zara Steiner. My colleague, Dr David Dinwoodie, has been decidedly generous in his comments. I also appreciate the kindness of the present Lord Howard of Penrith who offered me the hospitality of his home and discussed his father's embassy with me. Two people deserve special thanks: Professor Ian Nish, the past chairman of the Centre for International Studies, who suggested that I consider submitting my manuscript to the CIS; and Dr Keith Neilson, my friend since our under-graduate days at the University of Alberta and, later, as doctoral students in England, who knows how much I owe him. I must also acknowledge my immeasurable debt to Professor D. C. Watt who, as my doctoral superviser and then my friend, provided positive criticism and encouragement to my work. This book reflects in part his confidence in me.

Finally I would like to thank Professor Michael Leifer, chairman of the CIS, Mrs Elizabeth Wetton of Cambridge University Press, and Bonnie Kyle, who read various drafts for errors. The Hurst family – Paul, Lynn, Kati, and Sally – were most helpful by letting me 'bunk in', sometimes for months, when I was staying in London. Most important, I would like to thank my wife, Cheryl, for the support she gave me when we lived in England and when I wrote this manuscript back in Canada.

LIST OF ABBREVIATIONS

ADM	Admiralty
AHR	*American Historical Review*
APSR	*American Political Science Review*
BJS	*British Journal of Sociology*
BLINY	British Library of Information, New York City
BM	British Museum (the British Library)
CAB	Cabinet
CHR	*Canadian Historical Review*
CID	Committee of Imperial Defence
CJH	*Canadian Journal of History*
CP	Cabinet Paper
DBFP 1A	*Documents on British Foreign Policy*, Series *1A*
EHR	*English Historical Review*
FA	*Foreign Affairs*
FO	Foreign Office
FRUS	*Papers Relating to the Foreign Relations of the United States*
HJ	*Historical Journal*
H of C Debs	*House of Commons Debates*
H of L Debs	*House of Lords Debates*
IA	*International Affairs*
IR	*International Relations*
JAH	*Journal of American History*
JBS	*Journal of British Studies*
JCH	*Journal of Contemporary History*
JCPS	*Journal of Commonwealth Political Studies*
JEH	*Journal of Economic History*
JMH	*Journal of Modern History*
JRIIA	*Journal of the Royal Institute of International Affairs*
na	no author
NB	*Foreign Policy Association News Bulletin*

nd	no date
PRO	Public Record Office, London
PREM	Prime Minister's Office
PSQ	*Political Science Quarterly*
Pub Admin	*Public Administration*
RP	*Review of Politics*
RT	*Round Table*
un	unnumbered

All private MSS abbreviations are listed in the bibliography.

1 . THE SECOND BALDWIN GOVERNMENT AND THE UNITED STATES, NOVEMBER 1924–JUNE 1929

Hitherto, so it seems to me, we have been inclined to deal with the United States from a wrong angle. We have treated them too much as blood relations, not sufficiently as a foreign country . . .

Foreign Office Memorandum, November 1927

The essence of diplomatic history is not so much to discover what was actually happening in a period under study but, rather, to understand the way in which diplomatists beheld that reality. The key to understanding why the makers of foreign policy chose particular courses of action, that is, to see how they perceived the world and how in turn these perceptions led to policy, lies in an appreciation of their attitudes. A case in point concerns those who made British foreign policy during the period of Stanley Baldwin's second government and their attitudes towards the United States.[1] During the life of that ministry, in the two years following the failure of the Coolidge naval conference in the summer of 1927, Anglo-American relations fell to their lowest point in this century.[2] The discord that arose was political in nature and, as far as the Cabinet and the Foreign Office were concerned, derived from American foreign policies which threatened Britain's ability to defend itself and the Empire. Since the resolution of these differences was believed by the leaderships of both countries to be decisive for their futures as great Powers, an atmosphere of mutual suspicion and mistrust developed in which attempts at compromise became difficult.

Baldwin's second government actually took office at a time of unusual quiet in Anglo-American relations. For most of the preceding five years, since the Senate had failed to ratify the Treaty of Versailles in late 1919, these relations had been strained by a range of economic, diplomatic, and strategic issues, the legacy of the war and the Paris Peace Conference. Successive American administrations in the 1920s, with the Republican Party controlling the White House and Congress throughout, sought to remain isolated from international politics outside of the western hemisphere. In practice, however, the United States could not isolate itself from Europe's financial difficulties, and this affected Anglo-American economic relations. There were two inter-twined issues: war debts owed the United States and German reparations. The British had borrowed heavily in the United States between 1914 and 1918 to finance their war effort and that of their allies.[3] The sum was immense, almost £1,000 million, though the British were owed far more by their former allies. In 1922 the poor state of Europe's economy led the British government to announce that it would cancel the debts owed it and collect only the amount needed to pay the Americans; if the Americans cancelled their debts as well, so much the better. It was felt that with this issue removed, despite the losses to Britain and the United States, the more pressing problem of European economic reconstruction could be tackled.[4]

But American policy and the German ability to pay reparations now touched the debt question. In 1922 Germany's economy was crumbling, in part because of the reparations régime imposed at Paris. A new, less stringent agreement tied to an American loan to Germany was needed, but this depended on the debt settlement: Britain owed the United States; France and the other allies owed Britain; and Germany owed France and the Allies. However, the Harding Administration saw no connexion between what the former allies owed Britain and the Anglo-American debt, nor between reparations and war debts, and it indicated it would collect what was owed the United States.[5] This created ill feelings on both sides of the Atlantic. The Americans felt a debt was a debt and had to be honoured. The United States government stood as the guarantor of the war loans which had been raised by selling bonds to the American public. It was impossible electorally for the American government to cancel the debts. This piqued the British. They believed they had fought the war to uphold broad democratic ideals, that America had benefited as a result, and that Britain had sacrificed far more in blood and treasure – in 1919 Britain was a net debtor, the United States a creditor, the opposite of 1914. However, the Americans remained intractable, and negotiations ensued that led in 1923 to the Anglo-American debt settlement.[6]

As the then chancellor of the exchequer, Baldwin took a prominent part in this diplomacy. The settlement brought Anglo-American economic relations back on an even keel; work began immediately on a new reparations agreement to be coupled with an American loan to

Germany, spurred on by the French occupation of the Ruhr as punishment for German default on their payments. In April 1924, just six months before Baldwin's second government took office, an international committee under the chairmanship of Charles Dawes, an American banker, arrived at a new reparations scheme to take the pressure off Germany. In this way, by November 1924, Europe's economic troubles were ameliorated and, for the duration of Baldwin's ministry, never upset Anglo-American relations. This is not to say that British and American financiers, industrialists, and traders failed to compete with one another in various parts of the world; they did, and with decided vigour. But this rivalry was dominated by discernible 'patterns of cooperation and compromise', at least until the end of 1928.[7] In tandem with the debt settlement, these patterns dominated Anglo-American economic intercourse, preventing the injection of pecuniary poison into purely political diplomatic relations.

An over-riding problem for the British in the period between the end of the war and the formation of Baldwin's second government was European security. In terms of Anglo-American relations this had both a diplomatic and a strategic dimension. At the Peace Conference President Wilson had undertaken to join with the British in guaranteeing France from a resurgent Germany; indeed, this allowed the French government to overcome some of the more extreme demands of the French Army. But the Senate's failure to ratify Versailles meant the collapse of the guarantee and all of the political commitments which Wilson made, including American membership in the League of Nations, the proposed guardian of international security. This American abdication of political responsibility in Europe created strategic problems for the British who decided they could not guarantee unilaterally French security.[8] Anglo-French relations suffered and the French, fearing restored German power, used their military and diplomatic preponderance between 1919 and 1924 to encircle and enfeeble Germany. This occurred through treaties negotiated with Germany's eastern neighbours, most of whom had benefited territorially at German expense at the Peace Conference, and the threat and use of military power to assure Germany honoured the obligations imposed at Versailles; the Ruhr occupation was the high point of this latter policy. To a large extent British leaders laid the blame for Europe's security problems on American isolation.[9] By mid-1924, however, the American element in

Europe's security problems had receded, at least for the British, as Baldwin's Labour predecessors were promoting 'the Geneva Protocol' as the panacea for European, as well as international security. As an ostensible League endeavour, it was going to ignore the United States in enforcing its particular vision of international peace.

The only unresolved problem in the period before November 1924 centred on the lack of a comprehensive Anglo-American agreement on the possession and use of naval power. This brought decided discord to Anglo-American relations.[10] It was not the technical aspects of naval competition, like disputes over gun calibres, that created difficulty; these were simply the visible manifestations of a deeper political problem: the incompatibility of the British doctrine of maritime belligerent rights with the American theory of the freedom of the seas. During the war, until April 1917 when the United States joined the Allies, neutral American commerce had been hurt by British maritime blockade of the Central Powers. This issue dominated Anglo-American relations from the armistice until 1921 – during the period of their belligerency, the Americans joined their British allies in enforcing firmly maritime blockade. In November 1918 the Americans sought British assurances that there would be freedom of the seas in future wars. These were not forthcoming as they struck directly at the heart of British policies of Imperial defence, the basis of which was a powerful navy with the ability to keep open maritime lines of communication whilst blockading the sea routes into the enemy's homeland.

This British determination not to relinquish their place as the world's greatest naval Power led to an equally strong American resolution to secure formal equality. This mutual antagonism remained at the fore until, at the Washington Conference in late 1921, Britain and the United States agreed to parity in capital ships. For the moment this took the urgency out of the naval issue. In reality, though, the Washington Conference did not do what it was supposed to do in terms of relieving Anglo-American tensions. American admirals still were suspicious of the Royal Navy – technical improvements in vessels and guns, the method of getting around the strictures imposed at Washington, as well as worry about protecting sea routes, were not eliminated.[11] The Washington Conference had not limited lesser warships, especially cruisers, the chief weapon for defending maritime routes and imposing blockade. Although dormant when Baldwin's government took office, it was this which, when tied to corollary issues after 1926 like the League's pursuit of disarmament and American desires to have a new arbitration agreement – the former would limit naval arms and the latter their use in defending British interests – brought Anglo-American relations to their low point.

In this way broad economic and political issues, and the technical aspects of naval rivalry, did not produce Anglo-American disharmony after late 1924. The debt settlement removed the main financial block to good relations, and trade rivalry was dominated by those 'patterns of cooperation and compromise'. Though lamentable, isolationist policies effectively removed the United States from efforts touching European security. It was the political side of the naval question – belligerent rights versus the freedom of the seas – that was problematical. Belligerent rights had to be upheld if Britain was to preserve its maritime supremacy. Hence the American question gradually assumed greater importance for the second Baldwin government; resolving the predicaments it spawned became a matter of maintaining Britain as a Power of the first rank.

Austen Chamberlain, the Cabinet, and the United States

Because of its special nature, foreign policy has rarely been the province of the full Cabinet; instead it has tended to be the preserve of two men, the prime minister and the foreign secretary. Whilst some prime ministers have from time to time doubled as their own foreign secretaries, for the century between the Congress of Vienna and the July Crisis the careers of Canning, Castlereagh, Palmerston, Salisbury, and Grey underscored a continuity in British foreign policy.[12] David Lloyd George's rise to the premiership in December 1916 disrupted that continuity. He rose to power on the assumption that he could inject vitality into flagging British war effort, and at the centre of his attempt to do so was the creation of the War Cabinet. But when this new body was established the foreign secretary was not considered important enough politically to merit a place in it, the result being Lloyd George's assumption of control over foreign policy and diplomacy. Once the war ended and the War Cabinet was phased out, the prime minister and a few of his private secretaries had dislodged the foreign secretary and the Foreign Office from the formal processes which made foreign policy.[13] This situation remained essentially unchanged until the advent of the second Baldwin government.

At that time two unique factors reaffirmed the traditional pre-eminence of the foreign secretary in foreign policy matters. First, Baldwin was indifferent personally to international politics, which resulted in a willingness to allow the foreign secretary, Austen Chamberlain, to lead in these matters. In effect the prime minister became merely another Cabinet member who considered British external relations as they appeared on the Cabinet agenda. Baldwin's personal disposition to allow Chamberlain this independence was reinforced by a dislike of Lloyd George and of the manner in which the power of the foreign secretary had been subverted during Lloyd George's premiership. Baldwin did not want to imitate Lloyd George nor repeat his mistakes.[14]

The second factor was political, and it concerned the unity of the Conservative Party. Baldwin offered Chamberlain the post of foreign secretary, still considered the most prestigious Cabinet position next to the premiership, in an attempt to heal a rift within the Conservative Party that had sapped its political strength and effectiveness for two years. Chamberlain had been the party leader in October 1922 when a group of his younger colleagues and junior ministers, including Baldwin, rebelled against the party policy of sustaining Lloyd George's coalition government in the House of Commons. When the rebels triumphed, Chamberlain resigned the leadership and led a faction of Conservative MPs loyal to him into the political wilderness.[15] Baldwin's short-lived first government had suffered as a result of this division and, by offering Chamberlain the Foreign Office after the Conservative electoral victory of October 1924, he hoped to avoid a repetition of his earlier difficulties.[16] It followed that Chamberlain could have a preponderant influence on foreign policy if he chose to exercise it. He did.

Chamberlain remained the most important member of the foreign-policy-making élite that existed during Baldwin's second government, so that his character – his private disposition and public image along with his aims and abilities as a leader – set the tone of British foreign policy in the latter half of the 1920s. A problem common to most studies that discuss Chamberlain's direction of British foreign policy is a tendency to concentrate heavily and somewhat simplistically on his public image. Too much is accorded to his formality and correct bearing, so that important aspects of his personal and political development prior to November 1924 are ignored.[17] His most severe critic is conspicuous in failing to consider these antecedents.[18]

Chamberlain was a more complex individual than is generally assumed. Throughout his political career he consciously maintained a dual personality: to his family he was a warm and devoted son, brother, husband, and father; to the rest of the world, including even his closest political colleagues, he embodied Victorian propriety – always correct and formal, loyal, and adept at keeping his innermost thoughts private. Chamberlain was not unaware that his public manner affected his relations with those outside his family. He believed that he and his brother, Neville, were similar in many ways and, in once evaluating Neville's personal and political shortcomings – 'N's manner freezes people ... Everybody respects him and he makes no friends' – he observed that 'it is precisely my weakness in the House today'.[19]

His personal and political relationship with his father, Joseph, was the dominant feature of his life. Joseph Chamberlain was politically influential for nearly thirty years, achieving his greatest prominence in the decade and one-half following the Liberal Party split of 1886. Early on the elder Chamberlain selected Austen to be his political heir, a role the son willingly assumed, and the boy's education in England, France, and Germany was the preparation for a life to be devoted to public service. He served his apprenticeship in the House of Commons – he entered in 1892 – as his father's assistant. His father's position naturally opened political doors and, showing promise, young Chamberlain achieved junior ministerial rank within three years. As his public career advanced, his close association with his father continued. He lived in the family home until he was forty when, in accepting the exchequer, he followed precedent and took up residence at the Treasury Chambers in Downing Street. Even after Joseph's active political life ended suddenly in 1906, the result of a stroke, Austen regularly discussed politics with him and, until his death in 1914, the elder Chamberlain remained his son's political mentor.[20]

Because Chamberlain tended to be less flamboyant in his politics and more faithful to his party than was his father, some of his critics assert that he was not at all like Joseph.[21] The implication seems to be that whilst 'Radical Joe' would do anything to achieve his political goals, Austen, by being more conservative and less flashy, was not as dynamic and innovative a leader. This is not correct. Of course, the policies pursued by both men during their combined span of sixty years in Parliament obviously differed. Particular political concerns, the demands of the electors, and the nature of the political environment did not transcend time unaltered. New situations required new policies. But whilst specific political goals were mutable, the philosophy underlying them was not. Three constant aims guided both Chamberlains, and the son conformed to the pattern established by the father. These aims were to improve the lot of the common man, to maintain the Empire and Imperial unity, and to work to ensure international peace as the best assurance of continued British prosperity.[22]

When Chamberlain accepted Baldwin's offer of the Foreign Office, he already possessed a distinguished parliamentary and ministerial career spanning thirty years. He obviously had an acute political acumen, not rising to the forefront of political life and retaining a prominent place there for so long without demonstrating an ability to lead. Interestingly, criticism of his political career centres more on his personal defeats than on any analysis of his record in office. Lord Beaverbrook, the newspaper proprietor, was the chief amongst his detractors, a situation deriving from the antipathy that existed between Chamberlain and Bonar Law, Beaverbrook's patron.[23] Beaverbrook's petulance has been repeated mindlessly by his disciples since,[24] so that Chamberlain's capacity to lead has been misrepresented.

Austen Chamberlain was an astute politician whose skills were the combination of his innate faculties and the lessons he learned from his father. From his father he acquired what can loosely be called 'work habits', and these entailed the high Victorian virtues of 'clear thinking and hard work'.[25] When confronted with a new political problem, Joseph Chamberlain decided clearly on his goal – assessed in terms of his general aims – and then planned carefully the route by which he could move to secure it.[26] With a few exceptions, such as the failure to contain the rebellion of his party in 1922, Austen profitably applied his father's formula to his own unique situation. The elder Chamberlain also added much to his son's capacity to lead when he was able to refine one paramount skill within Austen: the use of pragmatism. If the utility of a particular set of tactics faded suddenly, as it could if the mood of public opinion altered, the desirability of securing its objective might not. Hence it was perfectly acceptable to devise a new strategy to secure that goal, a line of reasoning that added the critical element of realism to Austen Chamberlain's politics.

These acquired skills were supplemented by natural ones. Chamberlain possessed neither the intuitive brilliance of Lloyd George nor the dialectical prowess of Birkenhead, faculties that contributed much to the capacity of these two men to lead. But he did have an uncanny knack of being able to see to the heart of a problem, to reduce, quickly, complicated questions into easily digestible portions.[27] More important, he was, and was recognised to be, an honest man, loyal and incapable of duplicity.[28] These traits coloured all of his private and public dealings to such an extent that no one, whether his friend or enemy, could have delusions about where he stood on issues. Dismissed casually by some as 'boyish traits',[29] the fact remains that Chamberlain supported genuinely his colleagues and whatever causes he took up. He was not prone to equivocate to the detriment of his party, Parliament, or any ministry of which he was a member.

His first foray into international politics as foreign secretary resulted in a striking victory that provided proof of his diplomatic genius and assured his ascendancy in foreign policy matters. This derived from the role he played in the delicate and complex negotiations leading to the conclusion of the Locarno accords, the series of treaties that guaranteed the Franco-Belgian–German border whilst simultaneously attempting to stabilise Germany's eastern frontiers with several arbitration agreements.[30] Soon after he came to the Foreign Office, Chamberlain became convinced that with the amelioration of Franco-German animosity lay the basis for future European peace and security. He believed that if another continental war broke out Britain would willy-nilly be drawn in. He argued persuasively that if Britain played the honest broker in reconciling divergent Franco-German views on security, British interests could be better protected in the event of a continental crisis.[31] Baldwin gave him unstinting support and, as a result, Chamberlain garnered Cabinet approval of his policies. It is true that the Cabinet debated the implications of a Franco-German security pact to be guaranteed by Britain, and that it succeeded occasionally in shaping British notes.[32] But the foreign secretary's formula for maintaining European security remained unsullied and the credit for bringing France and Germany together in a spirit of cooperation, however cautious it might have been, was accorded to him;[33] he was given the Garter and won the 1925 Nobel Peace Prize.

Because of his instrumental part in effecting a Franco-German *rapprochement* within a year of coming to the Foreign Office – a goal which had eluded his predecessors for seven years – his initial stature within the Cabinet was enhanced further. It resulted in his authority on foreign policy issues becoming almost unshakeable for the duration of Baldwin's second ministry. It also meant that with the emergence of a foreign secretary who was influential in both his party and the Cabinet, the power of the Foreign Office in devising and implementing policy increased accordingly. With Chamberlain as foreign secretary, the Lloyd George experiment in controlling foreign policy was abandoned. The traditional pattern of control was reestablished, but with one subtle difference: through unique circumstances the foreign secretary stood alone at the centre of the policy-making process.

The members of Baldwin's Cabinet who, with their civil service advisers, contributed to the making of foreign policy remained a small group. This derived not only from Chamberlain's dominance in diplomacy but also from the major domestic, economic, political, and social problems that beset Britain after 1924, and which took the majority of Cabinet time.[34] What was true of foreign policy in general was even more so with respect to British American policy.

Baldwin's personal indifference to international politics has been noted earlier. Between November 1924 and June 1929 he only made public utterances on foreign affairs when the prestige of the prime minister was required to give added weight to policy. Only twice did Baldwin contribute behind the scenes to the direction of foreign policy. The first was abortive. Soon after his second ministry took office he suggested to Miles Lampson, a Foreign Office official, that a tripartite Anglo-American–Japanese peace treaty for the Pacific might have merit. When the Foreign Office rejected the idea out of hand because it would reopen issues buried at the Washington Conference,[35] he withdrew from making suggestions about foreign policy until shortly before the 1929 general election. At that time he succeeded in delaying Cabinet discussion of Anglo-American relations, which was being pressed for by Chamberlain; he did this to postpone what was sure to be a heated debate until after the anticipated Conservative victory.[36] But throughout his second government Baldwin gave Chamberlain his unflinching support.[37]

The most vocal Cabinet member, not only regarding foreign affairs but all number of issues, was Winston Churchill, the chancellor of the exchequer. The product of a trans-Atlantic marriage, his blood ties to the United States did not prevent him from becoming on occasion one of the most vociferous anti-Americans in Cabinet. To be fair, soon after becoming chancellor, Churchill wrote Chamberlain warning him that the Treasury would not be reticent about foreign policy if it in any way touched on economic matters.[38] But after inducing Chamberlain to make a statement that the possibility of an Anglo-Japanese war was remote, at least for ten years,[39] Churchill settled in to enforce Treasury parsimony in every aspect of government. Although his constant bickering with the Admiralty over naval construction remains the most visible example of his attempt at imposing fiscal restraint, his actions did not impinge much on Chamberlain's work. Indeed, the few times that the Treasury attempted to trespass on the purely political domain of the Foreign Office, Chamberlain had little trouble in fending it off. Treasury incursions into the American question were attempts simply to find some excuse to avoid the bi-annual payments of the British war debt to the United States.[40] However, by the last year of Baldwin's second government Churchill had become a gad-fly in any foreign or defence policy deliberations, especially when these entailed questions of expenditure and national honour. He was always ready to criticise but rarely offered constructive alternatives. During the period of Anglo-American naval deadlock he even came to advocate two paradoxical policies simultaneously: resistance to demands for increased naval construction and the need for continued British maritime supremacy. Churchill was nothing more than a political opportunist whose every move was designed to bring him closer to the premiership.

Since the cruiser question represented the most conspicuous aspect of Anglo-American enmity in the late 1920s, William Bridgeman, the first lord of the Admiralty, was important in making foreign policy. His struggles with Churchill over funding for naval construction took a large amount of his time, and Admiralty–Treasury disagreements led to strained relations between Bridgeman's staff officers and Churchill's officials. But the Admiralty suffered from a siege mentality at that time. Just as much as the Treasury, the Foreign Office became an object of Admiralty obloquy. Bridgeman and several of his advisers, notably Rear-Admiral Dudley Pound, the assistant chief of the Naval Staff, believed that the Foreign Office was soft on the United States and, moreover, that Chamberlain and his subordinates were too willing to compromise in order to pacify American sensitivities.[41]

There is no doubt that Bridgeman dealt honestly with Cabinet colleagues, including Chamberlain, in presenting the Admiralty case. But he knew little of international politics and had had nothing to do with the United States until the summer of 1927 when he represented Britain at the Coolidge conference. He disliked immediately the Americans he met: 'I don't think people at home have the faintest notion of the difficulty we have with these cursed American Admirals. They understand nothing of our position and very little of their own.'[42] Although Chamberlain followed willingly Admiralty wisdom in matters relating to the technical aspects of arms limitation, and he submitted all questions relating to these questions to Bridgeman,[43] neither he nor his advisers would allow similar freedom on political issues judged to be the Foreign Office's responsibility. This stance did not stop Bridgeman and the Admiralty from trying to influence British American policy concerning belligerent rights; the defence of the Empire was their principal preoccupation and, as they tended to regard the Empire as a static entity, perceived threats like an American call for naval equality had to be resisted.

Leopold Amery, the secretary of state for both the colonies and dominions, became preoccupied with the American question after the 1926 Imperial Conference. He had risen to prominence in the period after the Boer War by working assiduously to strengthen Imperial ties and promote better Imperial understanding.[44] The 1926 conference, both the run-up to it and the implementation of its resolutions, became the focal point of his endeavours during Baldwin's second government as he sought to use his position to bind Britain and the Empire closer together. But after 1926, in an attempt to demonstrate autonomy in foreign policy, the Canadian government arranged to exchange permanent diplomatic missions with the United States government for the first time. Several influential British Imperialists responded with dismay, believing that the Americans were intent on prying Canada away from Britain and the Empire.[45] The matter became critical in 1928 and, coming at the same time as Anglo-American differences over arbitration, belligerent rights, and the question of naval disarmament, the problems of preserving Imperial unity forced themselves on the making of British American policy at a crucial juncture. To ensure that his American policies were neither deflected from their course nor diluted in any way,

Chamberlain – who was not on the friendliest terms with Amery as the latter had played a prominent part in the 1922 revolt against Chamberlain's leadership of the Conservative Party – had to work to assuage the fears and worries of the colonial and dominions secretary and his supporters.

James Edward Cecil, the fourth Marquess of Salisbury, sat in the Cabinet as lord privy seal and, though tied to Baldwin by political rather than personal bonds, he was one of the prime minister's closest associates. Since Salisbury's family had been involved at the highest levels of political life since the reign of Elizabeth I, the association of the Cecil name with Baldwin's Cabinet gave the government an aura of prestige.[46] But the fourth Marquess had also gained the respect of his political colleagues by earning a reputation for evenhandedness and adherence to principle. His value derived from the respect that that equanimity engendered in his associates, opponents, and the civil service. It became Salisbury's function to mediate between opposing ministers in order to resolve differences that could split the Cabinet and weaken the party. He had demonstrated his worth in 1923 when he presided over a CID sub-committee that sought to resolve a vituperative Admiralty–Air Ministry disagreement over control of the Fleet Air Arm.[47] He did this with patience and non-partisan judgement. During Baldwin's second government Salisbury was called on a number of times to add his weight to the consideration of crucial political problems. Two directly concerned foreign policy towards the United States. He became the chairman of two policy groups: the Cabinet committee on disarmament and the CID sub-committee on belligerent rights. Salisbury's dispassionate handling of these two committees, especially of the belligerent rights sub-committee which witnessed the Foreign Office and Admiralty divided completely over how best to respond to the United States, permitted a crucial foreign policy debate to progress without causing a rupture in either in the Cabinet or between the competing departments of state.

Salisbury's younger brother, Robert, Viscount Cecil of Chelwood, held the chancellorship of the Duchy of Lancaster until August 1927. Unlike Salisbury, Cecil could not approach politics in a calm, detached manner. Moreover, he was preoccupied with British foreign and disarmament policies; ultimately this made him one of Chamberlain's and the Baldwin government's strongest critics. A lawyer by training, a devout high churchman by conviction, and a stubborn man by temperament, he seemed to embody the most extreme tendencies of each. Cecil saw all questions only in terms of right or wrong, holding his views to be the only correct ones; hence, those who disagreed with him were either misguided or malevolent and he attacked each with equal ferocity. Passionately committed to the League of Nations – he had led that section of the British Delegation to the Paris Peace Conference which had helped draft the Covenant – he believed that with universal disarmament would come universal peace. These notions were not incompatible for Cecil, as they were for most others, since he saw the League as the instrument for effecting disarmament.[48]

In the 1920s Cecil's view of international politics was based on two beliefs: the need for positive British participation in the League, as well as the desirability of Anglo-American accord. When he joined Baldwin's Cabinet in November 1924, Cecil anticipated that he would be made responsible for League affairs since, until then, they had been the province of either the prime minister or some Cabinet minister with an interest and enough political clout to take charge of them. But Chamberlain decided that League policy devolved from foreign policy, and Cecil lost an intra-Cabinet struggle over the direction of League affairs.[49] This was a blow, and from that point Chamberlain's League policies became the object of Cecil's bitterness. Baldwin attempted to placate Cecil over his loss of control of League policy by giving him the direction of disarmament affairs. Cecil consequently became the minister responsible for disarmament, leading the British delegation to the various meetings of the Preparatory Commission and accompanying Bridgeman as a senior delegate to the Coolidge conference. When that conference failed because of Anglo-American differences over the cruiser question, Cecil blamed his Cabinet colleagues for the impasse, especially Churchill, and left the government. Although his dislike of Chamberlain increased with time, those who have criticised the foreign secretary since over his League and American policies have relied heavily on Cecil's jaundiced views.[50]

Ronald McNeill, created Baron Cushendun in 1927, succeeded Cecil as the minister responsible for disarmament. His early career had been in journalism – he had been the editor of the *St James Gazette* from 1900 to 1904 – but after becoming an MP in 1911 he devoted himself totally to politics. As an Irish MP, Cushendun was preoccupied with Irish home rule and, later, with Ulster and, until chosen by Baldwin to follow Cecil, he had never held Cabinet office. Although he had been parliamentary under-secretary for foreign affairs twice and financial secretary to the Treasury before his rise to the Cabinet, Cushendun does not seem to have had any contact with the United States prior to replacing Cecil. Once he entered the Cabinet, however, he recognised immediately that he was doing so at a critical time in Anglo-American relations. He wrote to Chamberlain in November 1927 to express diffidence about the work he had agreed to undertake and to discuss the problems in fashioning naval disarmament policy in the aftermath of the Coolidge conference.[51] Preoccupied with Anglo-American relations, Cushendun asked bluntly: 'Has the time come when it would be wise for us to abandon, or modify, our traditional doctrine of Blockade in time of war?'

Cushendun's importance was enhanced by his assumption of Chamberlain's duties at the Foreign Office from August to November 1928. Chamberlain collapsed on 31 July 1928 of overwork and pneumonia, the day after the premature disclosure of an Anglo-French compromise on arms limitation. This precipitated the period of greatest strain in Anglo-American relations, with Cushendun directing the Foreign Office, coordinating the government's responses to both official and unofficial American displeasure with the compromise, supervising the publication of the White Paper that sought to explain how and why the compromise was struck, and attempting to maintain Anglo-American relations on an even keel when a violent press reaction concerning the agreement erupted on both sides of the Atlantic. At a time when American pique with British foreign policy caused a number of the Cabinet to display anti-American sentiment in the debate on how best to respond to the United States, Cushendun provided balance to the policy-making process.

Arthur Balfour, the first Earl Balfour, a cousin of the Cecils, was seventy-six years old in November 1924. As one of the most respected and distinguished British statesmen, he had been at or near the very highest circles of political life for fifty years. He became leader of his party and prime minister in 1902 and, whilst his tenure as leader was one of personal and political failure, his stature within both the party and the country did not diminish even after he resigned the leadership in 1911.[52] During the war and its immediate aftermath Balfour held the major posts of first lord of the Admiralty and foreign secretary, and his counsel was sought on all kinds of issues. When Baldwin formed his second government, Balfour attempted to remain outside of the Cabinet and, when he was enticed in in 1925, to concentrate on domestic affairs. Once the American question became critical, however, and despite growing infirmity, Balfour was pressed to contribute to the fashioning of British American policy.

Balfour was a staunch believer in the need for strong Anglo-American ties – he was the president of the London branch of the English Speaking Union.[53] More significant is that of all Baldwin's Cabinet he had had the greatest experience in dealing with the Americans. In 1917 when he was foreign secretary and just after the United States declared war on the Central Powers, he led a British mission to the United States to promote better Anglo-American understanding and facilitate a more effective Allied war effort.[54] In the autumn of 1921 Balfour again led a British delegation to the United States, this time to participate in a multilateral conference at Washington which was to effect some sort of naval limitation and affirm the existing naval and political *status quo* in the Pacific Ocean and Far East. As far as Britain and the United States were concerned the Washington conference formalised Anglo-American parity in capital ships, the largest vessels comprising battleships and above. But Balfour and Charles Evans Hughes, the American secretary of state and chief delegate, studiously avoided the nettled question of cruiser equality.[55] Thus, when the Coolidge conference foundered on the rocks of cruiser construction levels five years later, the necessity of Balfour's views in the discussion of British American policy was evident.

Because of the exigencies of politics Lord Eustace Percy, the president of the Board of Education, perhaps the one Cabinet post most removed from foreign policy, contributed substantially to the Baldwin government's consideration of British American policy. Percy's family, the Dukes of Northumberland, rivalled the Cecils as one of Britain's ancient political clans. When Percy decided to involve himself in discussion of any subject, his name guaranteed that his voice would be heard. But his family connexion was secondary to why the Cabinet listened to his views on the American question. Not only was Percy recognised to be one of the most gifted Cabinet ministers – he took the Board of Education by choice – he had had considerable experience with the United States and American diplomacy.

Born in 1887 with what he admitted to be 'the biggest of all possible silver spoons in [his] mouth', Percy decided to enter the diplomatic service after he came down from Oxford in 1907.[56] In May 1910 he arrrived at the Washington Embassy and remained there for four years, leaving just two months prior to the outbreak of the Great War. After serving briefly on the western front, he worked at the Foreign Office in a number of positions, gradually concentrating on the commercial aspects of Allied war effort. In April 1917 he accompanied Balfour to the United States to help set up Anglo-American commercial cooperation and, when the mission returned to London, stayed at Washington as the local representative of the Ministry of Blockade attached to the Embassy. Percy left the Foreign Office after the war to pursue a political career; once Anglo-American naval deadlock set in, with the attendant problems of arbitration, disarmament, and belligerent rights, he threw himself into the debate on British American policy. Percy felt that the best method to avoid inflaming American opinion was for British leaders to explain their position in calm, reasoned terms and to abstain from appearing to dictate: 'The really unpardonable offence in public life is to pontificate in the territory of a rival pontiff.' Percy was impressed with the dangers that an Anglo-American rupture could have for British security;[57] he approached the formation of British American policy intent on precluding a rupture.

The principal civil service advisers outside the Foreign Office who were interested in the American question at this time were a relatively small group. They can most easily be categorised as navalists, those seeking to preserve and possibly extend the potency of the Royal Navy. Although most of these men were naval officers seconded to the Admiralty in administrative roles, Sir Maurice Hankey, the secretary to both the Cabinet and the CID, and an ex-officer in the Royal Marines, was the most effective naval lobbyist in government. Navalist opinion coalesced around Hankey, and it was through him that this opinion was most forcefully presented. He had joined the CID as an assistant secretary in 1907. Five years later he was appointed secretary and, when Lloyd George implemented his reform of wartime decision-making, Hankey became head of the new Cabinet secretariat. His rise within the bureaucracy derived from awesome analytical, intellectual, and organisational abilities; by late 1924, entrenched firmly at the centre of government,[58] Hankey was able to involve himself in a major way in the debate on British American policy.

Hankey's attitude toward foreign and defence policy derived from a belief that a great Britain was only possible through the maintenance of a powerful and unified Empire. His views reflected those of other military and naval men whose sole preoccupation centred on Imperial defence.[59] As a student of history, Hankey drew the lesson from the collapse of past empires that 'national virility' could be sapped if disarmament was implemented too quickly and made national defence impractical. For him, the League of Nations existed as the manifestation of the tendency for rapid and complete disarmament. Tied to this was his certainty that that organisation would draw Britain into the affairs of Europe to the detriment of the Empire. The less Britain had to do with Europe the better:

I think people are beginning to see that, though we cannot disinterest ourselves in European affairs, our best attitude is one of aloofness, rather on the lines of the United States, though for geographical, commercial and other reasons we cannot segregate ourselves so completely as they. In fact our policy is, I think, one of helping Europe as much as we can without undertaking commitments.[60]

But Locarno[61] and the onset of Anglo-American naval deadlock brought threats to the Empire that Hankey never before believed possible. He came to lay the blame for many of Britain's diplomatic problems after mid-1927 on the doorstep of the Foreign Office,[62] so that when the belligerent rights question brought matters to a head, he felt obliged to conduct a determined rear-guard action within the CID to stave off any concessions to the American demand for freedom of the seas.

The largest part of the second Baldwin Cabinet who were concerned with Anglo-American relations represented the old landed interests: the Cecil brothers, Churchill, Balfour, and Percy. But this Cabinet contained a much larger element of the industrial and trading classes, a result of Baldwin reducing purposely the landed elements in the upper echelon of the party after he became leader.[63] Consequently, it would be expected that this group of men would be extremely sensitive to American commercial, economic, and financial rivalry. But the occasional contributions of the bulk of the Cabinet to the formulation of British American policy did not consider to any great extent the American threat to Britain's economic position. Rather, just like the majority of people then and since who have concerned themselves with this period, attention was focused on the ostensible American threat to the power of the Royal Navy. For a number of reasons, principally those revolving around the domestic political and economic situation, and those tied to their ministerial responsibilities, the majority of the Cabinet contributed to the making of policy toward the United States only when it touched this particular aspect of Britain's national honour.[64]

The Chamberlain Foreign Office, the diplomatic service, and the United States

Between November 1924 and June 1929, the foreign secretary and his advisers assumed an independence in the devising and implementing of foreign policy that had not been the case since at least August 1914. The advent of a foreign secretary who was both influential in the Cabinet and who possessed a power base within his party brought the Foreign Office perforce back into its pre-Great War role in the formal processes which made foreign policy. Foreign Office independence was especially pronounced in relation to the American question. Until the breakdown of the Coolidge conference and the onset of naval deadlock, the question remained firmly in the second rank. Until then the dangers posed by European security, Chinese nationalism, and Egyptian self-government were most crucial.[65] After the summer of 1927, as the crisis in Anglo-American relations mounted, the Foreign Office remained the dominant force within the second Baldwin government that shaped British American policy, this because it had been the only department of state assessing daily the political aspects of relations with the United States prior to the onset of naval deadlock.

From his first days at the Foreign Office, Chamberlain relied on the advice and opinions of his subordinates in shaping policy. There developed a *rapport* between Foreign Office officials and their political chief that made their respective jobs that much easier. In accepting Baldwin's offer Chamberlain realised fully the burdensome task before him, and he approached his new position with typical diffidence and humility.[66] Except for one brief absence to attend a League Council in early December 1924, Chamberlain spent his first two months in office in a self-imposed isolation.[67] He devoted himself to learning as much as he could as quickly as he could about all aspects of British external relations, about the urgent problems confronting Britain, and about the day to day administration of his department. It was at this time, when Chamberlain worked closely with his senior advisers, that that spirit of cooperation and mutual respect developed.

Soon after Chamberlain became foreign secretary, Beaverbrook wrote:

[Chamberlain], I am sorry to say, has become frightfully prolix and boring. His colleagues find him tiresome, and the officials at the Foreign Office laugh at him. The trouble seems to be in part, that he knows French completely, and speaks it perfectly. His delight in showing off this accomplishment makes him keener on the side of France than the present French premier (or his predecessor).[68]

As far as gauging the attitudes of Foreign Office members, this report demonstrates more Beaverbrook's francophobia than the truth. Chamberlain's *rapport* with his advisers, as well as his ability to handle difficult people and situations with grace and tact, especially the French, was lauded in the Foreign Office. Lampson wrote to D'Abernon, the British ambassador at Berlin: 'When one contrasts the Chamberlain–Briand *régime* to the Curzon–Poincaré nightmare one can hardly believe it to be true. Work which used to be a sore trial has become a real pleasure to all of us.'[69] These feelings did not diminish over the next few years. Near the end of his tenure as foreign secretary, though not when it was apparent, Ronald Lindsay, then the permanent under-secretary, wrote an unsolicited tribute to Chamberlain and to the support which the foreign secretary had given to him and the rest of the office.[70] In the group that made and implemented foreign policy during Baldwin's second government, the Foreign Office stands next to the foreign secretary in importance.

Foreign Office handling of relations with the United States was a joint effort of Chamberlain, his senior advisers, and the American Department, the political section responsible for all western hemispheric questions unrelated to the Empire. The Chamberlain Foreign Office has been criticised severely for contributing to the very low point to which Anglo-American relations fell in 1927–29.[71] Foreign Office participation in the negotiation of the ill-fated Anglo-French disarmament compromise, the attempt to resolve the disarmament impasse in 1928, is usually singled out as a major contributor to strained relations. Although the angles of criticism differ, they all stem from one basic assertion: that Chamberlain and his advisers understood neither the United States nor its foreign policy. However, this is not the case.

The purpose of the Chamberlain Foreign Office's American policy during the last two years of the second Baldwin government was to ensure that the United States had no need to build 'a navy second to none'. The Foreign Office was almost alone in recognising that the United States could do this if pressed and, moreover, if such a navy was built, that the British doctrine of maritime belligerent rights would be worthless. The Republican America with which the Chamberlain Foreign Office dealt during the period of naval deadlock was the same one with which it had had to contend in the two and one-half years preceding that unhappy period. Equally important, those whose job it was to consider the American question during Baldwin's second government had not begun their task in November 1924 lacking previous contact with the United States. Even Chamberlain, very much the new boy, had had some contact. During the Great War he had been exposed to the Cabinet's discussion of British dependence on United States finance to conduct the war and to the problems that arose during the financial crises of 1916 and 1917. He had been the chancellor of the exchequer when the first post-war discussions began concerning the payment of the British war debt to the United States. On a more personal level his surviving step-mother, Mary Carnegie, was an American whose father had been the secretary for war during Grover Cleveland's first Administration.

But the Foreign Office advisers are the key. Sir Eyre Crowe was the permanent under-secretary when Chamberlain took office and, though he and Chamberlain got on well, he died in April 1925, before the American question became critical. After Crowe, two seasoned diplomats, Sir William Tyrrell and Lindsay, held the permanent under-secretaryship. Tyrrell was Crowe's immediate successor and, when he became permanent under-secretary, his career spanned thirty-five years. Half of Tyrrell's time had been spent at or near the highest levels of policy formulation. For eight years, from May 1907 to June 1915, he had been the private secretary to Sir Edward Grey, then the foreign secretary. Tyrrell used this position to his advantage and so enhanced his subsequent promotions. At no time was he ever posted abroad for any length of time:[72] he had been an acting second secretary at Rome for less than a year in 1904; he had served at the Paris Peace Conference as a minister plenipotentiary in January 1919; and he had accompanied Grey on the latter's fruitless mission to the United States in late 1919 that was designed to remove Anglo-American differences over League, naval, and Irish questions.

Interestingly, the Grey mission coincided with that acrimonious period in American politics when the Senate failed to ratify the Treaty of Versailles.

A crucial aspect of Tyrrell as permanent under-secretary was his friendship with Baldwin. Tyrrell was so close to Baldwin that he apparently spent at least one social weekend a month with the prime minister,[73] far more than almost anyone else, including some of Baldwin's closest political colleagues. This intimacy with Baldwin did not undermine the *rapport* between Tyrrell and Chamberlain. Indeed, Tyrrell shared a number of interests with the foreign secretary, notably a decided francophilia. Affable, witty, and friendly even to the press, though somewhat reliant on strong drink, he served Chamberlain loyally for over three years. The reward for such service was the Paris Embassy. Tyrrell's admiration for Chamberlain was mutual, and he wrote to him just before leaving for Paris: 'Never have I served a master who has had such a personal knowledge & grasp of continental things & people as you have.'[74]

Unlike Tyrrell whom he succeeded in July 1928, Lindsay had spent nearly all of his career in the diplomatic service, principally in the eastern Mediterranean region, in Cairo, Constantinople, and Teheran. His selection as permanent under-secretary had come as the reward for two profitable years as ambassador at Berlin, where he worked well with the German chancellor, Gustav Stresemann, and, in representing British interests with force, ensured that troubles with Germany did not arise to endanger Locarno.[75] In all of this Lindsay was not unfamiliar with the United States. Twice he had been posted to Washington, for two years between 1905 and 1906, and for one year in 1919–20. During his first tour of duty, a politically uneventful one, he married an American. Though shorter, his second one occurred at a critical juncture, coinciding with both the Senate rejection of Versailles and the genesis of the Republican ascendancy that was to last until 1932. His time as the second man in the Foreign Office was coextensive with the period when Anglo-American relations were at their worst. He took up his appointment two weeks before the announcement of the Anglo-French disarmament compromise, relinquishing it a month before the signature of the London Naval Treaty of 1930, the recognised end of Anglo-American naval deadlock. More to the point, Lindsay gave up the permanent under-secretaryship to become British ambassador at Washington.

The deputy under-secretary after April 1925, Sir Victor Wellesley, resembled Tyrrell in that almost all of his diplomatic life was spent at the Foreign Office. Unlike Tyrrell, Wellesley was channelled first into the administrative rather than the political side of British external relations. A descendant of the Duke of Wellington and the grandson of the first Earl of Cowley, the British ambassador at Paris in the 1850s, he entered the Foreign Office in 1899. His work came gradually to centre on commercial and consular affairs and, in September 1916, he became their controller. Political questions began immediately to encroach on his work, with his initial exposure to the weighing of political considerations concerning the United States. After the Americans declared war in April 1917, Wellesley's position dictated that he help in arranging Anglo-American commercial cooperation. This contact with political affairs did not end after the war; it continued apace and in other directions. His expertise developed rapidly, coming to focus on East Asia, a sphere where American ambitions were not meaningless. At the time of his appointment as deputy under-secretary, he was head of the Far Eastern Department. This balance of administrative and political experience obviously contributed to Wellesley's rise within the Foreign Office and, with his brand of calm and reasoned advice, benefited Chamberlain's administration of foreign policy.[76]

These senior Foreign Office members, the foreign secretary, the permanent under-secretary, and the deputy under-secretary, dealt only with important matters. Those, therefore, who staffed the individual departments gained an authority in their areas of concern because of the daily monitoring of all questions relating to these areas, whether of consequence or not. Courses of action proposed by individual department members as minute sheets made their way upward in the Foreign Office, and specialist advice tendered to superiors when requested, put these men in a pivotal position in devising and implementing foreign policy. Nowhere was this more so than in the American Department during Chamberlain's tenure as foreign secretary, a situation attributable to the relative unimportance of the American question from 1924 to mid-1927.

Robert Vansittart, the American Department head from February 1924 to February 1928, lamented about the relative unimportance of the American question until late in his tenure: 'To the American Department, tucked away under the roof, few ascended and the powers that were downstairs troubled us little.'[77] But this was due to Vansittart. The one serious threat to good Anglo-American relations in the two and one-half years prior to the onset of naval deadlock, a controversy about the presentation of American blockade claims dating from the Great War, was removed by Vansittart and his staff.[78] Thus by the time the American question assumed critical proportions, there was perhaps a greater reliance by senior members on the opinions and advice of this department than on those of others.

Four members of the American Department were concerned with the United States. Vansittart was suited admirably for handling Americans and their unconventional brand of diplomacy. Possessing all of the attributes of the stereotype English diplomat of the time – poise, wit, charm, and the refined arrogance of the upper classes – he was atypically competitive and pugnacious. When pushed too far by his adversaries, a group including even those in the British government who opposed his views, that cloak of civility could be removed quickly to expose a most recalcitrant and combative man.

He entered the diplomatic service in 1902 and soon became identified with the anti-German element in the Foreign Office that was influential in shaping foreign policy prior to the Great War. During the war he sat on a committee that enforced the blockade of the Central Powers and, as the Americans argued loudly for upholding neutral trading rights, this brought him into contact with the United States. He rose to prominence after the war by serving as the private secretary to Lord Curzon, the foreign secretary, and he went from there directly to the head of the American Department. Vansittart was pro-French, yet in retrospect he criticised Chamberlain's francophilia, which he felt had precluded closer Anglo-American relations.[79] But at least whilst he headed the American Department, he supported the views of his political superior. His success at the American Department in producing policies that reflected to some extent the ideas prevailing in the senior levels of the Foreign Office, that is, in protecting Locarno, led directly to his selection in February 1928 as the prime minister's foreign policy adviser.[80] After two distinguished years at Downing Street which coincided with the nadir in Anglo-American relations, Vansittart returned to the Foreign Office to succeed Lindsay. Like Lindsay, Vansittart had an American wife – she died in 1928 – and this link with the United States aided him in his diplomatic endeavours.[81]

Robert Craigie became the American Department head after serving as Vansittart's number two for three years. Craigie had entered the Foreign Office in 1907 and, after a varied initial service, was posted to Berne in September 1916. Swiss neutrality during the Great War led to that city becoming a major diplomatic post, as both belligerent and neutral Powers maintained missions there.[82] Craigie remained at Berne until 1920 – he left with an American wife, the daughter of the United States minister. His war duties were increased by his selection as the British representative on the Inter-Allied Blockade Committee, an appointment which brought him into close and constant contact with American officials. He served as first secretary at the Washington Embassy from July 1920 until July 1923 and, before beginning work on the American Department in January 1925, he was seconded to the Department of Overseas Trade for a year and one-half.

As gifted a diplomat as Vansittart, Craigie differed in temperament. Whilst lacking Vansittart's pugnacity and combativeness, this did not mean that he was any less resolute in his foreign policy planning. Rather, it meant that if particular avenues were blocked suddenly or if new situations arose to prevent the execution of strategies, he neither was angered nor embittered by setbacks. Craigie possessed a flexibility of attitude that injected subtlety and ingenuity into his diplomatic methods. He was the eternal optimist, probing continually every aspect of a problem until he could discover a solution. He also came to be the Foreign Office expert on naval affairs.

Until April 1927 the junior member of the department responsible for monitoring the United States was Ronald Ian Campbell, whose short career had almost totally been concerned with the American question. He had entered the diplomatic service in November 1914 and two months later arrived at Washington. He remained there five years – until December 1919 – the period of American neutrality through American belligerency to the Senate rejection of Versailles. In June 1923, following two short stints at the embassies at Paris and Brussels, he was transferred to the Foreign Office and the American Department. After four years he was reassigned to the Washington Embassy, arriving as first secretary just before the Coolidge naval conference convened at Geneva. Whilst a junior member of the Foreign Office, Campbell did not show diffidence in suggesting courses of action to his superiors. His intimacy with both the United States and the types of problems posed by American foreign policy permitted this; thus, though the senior members occasionally judged his proposals to be inappropriate, his voice on the American question was not without weight.

Geoffrey Thompson, a diplomat who had never served in the Foreign Office and whose career by mid-1927 spanned less than seven years, replaced Campbell as the junior department member. His role, though, must not be under-estimated. He went to the department fresh from five years at Washington, and the coincidence of his exchange with Campbell on the eve of Anglo-American naval deadlock provided the Chamberlain Foreign Office with a continuity of expertise for evaluating the American question. Thompson returned to London convinced about the need for strong Anglo-American ties; he later reflected that he left Washington 'a firm believer in Anglo-American friendship based upon mutual dependence and mutual respect'[83] – he also left with an American wife. But once difficulties with the Americans developed over arbitration, disarmament, and belligerent rights, he was just as resolute as his senior colleagues in defending British interests.

In some cases senior Foreign Office members and the American Department did not have exclusive jurisdiction over matters relating to the United States. The chief legal adviser to the Foreign Office, Sir Cecil Hurst, had often to provide his superiors and the American experts with essential specialist advice. He had been called to the bar in 1893 and after eight years in private practice became attached to the Post Office. He joined the Foreign Office as assistant legal adviser in 1902, rising to become the chief in August 1918.

Hurst had had a fair amount of professional contact with Americans, mainly State Department officials. He had been the British agent for the Anglo-American Claims Arbitration Tribunal from 1912 to 1923 and, in serving on the British drafting committee at the Paris Peace Conference in 1919, had joined with his American opposite, David Hunter Miller, to write the first draft of what became the League Covenant.[84] More important in terms of arbitration and belligerent rights, Hurst was a member of the committee of jurists appointed at the Washington Conference of 1921–22 to reexamine and report on the laws of war. He reached the peak of his influence within the Foreign Office whilst Chamberlain was foreign secretary – he left the Foreign Office in late 1929 to join the International Court at The Hague; included in the delegation that travelled to Switzerland to negotiate Locarno, he so impressed the foreign secretary that he was included in the select Foreign Office group that Chamberlain called fondly the 'Locarnoites'.

Because of his intimate connexion with the origin of the League, coupled with a devout belief in the need for the arbitration functions of the International Court and League Council, Hurst became attracted to Geneva and the potential a strong League could have for the maintenance of international stability. American rejection of Versailles and the League Covenant made him distrust American diplomacy. The inability of American leaders to deliver on their promises – Woodrow Wilson's egregious failure to transform his rhetoric about the need for a League into practical politics was a vivid memory – indicated that United States foreign policy represented an unstable element in international politics. To maintain international stability Hurst advocated a British leadership role within the League, and, hence, within Europe, whilst having little to do with the United States.

The American press has always been one of the major arbiters of United States public opinion and, in the 1920s, it could and did exercise this capacity to influence; the power of the press was not lost on either the Coolidge Administration or the State Department.[85] It follows that the Foreign Office News Department, responsible for interpreting British diplomacy to both domestic and international journalists, played a pivotal role in developing Chamberlain Foreign Office American policy. No one was better suited to this job than Sir Arthur Willert, the head of the News Department after 1925.[86] He had joined *The Times* in 1906 and, in 1910, went to the United States as the chief *Times* correspondent, remaining for eleven years and leaving only to join the News Department. During the Great War he had worked as a secretary for the Balfour Mission in 1917, as well as doubling as the local representative of the Ministry of Information. Though returning to London as a pro-American,[87] his counsel was always sober, temperate, and, because of his familiarity with the United States, rarely questioned.

His principal function was to explain British policies to newspapermen so as to avoid distortions and to place those policies in the best light. In this he did a first-rate job. One example occurred when he attended the annual meeting of the Institute of Politics at Williamstown, Massachusetts, just when the Coolidge conference sputtered to a halt. Malcolm MacDonald, the son of the leader of the Labour Party, who was also there, reported to his father that 'Sir Arthur Willert gave six lectures on "British Foreign Policy Since the War" . . . I could not find anything to quarrel with them.'[88] Young MacDonald added humorously that the American audience was somewhat disappointed in Willert as he had not given away 'enough Foreign Office secrets'. But Tyrrell had selected Willert to give the lectures for this reason.[89] During the period of strained Anglo-American relations this was the key to Willert's deft handling of his explanatory duties: to combine sympathy for the American viewpoint with a reasoned exposition of the British case that did not give the game away.

Of course, all of these men were practical and realistic diplomats in that their American connexions did not necessarily create unalterable images of what the United States was or what its foreign policies could achieve. Hurst could become more accommodating if required whilst Thompson, usually more sympathetic to American problems, could assume a more intransigent guise. However, the essential point remains – those who point their fingers at a lack of Foreign Office understanding about the United States are completely off the mark. The United States was not an unknown quantity within the Foreign Office when Austen Chamberlain became its head in November 1924.

It is axiomatic that in the 1920s the foreign secretary and his advisers worked in a world of images. Unlike other ministries whose work centred chiefly on domestic affairs and who could test easily Britain's political climate before devising and implementing policy, the Foreign Office had a more difficult task in assessing the constantly changing *milieu* in which international politics were conducted. Its members relied heavily on a mass of second-hand information that reached them by despatch bag and telegraph from abroad and, less often, by personal interview with British diplomats at home on leave and with the foreign diplomatic corps and others at London. But as all of this amounted to impressions of reality, it follows that the Foreign Office was to some extent detached from that reality. Hence the clearer and more distinct the images that came to the foreign secretary and his advisers, the closer they were to what was actually happening in international politics, and the better able they were to initiate responses and coordinate strategy. In this equation the British diplomatic service was fundamental to the development and implementation of sound foreign policy. Individual British ambassadors and their embassies linked the Foreign Office to the international *milieu*, thus the strength of that link depended on the competence of those men in gauging opinion within their host country and in explaining forcefully British policy.

For the duration of Baldwin's second government, Sir Esme

Howard served as the ambassador at Washington. This was fortunate. Howard was a talented diplomat, gifted in the social arts and adept at presenting the most unpalatable subjects in an anodyne way. Prior to 1924 he had had substantial experience with the United States and its foreign policy; he also knew its Republican leadership well. More important, he and Chamberlain established a close professional relationship during the early days of Baldwin's second government when Britain's accession to the 'Geneva Protocol' was being considered. In combination these elements forged a strong link between the embassy at Washington and the Foreign Office, the result of which was that Chamberlain and his advisers had confidence in the clarity of the image of the United States despatched to them.

Thompson comes closest in explaining Howard's value with the succinct comment that he was at once 'a great ambassador and a charming person'.[90] His diplomatic prowess derived from the ability to employ consummate skill in the social graces – Chamberlain called him 'the gentle Sir Esme' – as a means of making difficult tasks easier. When the occasion demanded, however, Howard did not shirk from raising disagreeable topics, though he always managed to do so with reasonableness and a hint of sophistry that did not offend. In 1925 he spoke to a gathering of American political scientists about the value of the so-called balance of power in preserving international peace and security. At a time when Americans generally were condemning this concept as an outmoded aspect of Europe's 'old diplomacy', this was a courageous stance.[91] Howard confided in his audience that he too deprecated the idea of the balance, but he argued persuasively that as yet no other practical alternative existed. This ability to empathise with American views, but to do so with a pragmatic appraisal of international politics as it reflected on Britain, typified his embassy.

Howard had joined the diplomatic service in 1885 and after a variety of postings became counsellor at the Washington Embassy in 1906.[92] Though in Washington for slightly less than two years, his experiences proved to be of immense value when he returned as ambassador in February 1924. In 1906 the Republican Party controlled both houses of Congress and the White House – Theodore Roosevelt was president – and during the obligatory social rounds Howard naturally met influential Republicans. He and his wife formed a number of durable friendships with people like James Garfield, Roosevelt's secretary of the interior and the son of the assassinated president, and Mabel Boardman, whose family had

State Department connexions and in whose Washington *salon* members of the select 'Eastern Establishment' congregated.[93] These friendships were renewed when Howard returned as ambassador, permitting him once more to gain access to Washington's patrician social and political circles. In addition, in the 1920s his Republican acquaintances were older, more respected, and more influential; he did not hesitate to use social connexions in his diplomacy.[94]

Howard's contact with the United States did not cease in the interim between his two Washington appointments and, significantly, that which he did have centred on American reaction to British blockade policies pursued during the Great War. In May 1913 Howard went to Stockholm as the head of the British Legation, remaining there until late in 1918. During the Great War Sweden remained neutral but, because of its proximity to Germany and the pro-German tendencies of the government of the day, it became one of Germany's main economic links with the outside world. The Stockholm Legation became responsible for identifying contraband cargoes destined for Germany and for coordinating British blockade policy in the region. In the early stages of the war Howard's work concerned the Americans as much as the Swedes. Until United States entry into the war, American trade with Germany amounted to a substantial portion of that which passed through Sweden, and with the stringent application of British belligerent rights came protests from American traders and anglophobic groups about interference with the freedom of the seas.[95] After April 1917 Howard witnessed an American about-face on this issue as United States authorities became more zealous than their British allies in applying maritime blockade, even going so far as introducing new doctrines about contraband.[96] For all their bluster about the freedom of the seas, American leaders were as realistic and hard-nosed as any people in defending their national interests. This lesson was not lost on Howard.[97]

It is impossible to over-estimate the importance of Chamberlain's relationship with Howard in the process that made British American policy. Although Howard had close friends in the upper levels of the Foreign Office,[98] there is no doubt that he would have been replaced if the foreign secretary had lacked faith in him;[99] this did not happen. Of all the ambassadors serving at major posts during the second Baldwin government, Howard was one of the only two who were not transferred or released from the service. Although transfers and releases did not necessarily indicate incompetence – most concerned the normal round of promotions and retirements – Chamberlain had ample opportunity to remove Howard once the American question became critical. That he did not indicates the confidence he had in Howard's ability to interpret American events and to defend British interests.[100]

The pattern of Chamberlain's relationship with Howard developed in the first few months of the Baldwin ministry, when the Cabinet deliberated over its first major foreign policy problem: whether to accede to the Geneva Protocol.[101] This proposal had been fostered by Ramsay MacDonald, Chamberlain's predecessor, as a means of reconciling differing Anglo-French views on ensuring European security. Designed to remove weakness in the League Covenant, the Protocol was a three-part initiative by which League members would accept arbitration in all international disputes, disarm by agreement, and undertake mutual support in the event of unprovoked aggression. Its chance of success lay with the attitudes of Britain and France, respectively, the most powerful naval and military League members, since enforcement of its mutual support provisions would fall chiefly to them. MacDonald had been concerned primarily with effecting a Franco-German reconciliation, but the Protocol's universal application assumed that Britain, by acceptance, would employ willingly its diplomatic or naval power with equal force in Eastern Europe, the Far East, or South America.

Chamberlain joined the CID sub-committee which was to examine the Protocol and recommend either its acceptance or rejection and, in gathering information privately on the subject, he instructed Howard to ascertain American reactions.[102] This was necessary because the United States stood outside the League and, as the application of British naval power to enforce the Protocol would mean blockade, the lessons of the Great War could not be ignored. Chamberlain believed that Americans tended to put trade and financial matters above 'those larger interests and general principles of equity in the international sphere'. Although he made it clear that he was not criticising or complaining of American policy, the possibility of British blockade action affecting United States maritime commerce had to be assessed.

Howard responded with two reports. The first recorded official disfavour with which the Coolidge Administration regarded the Protocol's mutual support provisions.[103] Howard met with Hughes, Coolidge's departing secretary of state, who emphasised that League interference through the Protocol could never be permitted by the United States in areas of the world where American interests were judged to be vital. He was concerned principally with Latin America, arguing that any League action in Central or South America would see an 'explosion of opinion' in the United States. To soften the impact of these words, Hughes indicated that, although governments might be drawn easily into conflict 'in a moment of national excitement', business interests would not allow their relations to be severed at the whim of the League. In Hughes' estimation the Protocol remained unenforceable for this reason; he hoped it 'would die a natural death'. Howard's second report assessed general American views, the tone of which was set with the observation that 'nervousness' about the Protocol was not confined to the White House and State Department.[104] Americans, he observed, feared the League might drive a wedge between them and Latin America:

People here have got to look on the Pan-American idea and the Monroe Doctrine as one and the same thing. If you touch the Pan-American idea you threaten the Monroe Doctrine, and if you threaten the Monroe Doctrine you are a danger to the United States.

Although official American opposition was not the over-riding factor in the eventual British decision to reject the Protocol, Chamberlain added to the anti-Protocol sentiment by circulating a memorandum that was based on the Howard–Hughes conversation.[105]

As far as cementing a firm relationship with the foreign secretary, Howard's efforts over the Protocol meant three things. First, he demonstrated that he could record and assess quickly a wide spectrum of American opinion, thereby assisting Chamberlain and the Cabinet in making difficult political decisions. Next, his reports not only reinforced Chamberlain's opinions about the United States, for instance, the sanctity of trade and commerce, they showed there were obstacles blocking a smooth League–United States relationship.[106] Last, Howard demonstrated that he could tread on dangerous political ground without upsetting his hosts or compromising his government.

The principal drawback of the Washington Embassy was its geographic isolation on the American east coast. As the nature of the work done by Howard and his staff required speedy evaluations of issues and their immediate despatch to London, views prevalent in Washington's political and social circles, and in the major eastern newspapers, formed the basis of Embassy analyses.[107] Since time, expense, and distance mitigated against extensive Embassy travel, Howard recognised that he and his subordinates were detached in many ways from American life in the South and west of the Mississippi Valley.[108] Thus, a subsidiary branch of the diplomatic service, the British Library of Information at New York City – BLINY – supplemented the embassy's political appraisals with valuable assessments of national press opinion.[109]

Because of Willert, the Foreign Office tended to equate American public opinion with press opinion. BLINY reported directly to the News Department, though it did have liaison with the Embassy; its purpose was two-fold: 'to serve as a clearing house, where information on British affairs is made available to the American public, while information is secured from American sources on various matters of interest to the Foreign Office and other departments'.[110] BLINY received newspapers from all over the United States, summarised them topically, and sent these summaries weekly to London. Willert had great confidence in Robert Wilberforce and Angus Fletcher, the two principal BLINY staff who had spent nearly their whole government service in the United States. He established a regular correspondence with them, often having them conduct special surveys of press opinion on specific issues when the Foreign Office required help in creating diplomatic strategy. In this way the British diplomatic service in the United States, the tandem of Esme Howard at Washington and BLINY, was fundamental to the formal process that created and implemented the American policy of the second Baldwin government.

2 . FOREIGN OFFICE PERCEPTION OF REPUBLICAN FOREIGN POLICY, NOVEMBER 1924–MAY 1927

In view of the general odium in which America is held, it is fully as important to her to remember what we think of her as it is for us to worry about what she thinks of us.

Vansittart, August 1926

The blockade claims controversy

Three months after Chamberlain became foreign secretary, Cecil Hurst travelled by ship to the United States. On board he met Frank Kellogg, the American ambassador at London who had just resigned and was returning to Washington to take office as Coolidge's new secretary of state. In the course of a general conversation, the secretary-designate commented on the subject of outstanding claims that his government had against the British government; Hurst understood him to include with these blockade claims dating from the Great War. Between August 1914 and April 1917 a large number of American industrialists, shippers, and other traders, who lost cargoes that were intercepted and seized as war contraband or who believed that the British blockade had interfered with their neutral right to trade and as a result had lessened their profits, filed private complaints against the British government through the State Department at Washington. These were the blockade claims. In reporting this conversation to the Foreign Office,[1] Hurst suggested that he might have been mistaken in assuming that Kellogg had included blockade claims; nevertheless, he recommended that preparatory work on this question should begin.

Coolidge's selection of Kellogg as secretary of state in January 1925 had surprised the Chamberlain Foreign Office. It was an unwelcome choice as far as the foreign secretary and his advisers were concerned because they had been provided with the rare opportunity, albeit a short one, to assess first-hand the capabilities of a man who became one of their most powerful opposites. A senator during the war and peace conference period, Kellogg had risen to prominence as a formidable legal strategist. He had served as Theodore Roosevelt's 'trust-buster', and he had been the architect of the successful dismemberment of the Standard Oil Company and the Union Pacific Railway.[2] But at the time of his appointment as secretary of state, Kellogg was sixty-eight years old and had completed a rather unspectacular year as the American ambassador at London. He was an irascible individual who possessed an extremely short temper, a combination which did nothing to help him in his ambassadorial duties.[3]

In a letter to Howard written a few days after the announcement of Kellogg's promotion, Chamberlain expressed the Foreign Office's surprise at Coolidge's choice.[4] Admitting that he might be under-estimating the man, Chamberlain confessed that 'what little I have seen of Kellogg in business relations had left me with the impression that he was a somewhat tired man, who had lost his power of grip and decision'. The foreign secretary was also of the opinion that Kellogg had a tendency to rely too heavily on his subordinates. Howard echoed Foreign Office misgivings after assessing Washington's reaction to the appointment.[5] As far as the ambassador could determine, general Washington opinion held that the new secretary represented a 'stop gap' in Coolidge's political planning. It was felt that the president required an individual at the State Department, at least for the first part of his new Administration, who could work well with the Senate whilst having first hand knowledge of European problems.

After Hurst returned from the United States, he submitted a minute providing background to his initial report.[6] Because of Kellogg's remarks, he had taken the initiative collecting information on American blockade claims, unofficially and informally, from 'anybody who was likely to be well informed'. The situation's seriousness emerged with his disclosure that three State Department officials, under the direction of the legal division, had been assigned to devote full attention to a 'careful and exhaustive consideration' of all American claims against the British government.[7] The thrust of this examination was to determine which claims, including blockade claims, were valid and then to prepare these for presentation. Hurst remained convinced that the Americans would not be dissuaded from submitting blockade claims by virtue of United States entry into the war as a British ally. But because of anticipated changes in the State

Department's legal division, scheduled for July, he believed that there would be no reason to expect an early presentation. He recommended once again that preparatory work commence. He further suggested that a CID sub-committee that had been set up in 1924, with responsibility for formulating principles of British blockade policy in the event of future war, advise on analogous questions.[8]

Seven months elapsed between the submission of Hurst's clarifying minute and the first report from Washington that the Americans would present their claims. In the interim the Foreign Office began to prepare the British case. Essentially this entailed the creation of diplomatic 'make-weights', for the obvious counter to the American claims was to determine what outstanding ones British authorities had against the United States government, to collect them, and to have them ready to off-set the American presentation.[9] There was no sense of urgency in this period, even though Hurst discovered in August, after attending the Institute of International Law at The Hague and meeting with American delegates, that a new assistant under-secretary of state, Robert Olds, had been appointed specifically to supervise all of the international arbitration work for which the State Department was responsible.[10] When Howard's message arrived in late October 1925 announcing that the Americans were intent on pressing their claims,[11] the Foreign Office preparatory work was almost completed.

Two weeks before Howard's message, Craigie wrote a memorandum which discussed the entire claims question in terms of the options facing British policy if the blockade claims were put forward.[12] Vansittart requested this paper as he felt 'that it was futile to attempt to advise on the details of claims policy until [the Foreign Office] had reached a firm decision on the question of principle'. Craigie envisaged three practical responses to an American presentation. There could be an agreement to enter into negotiations and, in the process, present the 'make-weights' to off-set the blockade claims. On the other hand, there could be an outright rejection of the American claims coupled with the assertion that the thesis on which they were based, if acknowledged by the British government, could jeopardise the application of British belligerent rights in any future war. Once this had been accepted by the Americans, the Foreign Office could agree to arbitrate any outstanding non-blockade claims. Last, all American claims could be rejected *in toto* with no question about arbitrating any one of them.

Craigie emphasised that there was no legal means by which the Americans could force an arbitration of blockade claims. Existing agreements providing machinery for the resolution of Anglo-American disputes – the 1908 arbitration convention and the 1914 peace commission treaty[13] – could be utilised only if Britain was willing. The desirability of avoiding arbitration stemmed from the certainty that, if the United States was successful in securing compensation, other former neutral Powers would press to have their claims handled similarly. Though unstated in Craigie's memorandum, two crucial factors had also to be considered in any arbitration of claims entered into with former neutrals. There was the possibility that if Britain lost, the already beleaguered Treasury would have to find additional revenues in difficult economic times. It also meant the chance that at a stroke the legal basis of the British wartime blockade, built around an Order in Council of March 1915, and the legal remedies designed to provide a fair hearing to foreigners with claims, for instance, the Prize Courts, could be questioned.[14] Hence, more important than mere money, British principles of maritime belligerent rights judged to be vital to Imperial defence could be compromised.

Craigie opined that the American blockade claims had to be headed off because, once they were put forward, a British refusal to arbitrate would be 'strongly resented' in the United States. In addition, he also felt that British resistance might be difficult after a presentation in the light of 'the existing drift in favour of arbitration for practically all international disputes'. He suggested that a blockade claims controversy could have a serious effect on British public opinion by feeding on the strong current of anti-American feeling that he maintained was prevalent in Britain. As he saw it, this was the result of the American rejection of Versailles and the hard bargain that had been driven during the settlement of Britain's war debt. He worried that an adverse reaction by the British public over this issue could undermine Anglo-American cordiality and prejudice seriously any prospect of useful cooperation between the two countries.

To stave off controversy he suggested that a direct appeal be made to Coolidge. If Howard could impress on the president that the idea of a presentation was not only 'preposterous' but that it could be detrimental to British public good will, the idea of a claims presentation might be abandoned. To Craigie, Coolidge appeared to be much stronger than Kellogg and, thus, better able to withstand the pressure to present claims that was coming from various quarters, notably the State Department's legal division. Craigie stressed that this preemptive action would best be undertaken after the British government's attitude toward an American presentation was decided.

Howard reported in his telegram of 26 October that Olds had said that blockade claims would be presented shortly. The ambassador sought permission to take up the question immediately with Kellogg and, possibly, Coolidge, and to prevent the matter going further he asked for legal arguments by which Britain could resist the claims. Campbell believed that the claims might still be headed off through Craigie's idea of a direct appeal to Coolidge and, as speed was crucial, he felt that valuable time should not be spent debating whether or not to refuse an American demand for arbitration.[15] He advised against supplying Howard with the relevant legal arguments, since he believed that this was the sort of thing in which the State Department revelled.

Hurst also supported Craigie's suggestion of a direct appeal to the president, though he was not sanguine about a positive result.[16] He contended that the American government lacked the courage to oppose any American claimant. Moreover, since the debt and reparations questions had been settled, those in which Washington had an interest, government support of private claims could not imperil other financial considerations. He noted that the legal arguments could not be forwarded as they had yet to be decided. He argued against Howard making much of Craigie's contention about the adverse effect of the claims on British public opinion. He commented bluntly:

It will not much alter the outlook of the average Englishman. The debt and similar claims on the part of the United States have already made the average Englishman think the Americans are dirty swine, and I doubt whether this will make him think them very much dirtier.

As the question of replying to Howard made its way upward in the Foreign Office, there was unanimous support for a Howard–Coolidge meeting.[17] Hurst's *caveat* about the futility of mentioning the adverse effect a claims presentation would have within Britain was ignored, as Craigie's suggestion to make much of the alarm with which the claims would be greeted in Britain was endorsed.

Chamberlain first looked at the blockade problem early on the morning of 31 October. For the preceding ten months he had been preoccupied with European security and had only returned to London the previous afternoon with the Locarno accords in his pocket. He reacted swiftly and decisively on the probable American presentation by endorsing the Howard–Coolidge meeting and the instructions to stress the negative effect such a policy would have on Anglo-American relations.[18] Coolidge was to be told point blank that differences on this issue could reintroduce wartime controversies, disturb international relations, and possibly defeat the purpose of Locarno. Howard was even to suggest that the president might be playing into the hands of those who sought to 'drive a wedge' between Britain and the United States over the issue of the freedom of the seas.[19] Privately, Chamberlain expressed surprise and dismay at the possibility of an American presentation; he wrote to his sister, noting that he agreed with his advisers that it was an issue of 'the very highest political importance'.[20]

To strengthen his position, the foreign secretary called in Alanson Houghton, the American ambassador at London, to discuss the matter. Chamberlain developed the points that Howard had been instructed to make to Coolidge, and Houghton replied that he had heard nothing from Washington. He failed to understand Chamberlain's concern: 'Debts were to him debts – they must be paid by somebody.'[21] But agreeing that there could be nothing worse than an Anglo-American dispute, Houghton gave assurances that he would do all possible to achieve 'an amicable settlement'. When he saw the report of this meeting, Craigie wasted no time in rebutting the attempt to equate blockade claims with debts:

It would be very unfortunate if the American public mind were allowed to become confused between war debts and blockade claims. The 'debt', if any, is by the United States to us, since these United States claims are in respect of losses incurred through the frustrated efforts of United States citizens to provide Germany with food and material during the war. If the transactions had materialised, the war would have been prolonged and more United States lives would have been lost.[22]

Howard had trouble in seeing Coolidge. Following precedent, he informed Kellogg that he wanted to see the president on an important matter; indeed, he read a paraphrase of the Foreign Office telegram to the secretary of state. Kellogg suggested that this meeting be postponed until he became conversant with the claims question, about which he professed ignorance. Howard reported this, adding that Kellogg believed there was no hurry about discussing the matter.[23] The State Department did not intend to press the claims at once. This was exactly what the Foreign Office feared. In a strongly worded reply that bordered on a reprimand, Howard was told to see Coolidge without delay.[24] Chamberlain did not want the president to be primed with State Department legal arguments nor did he want the British message to become diluted before it reached the White House. If the latter occurred, the State Department's case could possibly appear stronger. The key was to impress Coolidge with the seriousness of the matter, regardless of the validity of the claims, and to do this before Kellogg could discuss it with him.

Two days later Howard reported on his meeting with the president, a meeting which Kellogg attended.[25] After Howard read the initial Foreign Office message about the gravity with which London regarded the issue, he was told that these particular claims had not been brought to Kellogg's attention. Kellogg did understand, however, that there were a number of British government claims pending against the United States government and that the entire claims question would require much study. Howard countered quickly that there was a distinction between blockade claims, which were those of private citizens, and other types, for instance, inter-governmental claims existing between the British Board of Trade and the United States Shipping Board.

Coolidge remained friendly throughout the interview and appeared genuinely struck by what had been said. He did mention that he thought Chamberlain had been 'unduly alarmed' but, admitting his ignorance on the matter, promised that he would look into the question. Coolidge was unequivocal in stressing that there was no urgency in this and that his Administration would not present claims without prior consultation. He did not want to make the situation difficult for Britain as he had 'admiration and respect' for the way in which it had come forward to settle its war debt. He concluded by remarking that he valued good Anglo-American relations and would do nothing to damage them. When the meeting ended, Kellogg reiterated that a presentation would never have been made without prior consultation and, at least from Howard's description, appeared hurt that the British thought otherwise.

Foreign Office reaction to the Howard–Coolidge meeting was one of relief: the Americans were not ready to make their presentation.[26] Howard had redeemed himself by presenting the British case with such clarity that an American submission of claims could not be made in ignorance of the political consequences. Campbell discerned from this that it seemed as if the Americans had been waiting to see what the British position would be over unsettled inter-governmental claims.

Inter-governmental claims had been a simmering issue from about the time of Hurst's visit to the United States in February 1925. They were of consequence because the initial Chamberlain Foreign Office image of the Kellogg State Department was unfavourable and derived from the issue of blockade versus inter-governmental claims. In a letter to Thompson, then at the Washington Embassy, H. T. Kingsbury, a lawyer in the New York firm of Coudert Brothers, the British government's American legal advisers, reported that the State Department was attempting to stall inter-governmental claims which he was conducting.[27] He was representing the Board of Trade which was seeking £2.7 million from the United States Shipping Board for the 'German vessels claim'. This originated in 1919 when certain German vessels in the custody of the Shipping Board were allocated to Britain by inter-Allied agreement. Their delivery was delayed for some unspecified reason and, as a result, considerable British expense was incurred over the wages and subsistence of crews despatched to the United States to ferry those vessels to Britain. In early 1925, after lengthy wrangling, the Shipping Board admitted that the claim was one proper for direct settlement between the departments involved. But Kingsbury reported that the State Department disagreed and that it was moving to prevent these inter-governmental discussions from occurring. The Foreign Office perceived this as a State Department ploy to use the German vessels claim both as a peg on which to hang blockade claims and as a bargaining counter.[28]

To prevent this from happening, Vansittart met with Treasury and Board of Trade officials to curtail further inter-governmental discussion on the matter of these claims.[29] Pressure from these departments for settlement continued, especially from the Treasury which had to worry about the payment of British debt monies to the United States.[30] But the effect of outside interference in the settlement of inter-governmental business created the impression in the Foreign Office that the impetus for the presentation of blockade claims came from within the State Department. Once it appeared that such a presentation was imminent, Chamberlain demanded that neither the Treasury nor the Board of Trade discuss inter-governmental claims with American authorities without prior Foreign Office consent.[31]

After the Howard–Coolidge meeting, Anglo-American efforts on blockade claims centred on arriving at a mutually agreeable method for settlement. Kellogg preferred the establishment of a joint commission to consider all claims existing between the two governments, and this was repeated to Howard whenever he saw the secretary of state during the next six months.[32] It seemed that the State Department was intent on coupling American blockade claims against Britain with British inter-governmental claims against the United States. The Foreign Office took the opposite view, that all unsettled claims should be discussed separately, each on its own merit, and only by the departments concerned. It wanted shelved inter-governmental negotiations, such as those on the German vessels, to resume.[33] In this procedure of direct departmental discussion, the Foreign Office would be the British agency which would handle blockade claims.

The opposing British and American views were reconciled in a lengthy diplomatic correspondence, the precise details of which are not germane to this analysis. Of significance only are its main points and its result.[34] By May 1926 agreement was achieved whereby a joint examination of blockade claims was to be undertaken. The State Department had begun placing all of its claims on a single list in January 1926. In late March, since the Foreign Office refused adamantly to arbitrate and opposed a joint commission, Spencer Phenix, a member of the State Department legal division, mooted the idea of a joint examination to Howard. After much haggling, a result of Kellogg at first wanting a joint commission, then agreeing to a joint examination, and then changing his mind again,[35] it was agreed that a member of the British Embassy would examine the State Department list so that London would know precisely what the Americans meant by 'blockade claims'. J. J. Broderick, the commercial counsellor, was chosen, and Phenix, selected as the American examiner, was to accompany him. After the joint examination in Washington, which was to be unofficial and ostensibly for Broderick's information, Phenix would travel to London and likewise, unofficially and just for his information, examine British records to determine the status of the claims remaining on the list. The Foreign Office agreed to Phenix's suggestion – it was exactly what was wanted – because it had the potential of reducing the American list which supposedly contained several thousand claims. But the Foreign Office was determined that neither Broderick's enquiries nor Phenix's mission would commit Britain to the negotiation of blockade claims; both steps were to be considered as simply for the gathering of information and as preliminary to any further British consideration of the means of resolving the claims question. By securing a joint examination, the Foreign Office succeeded both in lessening the chance of an American call to arbitrate and in impressing on the Americans that there would be no negotiation of any claim which had the potential of questioning the application of British belligerent rights.

There was nothing altruistic in the American willingness to end the stalemate on settling claims. Kellogg was beginning to experience the pressures that Latin American problems could bring to bear on American diplomacy. His short temper and easily aroused irritability were becoming more pronounced as the Tacna–Arica dispute exacerbated his foreign policy[36] – so much so that his nick-name of 'Nervous Nellie' proved apt. As well, the spectre of possible Senate interference in blockade claims appeared in mid-March 1926. Senator William Borah, the chairman of the Senate Foreign Relations Committee, had introduced a resolution calling on Kellogg to advise the Senate on what steps he was taking to negotiate claims settlements with Britain and France. Even though they might have been well intentioned, Borah's endeavours worried the Foreign Office and frightened Kellogg.[37] Kellogg did not need the senator at his back, pushing him along, and complicating an already difficult task. Hoping to placate Borah somewhat, Kellogg again waivered, this time between supporting the notion of joint examination and Borah's desire to arbitrate all outstanding claims. Fortunately the senator was ignorant of the preliminary claims discussions then in progress and his concern about this matter lasted only as long as that Congressional session.[38]

Howard saw the president to impress on him British anxiety over Borah, and Coolidge again expressed concern about the necessity for healthy Anglo-American relations.[39] Obviously finding Borah and his antics distasteful, he commented dryly that the senator had no connexion with his Administration. Coolidge offered a very frank appraisal of the erratic Borah:

The Senator, he said, was by accident of seniority chairman of the Foreign Relations Committee of the Senate and the Government had naturally to have frequent communication with him, but that did not mean that they approved of his policies in foreign affairs. He often seemed, said Mr Coolidge, not to mind how much he antagonised the countries with which the Administration most desired to be on friendly terms.

When the president enquired about why British authorities persisted in believing that his government would present 'all kinds of claims arising out of the blockade', Howard explained that the State Department, especially its legal division, had made this quite clear.[40] From this conversation, it appears that the predominant support within the Coolidge Administration for a joint examination came from the president rather than the secretary of state.

In order not to add fire to the guns of critics to any Anglo-American deal on settling blockade claims, both the Foreign Office and the State Department wanted the Broderick–Phenix joint examination to maintain a low profile. It was Kellogg who suggested that Phenix's mission to London be undertaken secretly; he also thought that it would be advantageous if the mission occurred whilst Congress was in recess.[41] In this way the legislative activities of Borah and others would not upset a delicate diplomatic process and, Kellogg argued, the success of any agreement that the Administration could negotiate would be more certain if Congress was presented with a *fait accompli*. Significantly, Borah had made some comments about not caring if the United States realised 'ten cents' on a claims presentation as long as neutral rights in wartime were established.[42] At Kellogg's suggestion it was arranged that Phenix's mission be screened by his accompanying a United States Navy Department delegation that would be travelling to London sometime in the summer of 1926.[43] Secrecy in this matter sat well with the Foreign Office since Britain, too, had its Borahs.[44]

Adding to the need for secrecy were the actions of Herbert Hoover, the American secretary of commerce, during the rubber controversy of 1926. Hoover was a dynamic force within the Coolidge Administration and, in December 1925, he levelled charges that the British monopoly of crude rubber production 'mulcted' the United States of nearly $700 million per year.[45] There is no doubt that the British government at London, through the Colonial Office, did monopolise the production and distribution of over three-quarters of the world's crude rubber production or that the United States consumed this same staggering amount. But the control that existed in 1925 had not been there in 1918 when American rubber consumption was restricted to free shipping for wartime purposes, an action that depressed world rubber prices. After the war prices dropped further, the combination of an increased cultivation between 1914 and 1918 to meet wartime demand and a postwar fall in that demand.[46] By 1921 rubber prices had dropped below the costs of production, and the Colonial Office moved to regulate production and distribution. There were three main reasons for this: a substantial British capital investment, something approaching £100 million in Malaya alone, that had to be protected; the possibility that if planters abandoned large unprofitable areas plant diseases could spread; and the chance of British-controlled plantations being purchased at 'break-up' prices by foreigners, a situation that could lead to a reduction of British influence in the East Indies. A Colonial Office investigation by an *ad hoc* body, the Stevenson Committee, occurred in late 1921 and concluded that two different policies offered the hope of revitalising the flagging British rubber industry. The first entailed the simple control of production to an agreed annual level. The second envisaged a more complicated system whereby the government imposed a graduated scale of duties to prevent the export of more than an agreed percentage of production – 100 per cent would be the levels attained between November 1919 and December 1920. Because growers in the Dutch East Indies refused to restrict their production, the British were forced to adopt the second Stevenson proposal. It was the scale of duties attached to it that Hoover disliked; his activities to reduce them threatened to embitter Anglo-American relations.

Throughout 1926 tempers on both sides of the Atlantic rose over the Stevenson scheme strictures. Powerful American industrialists whose wealth derived from rubber followed Hoover's lead and funded propaganda campaigns that attacked vigorously British control. The Ohio tyre manufacturer, Harvey Firestone, lobbied with such intensity that by August, in a flurry of publicity, he was at the White House impressing on Coolidge the supposed threat to American interests. The president responded by endorsing Firestone's commitment to obtain independent American supplies of raw rubber. Firestone immediately began efforts, eventually successful, to purchase one million acres of northern Liberia for his plantations.[47] Equally influential men in Britain complained about American pique at the obvious American inability to manipulate the production and distribution of this one valuable natural resource when they did to so many others. Steel-Maitland, Baldwin's minister of labour, was so moved by what he saw as American bad taste that he wrote privately to Tyrrell offering to supply evidence of American efforts to monopolise world electrolytic copper production. Steel-Maitland indicated that he had documentary proof, if the Foreign Office required it, that the United States government discouraged American nationals after the Great War from participating in a venture to erect an electrolytic copper refinery in Britain.[48]

For whatever reasons, though assuredly to enhance his chances for the 1928 presidential election, Hoover's attack on the rubber monopoly continued intermittently throughout 1926. As a result the American and British press railed at each other on the subject, a situation that suggested that latent British and American animosities toward one another were aroused easily.[49] It also suggested that over a far more emotive issue, such as belligerent rights versus the freedom of the seas, the certain result of the inter-governmental examination of blockade claims becoming public, the chance to bring about a settlement calmly and rationally would evaporate in the heat of a chauvinistic press debate.

The Broderick–Phenix examination of claims on record at Washington saw the original three thousand pared down to about eleven hundred. This large reduction occurred because, as Broderick reported, 'the gentleman who compiled the index had used his imagination with some freedom, inserting, in many instances, various grounds for claim that had never occurred to the claimants themselves'.[50] Phenix's mission to London was designed to diminish the number further by examining British records; he began his task on 1 September accompanied by Broderick.

At this juncture Vansittart emerges as the dominant British personality in the events that led to the final extinction of the controversy. In two inspired papers written in late August and early September,[51] he outlined a strategy to resolve the issue that endangered neither the Treasury nor British principles of maritime belligerent rights. Endorsed by Chamberlain and Tyrrell, Vansittart implemented this scheme himself and by Christmas an agreement settling blockade claims was realised. Vansittart's attitude towards the Americans and their claims, typical of his competitive nature, is exemplified by his comparison of the controversy to test cricket, a game in which superior British batters could be brutal if provoked:

We don't want to score, but if America will persist in bowling vicious full pitches at our ribs, we shall be compelled to hit them out of the ground, & Europe will rise and applaud in the stands.

His strategy was to couple a personal frankness and openness towards the State Department and its problems with a Foreign Office resolve to preserve British interest at all costs. He could sincerely tell Phenix that 'I understand the Borah pressure', and at the same time minute: 'Mr Phenix is coming over here for information. He is going to get it; he is also going to get it in the neck if necessary.'

Vansittart suggested that the American examiner be given every opportunity to consult the British records pertaining to the outstanding claims remaining on the State Department list. At the same time nothing would be mentioned about the 'make-weights' that the Foreign Office had gathered. Vansittart believed that Phenix should be given his head in this examination and, after explaining to Phenix why the majority of claims were completely unacceptable to the British government, the one thousand or so could be reduced to somewhere around fifty. This was possible because Vansittart believed Phenix to be young, on the make, and hence desirous of proving to his superiors of how much work he was capable.[52] Vansittart contended that once the magic figure of fifty claims was attained, negotiation should occur between representatives of the two governments.[53] Through such negotiations the fifty could be reduced to five or six, a sum representing what was reckoned to be the number of 'meritorious' claims.[54] With this, the lowest level to which the American list could be taken, the Foreign Office could counter with their 'make-weights', the value of which could be fixed to approximate whatever was left on the American list.[55] This would be 'the material for a "deal" on condition of a total and final extinction of every other claim'.

The final negotiation was to be the most important part of the settlement. Phenix was to be told candidly that in no circumstances would the Foreign Office negotiate a final settlement with him. His mission was just to examine, and besides he did not possess the requisite authority. Olds, on vacation with his family in Europe, was scheduled to be in London on 20 September; Vansittart advised that he be approached about the negotiation of a final settlement.[56] Olds would be informed that any final negotiation could not occur in London – despite the secrecy enshrouding Phenix's mission, some articles in the *Morning Post* about the reasons for his presence at

London had caused enquiries to be made at the Foreign Office. Any departure from excuses given that he was there just for an enquiry could cause a serious reaction that might jeopardise a final settlement. Unknown to the Foreign Office, the *Times* correspondent at Washington, Wilmot Lewis, had been fully apprised of the reason for Phenix's journey – Broderick was his good friend – and he informed Geoffrey Dawson, the editor, at once.[57] But Dawson decided not to pursue the matter.

Vansittart calculated that the key to success was to have any claims negotiation 'done tidily and tranquilly on the other side after Mr Phenix has gone home with his reduced list and been partially forgotten'. Vansittart would suggest such a course to Olds, though declaring that he was speaking only for himself and for no one higher in the Foreign Office. Once Olds had departed and after the Phenix mission was completed, the claims issue would be allowed to stagnate until November. At that time, with Congress less than a month away from reconvening, Olds would be informed that higher authorities at London were willing to reconsider the meritorious cases. As Vansittart would be in the United States then, visiting his wife's family, he indicated that he would be willing to undertake these final negotiations for the British government.

This broad strategy succeeded.[58] Phenix received all of the assistance he required in working through his list, and from the beginning it was made clear that the Foreign Office would not entertain the possibility of his mission doubling as one for negotiation.[59] When Olds arrived at London he was approached about arranging a final extinction of the controversy, and the advantages of doing so in Washington were broached. Olds took this information back to the State Department, the notion of direct and secret negotiation was accepted, and Vansittart arrived at Washington in mid-November to begin the final liquidation of claims.

Although the Foreign Office handled the blockade claims question independently of other departments of state, it was decided to have Vansittart's actions monitored by an inter-departmental committee composed of representatives from the Admiralty, the Board of Trade, the Colonial and Dominion Offices, the Treasury, and the Foreign Office. These departments each had a stake in the final settlement. Occasionally it was judged necessary to instruct Vansittart on a particular point; thus, at every stage, his mission had the advantage of being endorsed by all interested government departments.[60] However, even though this inter-departmental committee was privy to the events going on at Washington, the Foreign Office was reticent about the conduct of this diplomacy even within the government.[61] On 11 December an agreement was reached whereby American meritorious claims were to be cancelled by the British 'make-weights'.[62] The agreement was to take the form of an exchange of notes, a sound diplomatic practice that avoided the whims and caprices of American legislative ratification. Since all that remained was the signature and exchange of notes, Vansittart departed after the negotiation was concluded; Howard was delegated as the British plenipotentiary. It was anticipated that the agreement would be signed by Christmas.

Howard saw Kellogg on Christmas Eve and learnt that a short delay was unavoidable as Coolidge's sanction to the settlement had yet to be obtained, and, more ominously, that it was decided for domestic reasons to consult Borah.[63] Sensing difficulty, Howard instructed Broderick to see Olds and ascertain the precise reasons for delay. Broderick discovered that Kellogg had not yet become 'thoroughly familiar' with the details of the settlement so as to discuss it with Coolidge. As well, the State Department had not yet agreed on whether to consult Borah, though Kellogg and, possibly, Coolidge were inclined to do so. Olds did not expect trouble, though if it arose he would inform the Embassy at once.

The signature and exchange did not occur until 19 May 1927, one month before the Coolidge conference convened at Geneva and, significantly, on the eve of Anglo-American naval deadlock. In the five months between the end of Vansittart's mission and the signature and exchange, Kellogg's stock and that of the State Department fell to new lows within the Foreign Office. The reason most often given to Howard excusing the delay was that the growing problems that Kellogg faced in China, Mexico, and Nicaragua diverted his attention from the claims settlement.[64] Instructed periodically to press for the formal conclusion of the agreement, Howard witnessed Kellogg's mounting irascibility that stemmed from the pressures of these problems. By March 1927 Kellogg was so exhausted that he was forced to take two weeks leave to regain his strength. When Kellogg was away, Howard met with Coolidge to impress on him British desires for an early signature; he became aware that the president had only the sketchiest idea of what had been agreed.[65]

An amusing though important event occurred at this time which showed the Foreign Office that coordination was lacking within the

American government on this particular foreign policy problem. In early March the Treasury received a cheque from the United States comptroller for $450 thousand which the United States Navy Department believed it owed the Admiralty. However, this particular sum had been waived during Vansittart's mission. The Treasury threatened to cash the cheque and put the funds in a suspense account pending the exchange of notes, and only under Foreign Office pressure returned the cheque uncashed.[66] Dismissed in Washington as a 'stupid mistake', this incident did not impress Chamberlain or his advisers with American efficiency.[67]

In the end the agreement was signed because of an unauthorised press leak. The *Baltimore Sun* had somehow discovered that a claims settlement was near and published this news on the morning of 19 May.[68] Howard was called in immediately and the claims agreement was signed and exchanged the same day. The speed by which American authorities moved to formalise the five-month-old agreement once there was a chance of the issues it raised being ventilated in public demonstrated Coolidge Administration fear of newspapermen scuttling the work of two years.

The lessons of the blockade claims controversy

The blockade claims controversy provided the Chamberlain Foreign Office with a number of valuable lessons about the Republican United States and its foreign policy. These derived from the obvious schism within the United States over this important aspect of government which went beyond the normal constitutional division of power. Besides the president and Kellogg, Borah, members of the State Department, and cabinet ministers seemed able both to influence markedly particular policies as well as to initiate their own. Complicating the situation was a vociferous press whose interest in foreign affairs sometimes led to interesting conclusions.

Coolidge appeared to be genuinely pro-British, and his often-voiced opinion about the need to preserve good Anglo-American relations clearly made a favourable impression on the ambassador at Washington and the Foreign Office at London.[69] Unfortunately the president seemed uninterested in international politics, and he seemed happy to abdicate the responsibility for this important aspect of his Administration's affairs.[70] In the two and one-half years preceding the period of Anglo-American naval deadlock, Coolidge did not originate a single foreign policy initiative – the naval conference bearing his name notwithstanding. Unless pressed by Howard, he never found it necessary to voice an opinion on the question of blockade claims. Quite often it looked as if the president had little idea about what his government was doing or attempting to do in the realm of foreign policy. Coolidge's incredulity at Howard's constant reference to the presentation of 'all kinds of claims arising out of the blockade' indicated either that he did not care about this crucial problem, with its grave economic and political implications, or that he was not being constantly informed by Kellogg. The Foreign Office tended to believe the latter, and the president's ignorance about the general lines of the final settlement as late as three months after its conclusion was accepted as proof.

Although the Foreign Office had a poor opinion of Kellogg as an ambassador, Chamberlain believed that he might show improvement once he returned to the United States and was surrounded by his own people.[71] The original Foreign Office assessment of Kellogg had not altered by May 1927. When Olds first mentioned to Howard that the State Department would present American blockade claims and Howard pressed Kellogg for a meeting with Coolidge, the secretary of state expressed genuine ignorance of what precisely this entailed. His vacillation between support of a joint examination and a joint commission, and, later, between a joint examination and Borah's idea of arbitration, did not endear him to the Foreign Office. His easily aroused irritability and nervousness that became more pronounced with each new crisis seemed to impair his ability to deal with other less critical but equally important matters. The five-month wait to sign and exchange the notes embodying the final settlement is exemplary. When the Foreign Office remembered that it was Kellogg's suggestion to conclude the agreement before Congress reconvened in December 1926,[72] its impatience with the man is understandable. In May 1927, as far as the Foreign Office was concerned, Frank Kellogg was a weak and indecisive secretary of state.

As perceived by the Foreign Office, the State Department represented a most influential element in the process that made United States policy toward Britain. It was within the State Department, specifically its legal division, that the thrust to present blockade claims originated. Hurst's clarifying minute in March 1925 had reported that three State Department officials under the legal division's direction were investigating blockade claims. State Department officials such as Olds and Phenix were constantly at the fore in this question, making it clear to the involved British diplomats that this issue was one which had to be resolved. Although the Foreign Office was unable to gauge precisely why the State Department wanted to press blockade claims – there was that early suspicion of a desire to link blockade and inter-governmental claims – Chamberlain and his advisers became convinced that the Coolidge Administration, represented by Kellogg, was unable to resist a determined State Department effort to pursue particular policies.

Borah's activities added an element of imbalance to American foreign policy. He had become chairman of the Senate Foreign Relations Committee in November 1924 on the sudden death of Henry Cabot Lodge. Although Coolidge could disclaim any Administration connexion with Borah, the senator was integral to the process that made American foreign policy; it followed that his endeavours determined to some extent the course that policy took. Borah was an honest, straightforward individual, but possessing the intolerance and stubbornness of one who believes that his answers are always correct. He once wrote: 'I do claim that I shall leave [the Senate] without having compromised on a single fundamental political belief which I entertain.'[73] This moral rectitude was united with an inflexible but brilliant political mind, a combination the Foreign Office recognised with regret.[74] Adept at using his position and the press to advantage, simultaneously fostering both his peculiar political beliefs and his career, Borah was a man with whom the Foreign Office had to reckon in pursuing its American policies.

During Coolidge's Presidency, American Cabinet members were much freer in their ministerial responsibilities than their British counterparts. It thus seemed to the Foreign Office that when individual American ministers pursued policies that encroached on the Administration's foreign policy, the chance existed that any diplomatic discussions in progress could be mauled severely. This is the way the Foreign Office viewed Hoover's attack on the British rubber monopoly. Hoover's assault also led the Foreign Office to form two conclusions about American politicians and foreign policy. First, Britain, its government, and its policies were easily identifiable scapegoats when an American politician appealed for support. Irish-American, German-American, and other domestic voter blocs could be depended on to uphold the basest anglophobic sentiments.

The Foreign Office had no control over this, appreciating that at any time Anglo-American relations could be disturbed by influential Americans exploiting domestic anglophobia for political advantage.[75] Second, the independence of Cabinet members and of men like Borah created the belief that most American politicians placed personal and party aims above the national interest in foreign policy.[76]

The Foreign Office also recognised the influence of the American press. Both the Foreign Office and the State Department succeeded in keeping secret the fact that Anglo-American discussions to resolve the claims question were being held. Hoover's appeal to the American public over the rubber monopoly demonstrated clearly that tempers on both sides of the Atlantic could be aroused easily by the press. The Foreign Office was realistic enough to recognise that the British counterparts to the Hearst press, Beaverbrook and Rothermere, could just as easily precipitate a press war with the Americans on a matter of national honour. The Coolidge Administration's sudden decision to formalise the claims settlement was significant, coming on the day that the *Baltimore Sun* published the leaked information about an imminent agreement. The connexion between the Coolidge Administration, the press, and American public opinion was not lost on the Chamberlain Foreign Office. But to the surprise of everyone, the claims settlement evoked little United States press comment.[77] This was puzzling: how could the American press, patriotic and chauvinistic to a fault, allow this important agreement to materialise without much comment or discussion? Howard offered what was accepted as the only plausible explanation: 'It is almost invariable practice on the part of the competing papers of this country to minimise the significance of an event in respect of which any one of them has achieved a "scoop".'[78]

The question arises about what lessons were deduced incorrectly from the blockade claims controversy. There was just one: that division over the creation of American foreign policy was endemic and could be counted on to stymie the unity needed for effective American diplomacy. This became an unspoken assumption in the Chamberlain Foreign Office since, after all, the blockade claims issue had demonstrated a lack of coordination between Coolidge and Kellogg, between Kellogg and his staff, and between the Administration and Congress; it had also shown an uneasy relationship between the government and press, the great arbiter of American public opinion. It was assumed that domestic American divisions had the potential of aiding British diplomacy.

Chamberlain and his advisers concluded that well-conceived diplomatic schemes, handled with subtlety, tact, and in reasonable secrecy, might preclude unity within the United States on foreign policy. Their attempt to effect a claims settlement at the departmental level was a good example; its success eliminated Congressional tampering at a stroke. Such ideas became fixed in the collective Foreign Office mind and, during the search to break the naval deadlock, led to initiatives like the Anglo-French disarmament compromise. By mid-1927 the Chamberlain Foreign Office felt it had come to grips with Republican foreign policy. To understand why certain British policies were formulated between mid-1927 and mid-1929, policies for which the Foreign Office has been blamed, understanding Foreign Office perceptions of American foreign policy on its eve is crucial. The delicate diplomacy involved during the blockade claims controversy is the key to that understanding.

3. THE ONSET OF NAVAL DEADLOCK, JUNE–AUGUST 1927

I am troubled about the cruiser question which seems to offer great difficulties. As far as I can make out, we are in the right on the basis of actual needs. America threatens to build for prestige an equal number, though her needs are not equal.

Chamberlain, July 1927

The cruiser question

In early 1927 President Coolidge called on the principal naval Powers to meet to complete the work of the Washington conference. At Washington these Powers – Britain, the United States, Japan, France, and Italy – restricted, respectively, the size and numbers of capital ships within a tonnage ratio of 5:5:3:1.75:1.75.[1] Although there had been heated exchanges about cruisers, it proved impossible to include them in the capital ship ratio. All that the delegations could do at Washington was to limit cruiser size to 10,000 tons and armament to eight-inch guns.

Only Britain, the United States, and Japan attended the Coolidge conference, which was held at Geneva between June and August 1927. It was anticipated that an agreement would be arranged to limit cruisers, destroyers, submarines, and auxiliary craft, such as mine-sweepers. The three Powers actually accomplished a great deal. They determined that there was no need to restrict auxiliary craft, and they succeeded in removing problems surrounding the limitation of submarines and destroyers – it was decided that there would be two classes of each type of vessel, squadron leaders and ordinary craft, and the appropriate maxima for each were established. Only over cruiser limitation was there disagreement, the result of an Anglo-American inability to compromise, and it was this that wrecked the conference, soured Anglo-American relations, and ushered in the period of naval deadlock.

The genesis of the Coolidge conference was one month after the

Republican Party's electoral success of November 1924. There is little doubt that Coolidge wanted to bring about some sort of international disarmament agreement; as the United States was essentially a maritime Power, this meant naval limitation.[2] He believed genuinely that a reduction in armaments would diminish the chances of war breaking out. Less idealistically, Coolidge was a devout Republican wedded to the principles of less taxation and less government spending. He could use an arms limitation agreement as a means of implementing policies of retrenchment. In December 1924, in a conversation with Curtis Wilbur, the United States secretary of the navy, Howard became aware of the president's desire for the convening of a disarmament conference. He reported this to the Foreign Office, indicating that the groundwork for such a conference would take a while to complete because of strained American–Japanese relations.[3]

Just at this time Congressional supporters of a large American navy attempted to force the pace in the matter of naval arms limitation. Some members of the House of Representatives began to agitate for the establishment of an enquiry into the feasibility of holding another naval conference along the lines of that held at Washington in 1921–22. Analysing this situation, and supported by Captain Francis Tottenham, the naval attaché at Washington, Howard concluded that the American navalists had two aims in mind.[4] If the enquiry decided that another Washington-type conference should be called because it could prove successful, the capital ship ratio might become universal, bringing with it Anglo-American naval parity. On the other hand, if convening such a conference seemed impractical or if it was allowed to meet despite the certainty of failure, Congressional navalists would be in a better position to wring money for increased naval construction out of a president who was disinclined to sanction such expenditure. Either way American navalists intended to secure United States naval equality with Britain.

The American Department supported Howard's contention, but it went further.[5] It saw the Congressional move as a strategy designed to remove by diplomatic means British superiority in light cruisers, that is, those smaller than the 10,000 ton maximum permitted by the Washington treaty. Despite this, the Foreign Office saw no urgency in the matter. Prior to issuing formal invitations to any conference, the American government would have to produce a specific disarmament programme, a project that would take time to accomplish. In

addition, once the Americans formulated their proposals, preliminary discussions with the interested Powers would have to be held to
see if any basis for agreement existed. It was suggested that hints
should be dropped to the Americans indicating that pre-conference
discussions would be necessary and indispensable to successful naval
limitation. As Vansittart reasoned: 'There is always a possibility that
America might go off at halfcock about another *naval* conference.'[6]

.When the House of Representatives passed a motion endorsing the
idea of a new naval conference, influential senators cautioned
Coolidge not to take precipitate action.[7] They felt that the European
Powers, preoccupied with the Geneva Protocol and Franco-German
security, were already considering disarmament. The president
would be unwise to involve himself at this early stage. Campbell and
Vansittart now believed that an American invitation to a new naval
conference was more remote than before. Coolidge would be unable
to move until the Protocol and the question of disarmament that it
raised had been resolved by the Europeans.[8] This assessment was
correct. In July the president indicated that he wanted to call a
disarmament conference but that he would wait until after the fate of
the security pact discussions then in progress – and which resulted in
Locarno – was known. In October, a week before the completion of
the security pact negotiations, press reports announced that Coolidge
wanted a disarmament conference to be held at Washington and that
he would take 'tepid interest' in one meeting elsewhere.[9] Once freed
from Locarno, Chamberlain assessed the American position. He
indicated that if the president's proposal entailed just naval
disarmament Britain would probably attend; if it included air and
land disarmament, Britain must respectfully decline as work was
already progressing on these two issues.[10]

The foreign secretary had in mind the anticipated general
disarmament conference that was to be held under the aegis of the
League. In the summer of 1925 the League Council had been
approached about establishing a body that would prepare the way for
such a conference.[11] In December the League Council established the
Preparatory Commission, indicating that it should meet as soon as
possible and posing a number of questions it had to resolve before the
general conference could convene. The British difficulty with all of
this was the matter of naval disarmament. As Chamberlain had noted
in October, Britain would have to confer with the United States on
this question. This was endorsed formally by the CID, which

concluded that proposals for naval disarmament would be 'useless' without American participation in the Preparatory Commission.[12] In December, under the prompting of Cecil and others, the League decided to ask the United States, the Soviet Union, and other non-League members to join the disarmament discussions at Geneva.

Chamberlain thought that the Americans would probably reject this invitation, and Cecil was instructed to yield to the proposal rather than to approve it.[13] To make the League understand the British concern over naval disarmament, and to ensure that the Americans would not be deluded into thinking that Britain would limit its naval forces unilaterally, Chamberlain informed the Council that the Baldwin government would be unable to discuss naval disarmament in a conference in which the United States was not present.[14] However, Kellogg did not dismiss the idea of American participation out of hand.[15] Coolidge had committed himself publicly to the aim of the Preparatory Commission, despite its intention to consider also air and land disarmament. Thus the Americans were forced to send a delegation to Geneva, and Kellogg selected Hugh Gibson, the American ambassador at Brussels, to lead the United States representatives. However, despite the tentative nature of the Commission, the Coolidge Administration manoeuvred to make certain that American attendance would not raise the matter of United States membership of the League. In approaching Congress for funds to send Gibson to Geneva, Coolidge stated plainly that: 'Participation in the work of the preparatory commission involves no commitment with respect to attendance upon any further conference or conferences on reduction and limitation of armaments.'[16] This not only conformed to the strictures imposed on the Administration by isolationist sentiment in the United States, it also provided the Americans with an easy way out in the event that the deliberations in the Preparatory Commission went against them. Until Coolidge decided to issue invitations for separate naval talks in February 1927, all international disarmament discussion centred in the Preparatory Commission.

Throughout 1926 the Americans tried to make a positive contribution at Geneva. This proved to be difficult as the Commission's two meetings in 1926 had done little more than push the date for convening the general conference further into the future. By the end of 1926 the possibility of an American call for separate naval talks loomed large. This had nothing to do with the international situation, rather it was a reflection of domestic American politics. During 1925 and 1926 Coolidge's Administration had been under attack by domestic critics on a number of fronts and, in November 1926, this had been translated into Republican losses at the polls.[17] In the House of Representatives the Democratic Party, the principal opposition, gained twelve seats whilst the Republicans lost ten. In a legislative chamber containing 435 seats and with a pre-election Republican majority of sixty, this was an unspectacular Democratic showing. With just ninety-six seats, the Senate was another matter. There a formidable Republican majority of sixteen fell to two. The lesson for the combined presidential–congressional elections scheduled for 1928 was obvious: if Coolidge wanted to repair Republican fortunes, a demonstration of effective government had to be the order of the day. International politics offered an easy option.

Although foreign affairs was a sphere in which the president had never involved himself and, indeed, had been one aspect of his Administration that had been severely criticised,[18] a coup here held the simplest, most effective means by which the Republican Party and Coolidge's electoral ambitions could be enhanced. By taking the initiative in the disarmament question, specifically naval disarmament, a number of political benefits could accrue to the Administration: government expenditures could be reduced; a breakthrough in naval arms limitation, inspired by the United States, could upstage the seemingly moribund, League-led Preparatory Commission; and the mantle of 'peace-maker' could fall on willing presidential shoulders. Coolidge's subsequent efforts to secure naval disarmament were geared solely to making a favourable impression on American voters and had little to do with allaying the fears that disarmament meant to other Powers.

On 7 December 1926, in his annual message to Congress, Coolidge announced that the extension of the Washington naval treaty to cover lesser craft remained a goal of his Administration.[19] He indicated that the other naval Powers had been apprised of this and that the American government would press for a naval conference when the time was right. Coolidge began immediately preparing the way for such a conference by indicating to the world that his Administration sincerely sought naval disarmament; he shelved appropriations from 1924 that were earmarked for the construction of three cruisers. On learning of this, Craigie discerned correctly that the president was 'becoming impatient with the Geneva proceedings and is turning again to the idea of a special naval disarmament conference'.[20]

The American Department was convinced that Coolidge would not propose such a conference unless United States public opinion believed that the Preparatory Commission had failed.[21] In January 1927 the shift in American public opinion occurred. Throughout that month, during the annual Congressional naval appropriations debate, a time traditionally reserved for the most xenophobic American outbursts, domestic pressures on the White House increased over the naval question. They were initiated by Thomas Butler, the chairman of the House Naval Affairs Committee, who suggested wildly that $400 million be set aside for the building of a new American cruiser fleet. Butler contended that the existing level of naval appropriations was insufficient to keep the American navy at adequate strength, especially, he charged, since the other principal naval Powers were cheating over the Washington capital ship ratio. Butler's attack was dismissed in London as one of a crop of 'venomous speeches on this subject'. When the 1927 United States naval appropriations bill was published, Howard reported that naval expansion had widespread support in Congress and the country.[22] The 1927 bill called for ten cruisers. Though the American navalists naturally welcomed any increase, surprising endorsement came from quarters which usually sought a reduction. Howard became convinced that these usually pacific elements saw the package of ten cruisers as a means of provoking a new naval disarmament conference. Clearly, domestic American opinion fretted about the naval question. In the last week of January BLINY reported that domestic criticism of the way the Coolidge Administration handled foreign policy was increasing; it was assumed that the president would be forced into moving to make up lost ground.[23] On 10 February Coolidge issued invitations to Britain, Japan, France, and Italy to discuss the limitation of naval armaments.[24]

Coolidge's original proposal did not envisage a full-scale naval conference running parallel to the Preparatory Commission. He merely invited the four principal naval Powers to allow their delegates to meet with those of the United States at the next session of the Preparatory Commission to consider naval matters. Pending the results of the General Disarmament Conference, Coolidge proposed that the five Powers could negotiate and conclude a naval limitation agreement that would supplement the Washington treaty by extending the capital ship ratio to lesser vessels. The American proposal did not expect the Powers to reduce their naval capabilities, that is, to disarm, rather, it sought to limit their construction within agreed maxima. These maxima were to be the fruit of the anticipated discussions. Coolidge did concede to the importance of holding the talks at Geneva, a reversal of his earlier intention to take 'tepid interest' in any held elsewhere than at Washington. The fact that the Preparatory Commission had been meeting at the League head-quarters forced him to retreat on this issue. As the Preparatory Commission was next to meet on 21 March, a quick reply to the invitation was necessary.

Responsible for general disarmament affairs, the Foreign Office Western Department examined Coolidge's invitation. R. H. Camp-bell, its head – and unrelated to R. I. Campbell – felt British difficulties would derive from deciding whether it would be an advantage to pursue a naval agreement that could potentially retard similar ones on land and air weapons. Land and air disarmament were tied firmly to the problem of continental security and the role that Chamberlain wished to play in maintaining the balance between France and Germany. Campbell observed that the American course was simple in comparison, deriving solely from the domestic political situation in the United States:

Coolidge has little to gain from the success of a general disarmament conference: he has much to gain from a naval conference, whatever the measure of its success. The presidential election is sufficiently nigh to influence every act of the administration from now onwards. The Republican electioneering cupboard is bare, and the President must shortly reach a decision in the matter of cruiser construction.[25]

Campbell suggested that the Coolidge plan, to succeed, would have to be adopted by the four invited governments; thus, the blame for rejection, if this was what the Cabinet decided eventually, might not be heaped solely on Britain.

The French and Italians refused to participate in separate naval talks, a situation deriving chiefly from Franco-Italian animosity.[26] To be fair to the French, from the beginning of their participation in the Preparatory Commission, they had argued that disarmament problems were indivisible. They felt that it would be retrogressive to consider naval limitation without reference to that of land and air. Mussolini demanded as a *sine qua non* for Italian participation that the Americans, in advance, guarantee that France's ratio would not exceed Italy's. When the Americans refused, Mussolini rejected Coolidge's invitation.

The Japanese expressed decided interest in the idea of further naval limitation talks. On 13 February Tilley, the ambassador at Tokyo, reported that the Japanese government did not object in principle to Coolidge's invitation, but that it would be unable to enter into talks in a month's time.[27] Tilley was told that the Japanese delegation to the Preparatory Commission, which had left Tokyo, had only limited instructions. Shidehara, the foreign minister, thought that it might be best if naval discussions were put off until the autumn, though he realised that Coolidge had been prompted by domestic political considerations. Tilley supplemented these official views with an evaluation of those of the Japanese press and 'naval opinion'. Press comment generally favoured a naval conference but deprecated the idea of a fixed ratio. In the opinion of the British naval attaché, Japanese 'naval opinion' was disinclined to accept a further extension of the 5:3 ratio against United States naval forces, but it saw nothing wrong with one of 6:3 *vis-à-vis* those of Britain. On 19 February the Japanese ambassador at Washington, Matsudaira, notified the State Department that his government accepted Coolidge's invitation.[28] He also expressed his government's hope that any discussion could be delayed until at least 1 June.

These events created a major diplomatic problem for the Baldwin government. Although the Franco-Italian failure to attend would produce a less than favourable result, the fact that the two principal naval Powers other than Britain were prepared to sit down together meant that an outright British rejection could not now occur. R. H. Campbell's hope that the blame for turning down the American invitation would be shared suddenly vanished. Since Japan and the United States were willing to discuss naval limitation, Britain's failure to join them, for whatever reason, would be interpreted as a deliberate scuttling of Coolidge's proposal. Therefore the Cabinet decided to accept the invitation, immediately communicating the draft acceptance to the Dominions for concurrence.[29] Howard informed the State Department on 21 February that the formal British reply would be delayed because of the need for Dominion consultation; however, he was empowered to say that his government had given the invitation 'sympathetic consideration'. Four days later Chamberlain called in Houghton to inform him of Britain's acceptance, though the formal announcement would have to be delayed until 28 February as the Dominion replies would not be in until then.[30]

Joseph Grew, the American under-secretary of state, interviewed Howard and Matsudaira separately on 5 March to broach the idea of separate Anglo-American–Japanese naval talks.[31] Grew asked the two ambassadors to ascertain informally their governments' views about the desirability of tripartite talks. With this information, the Coolidge Administration could more easily decide whether or not to suggest such talks in its reply to the four Powers. The Americans felt that once separate talks got underway the French and the Italians would consent to participate. As Chamberlain was at the March meeting of the League Council, Tyrrell consulted with Baldwin and Cecil about the British attitude toward tripartite talks. They both endorsed the idea, but they wanted Howard to make it clear that Britain thought that France and Italy should attend if possible. Cecil managed to include the proviso that separate talks should fit into 'the larger question of disarmament'.[32] Howard informed Grew of these views on 10 March; the next day Matsudaira communicated Japan's acceptance. On 11 March the Coolidge Administration announced formally that a 'Three-Power Naval Conference' would begin at Geneva about 1 June, and that it was hoped that France and Italy would join in some way.[33]

Contrary to Foreign Office expectations, no attempt was made to hold preliminary discussions prior to the opening of the Coolidge conference. Though much criticism has been levelled at this lack of preparation,[34] it could not have occurred any other way. The naval experts of the three Powers believed, first, that they knew the naval requirements of the other two[35] and, second, that the three positions with respect to naval limitation were not too far apart. This derived from the Preparatory Commission. At the Commission meetings in 1926 and early 1927 the naval delegates of the three Powers met regularly in the important Sub-Committee A.[36] This body dealt with all military questions and contained one military, one naval, and one air expert from each country represented on the main Commission. When two opposing draft disarmament treaties were placed before the Commission in March 1927, one British and one French, the United States and Japan supported the British scheme of limiting naval vessels by tonnage per class. That is to say, for every category of vessel, cruisers, destroyers, and so on, separate negotiations would be undertaken to set maximum size, numbers, and armament. The

French proposals suggested the establishment of a single tonnage total for each country and then letting each country decide how that tonnage should be distributed for its own purposes. This meant that a lesser naval Power, for instance, France, could steal a march on Britain, the United States, and Japan by concentrating on the construction of one type of vessel, most probably the submarine. Because of their greater maritime responsibilities, the three major Powers would be forced to distribute their allotted tonnages amongst a variety of vessels. The French scheme had the potential of placing them at a disadvantage. The majority of the Preparatory Commission, all lesser naval Powers, endorsed the French proposals. However, since the three major Powers were going to hold separate naval talks, London, Washington, and Tokyo felt that whatever decisions were reached would have an impact on the Commission's findings.

It was no secret that the possibility of reducing naval expenditures was the principal motive behind the three Powers meeting at Geneva. With this desire for reduction, each Power had specific strategic worries that had to be allayed before any commitment for limitation could be undertaken. Again, these were no secret. Japanese leaders were candid in their concern about British naval power in the Pacific and East Asia; this centred on the Baldwin government's decision to develop the Singapore naval base, a build-up permitted by the Washington treaty but seen in Tokyo as an anti-Japanese move.[37] United States policy in East Asia, especially in China,[38] was of even more concern to the Japanese. Although American leaders had for some time been reluctant to use force of arms to support China's independence and to protect American interests, in 1927 the Coolidge Administration was forced to despatch United States naval and military forces to China to protect American lives from the anti-foreign outbursts of Chinese nationalists. The focus of Japanese foreign policy at this time was to preserve Japan's favourable position in China, and this saw the creation of Japanese policies toward China which were also concerned with maintaining strength against the United States. A wide range of individuals recognised that the thrust of Japan's efforts at the Coolidge conference would concern the question of the United States.[39]

The general lines of the British and American attitudes were also well known. Since the war American leaders had plainly set their goal to be complete United States naval parity with Britain.[40] This derived from the desire to be able to enforce the freedom of the seas for neutral, that is, American, commerce in the event of another great war. In 1927 the assumption of this position meant that American naval limitation policies would concentrate on efforts to extend the Washington treaty ratio to include lesser classes of vessel, particularly cruisers. For their part, the British recognised the American claim to equality with them. However, the recognition of such a claim and concession to it were different propositions. British statesmen took the line that if the United States wished to build to the strength enjoyed by Britain, it had every right to do so. Since at least 1905 the British had conceded that their possessions in the western hemisphere were indefensible against expanding United States power.[41] But, in 1927, they wanted the Americans to acknowledge Britain's special needs in any naval limitation agreement. Because of Britain's insular position, its global commitments, and its dependence on naval forces to protect seaborne commerce and defend Imperial lines of communication, the special need found practical expression in a substantial cruiser fleet.

The Coolidge conference

Because the Japanese delegation had to travel so far, the Coolidge conference opened on 20 June, three weeks later than originally anticipated. Both the British and Japanese governments viewed these talks with the utmost importance, sending high-ranking men as their representatives. Kellogg admitted to Coolidge that both delegations were 'rather distinguished'.[42] The two principal Japanese delegates were drawn from the highest naval and diplomatic circles. The chief delegate, Admiral Saito Makato, was a former governor-general of Korea and had served as the minister of marine. His principal assistant was Ishii Kikijuro, a career diplomat and the doyen of the Japanese diplomatic corps, who was then beginning his seventh year as ambassador at Paris. Ishii's eminence derived from his service during the Great War, when he served for a time as foreign minister and was posted at both Washington and Paris.

The Baldwin government viewed the matter as one of first-class importance and decided to send Bridgeman and Cecil.[43] The choice of these two men was obvious. Bridgeman's department was responsible for the construction, maintenance, and deployment of the Royal Navy, whilst Cecil's special Cabinet responsibilities concerned all disarmament questions. Although Bridgeman and Cecil actually led an Empire delegation containing representatives from the five Dominions, the Dominion delegates did little more than endorse whatever their British colleagues suggested. As a consequence the bulk of the work fell to Bridgeman, Cecil, and their advisers. The Chamberlain Foreign Office were effectively excluded from the work of the delegation at Geneva. By mid-1927 British disarmament policy had become the responsibility of a Cabinet committee on arms limitation and reduction. Although Cecil chaired this committee, it continued to meet when he was attending the Preparatory Commission. In order to assuage Cecil's sensitivities about disarmament, Baldwin and Chamberlain persuaded Salisbury to chair Cecil's committee whenever he was absent.[44] This committee became the centre of British disarmament policy-making and, in tandem with the Cabinet, decided on all disarmament questions. The Foreign Office fulfilled a secondary role in this process. Its members advised about the probable repercussions of proposed policy and, once such policy was put into operation, monitored its effects. Throughout the Coolidge conference, Chamberlain abstained from interfering in the debate on limitation because he acknowledged that its technical aspects had little to do with foreign policy. He followed his habit of letting the experts do their jobs unhindered. The Foreign Office did perform a few minor duties for the delegation at Geneva: R. H. Campbell served as its secretary; a News Department member, George Steward, was provided to hold periodic briefings for newsmen; and the legation at Geneva coordinated all communications between the delegation and London.

Though competent, the American delegation lacked the distinguished bearing of its Japanese and British counterparts. This was a deliberate American move. Coolidge had asked Kellogg to select the United States delegation. The secretary of state did not report until 27 May, less than a month before the conference was to open and after the other delegations' personnel had been announced.[45] Hughes, the former secretary of state who had engineered the passage of the 5:5:3 ratio at Washington, had been considered as a possible chief delegate, but his candidacy was blocked.[46] This forced the Administration to look elsewhere. Kellogg concluded that sending prominent Americans would be inappropriate, and his rationale was curious in view of the Japanese and British selections:

I am a little afraid it would look like overloading the delegation and make it appear to the other countries that we were overanxious to have an agreement.

We are anxious to have an agreement . . . but we are in a rather independent position owing to the fact that we can accept as low a basis as any other country.

Kellogg recommended that the chief American delegates to the Preparatory Commission – Gibson, assisted by Rear-Admiral Hilary Jones, a member of the Navy General Board – double at the Coolidge conference. By sending men who could be controlled from Washington, Kellogg intended to preclude any independence on the part of the American delegates: 'It goes without saying that in our case every important move in the course of the proceedings will be either dictated from or approved here.'

The conference organisation became fixed at the first plenary session held on the afternoon of 20 June.[47] As the heads of their respective delegations, Bridgeman and Saito deferred to the fact that Coolidge had called the conference, and they agreed that an American should chair the proceedings. They nominated Gibson to be the conference president, a move which led to an American, Hugh Wilson, the head of the American legation at Geneva, becoming the chief of the conference secretariat. Once these formalities were dispensed with and each delegation made an opening statement, an Executive Committee, of which Bridgeman became chairman, was created so that the chief delegates could meet on a regular basis to debate the broad lines of limitation. At its first meeting the next day, the Executive Committee set up a special group of experts, the Technical Committee, where the minutiae of negotiation would take place.[48]

The British and American inability to compromise on cruiser limitation did not suddenly emerge at Geneva after 20 June. One week before the American announcement of 11 March that tripartite talks would be held in the summer, British and American naval experts met briefly to discuss the whole question of naval limitation. Admiral Jones arrived in London on 4 March on his way to the next meeting of the Preparatory Commission. He met with Bridgeman, Admiral Sir David Beatty, the first sea lord, and Vice-Admiral Sir Frederick Field, the deputy chief of the naval staff, to sound out official British naval opinion of Coolidge's proposed talks.[49] In a move that surprised Jones, the Admiralty officials indicated their approval of renewed naval discussions. But, at the same time, this exchange revealed the complete divergence of British and American views over cruisers. Whilst Field indicated that Britain 'would require an advantageous position in cruisers', Jones countered that the United States could never agree to 'a position of inferiority in any category of vessels'.[50] The discussions ended at this point and the two sides did not exchange views again until after the conference had opened. Besides the fact that the naval experts of both countries thought they knew a great deal about the naval requirements of the other, it was felt on both sides that there might be a tactical advantage in the subsequent negotiations if nothing specific was said prior to the opening of the conference. The Americans had rejected any discussion prior to the Washington conference, and it was widely believed that the success of the American proposals had resulted from the way Hughes had sprung them at the first plenary session in 1921. Beatty, for one, wanted to obtain a similar coup at Geneva in 1927 and successfully lobbied within the government to keep the British proposals secret until the Coolidge conference opened.[51]

The differences between the British and American positions over cruisers emerged in the statements delivered by Bridgeman and Gibson at the first plenary session. Because of his selection as president of the conference, Gibson spoke first.[52] As far as cruisers were concerned, the American scheme envisaged a total class tonnage of somewhere between 250,000 and 300,000 tons each for Britain and the United States and, in strict accordance with the Washington ratio, of 180,000 tons for Japan. There was nothing concrete about the limitation of gun calibres and displacement of vessels; hence, the Coolidge Administration saw the limitations placed on cruisers at Washington, 10,000 tons with eight-inch guns, as the basis for the limitation of cruisers at Geneva. In line with his government's proposals for limiting auxiliary craft, destroyers, and submarines, Gibson argued that the American plan would end competitive building since lower limits were set for all construction.

The British proposals, especially with regard to cruisers, were far more detailed.[53] Bridgeman announced that his government wanted the life of all vessels with eight-inch guns extended; that the Washington ratio be applied against 10,000-ton cruisers with eight-inch guns; that a separate class of cruiser be created with maxima of 7,500 tons and six-inch weapons; and, in not announcing what the total tonnage per class should be, that the number of cruisers for each country was open to negotiation. These proposals did not represent a new direction in the limitation of these important naval craft. In effect the British plan sought only to force the Americans and the Japanese to acknowledge formally the existing situation regarding cruisers. The Washington treaty maxima for cruisers had actually been the standard to which the largest of this class were subsequently built. By 1927 two very different sizes of cruiser were being employed by the principal naval Powers: the heavy, 10,000 tonners and lighter ones. All that the Admiralty wanted from the United States and Japan was an admission of the need to limit the displacement and armament of light cruisers.

Bridgeman's statement also contained a warning. He indicated that although the British government genuinely sought naval limitation by extending the life of vessels and restricting their size and armament, any new agreement would have to take into account two special British concerns: the nature of British commitments for Imperial defence and the position of Europe in the determination of British naval policy. Bridgeman noted that neither the United States nor Japan had equivalent concerns. In a veiled reference to France and Italy, he indicated that Britain's special position dictated that, if other Powers in future decided to expand their naval forces, any obligations assumed at these tripartite talks would be open immediately to revision. Whilst willing to limit naval armaments, Baldwin's government was not about to impair Britain's maritime defences.

The story of the Coolidge conference after its opening on 20 June is a familiar one.[54] The problem with a number of the studies that consider the conference is a failure to appreciate the real reason for the Anglo-American inability to agree on cruiser limitation: the British intention to maintain its ability to enforce maritime belligerent rights versus the American desire to assure neutral trading rights in the event of future war. The development of the attitudes of the second Baldwin government towards the United States in general and its leaders in particular, outside of the Foreign Office, began at this juncture. It was the cruiser question which polarised opinion within the élite and which made the political tasks of the Foreign Office that more difficult during the following two years.

It is impossible to underestimate the emotional significance of the cruiser issue in Britain. The Cabinet had nearly broken in two in 1925 when Churchill attempted to slash the cruiser construction programme.[55] Cruisers meant trade protection in wartime and that to a nation which had nearly starved to death only ten years earlier was a very real issue.[56] Before 1905 and the invention of the *Dreadnought*, the all big gun capital ship, cruisers came in two very different types, large, slow heavy ones of up to 11,000 tons and light 'scouts'. The post-*Dreadnought* naval race concentrated so heavily on capital ships that cruisers of the Powers were hardly affected. Britain had to build cruisers quickly during the Great War for blockade purposes and the usual process of scaling up in size, weight of armour, and range took place. By 1921 Britain had developed the 'E class' cruiser of about 6,000 tons and was developing four of a new and hybrid type of 9,250 tons with 7.5-inch guns. The hybrid cruiser proved to be unmanageable, but the Washington figure of 10,000 tons and eight-inch guns was promoted by United States naval experts as a means of over-trumping any British advance in heavy cruiser construction. Over the protest of his naval expert, Balfour accepted the 10,000 ton and eight-inch gun limit for cruisers at Washington, and after the conference the Italians, followed by the French and the Japanese, began modernising their cruiser fleets by building to the Washington level. The British Admiralty, obsessed by the Japanese, insisted on a British 10,000 ton cruiser programme. But it took them so long to get the Bonar Law and first Baldwin Cabinets to accept the building of two post-Washington battleships that the new cruiser programme was not approved until after Ramsay MacDonald became prime minister in 1924.

The United States began a 7,500 ton, six-inch gun cruiser class in 1920 but, in that same year, the Navy General Board overrode their experts, who said that was quite large enough, by evoking the lessons of the frigate-to-frigate duels during the War of 1812. The General Board insisted that, ship for ship, United States cruisers had to be as big or bigger than those of Britain. This led to the doctrinaire insistence of American naval experts at Washington and Geneva on the need for 10,000-ton cruisers with eight-inch guns. The Americans also argued that they needed long-range cruisers, because they had no overseas bases, and ones big enough to withstand armed merchantmen. The 10,000-ton cruiser also fitted these requirements.

The British cruiser proposals that had been outlined at the first plenary session were fleshed out in informal meetings among the delegates on 22 and 23 June.[57] The Americans were informed that Britain 'would require 500,000 tons of cruisers' and, as Bridgeman told Gibson, that London assumed that the United States would need far less. Reference was made to the susceptibility of Britain to blockade; such a large cruiser fleet would be necessary to prepare for the contingency of breaking a blockade. Nothing was mentioned about the fact that these same cruisers could be just as effective in enforcing belligerent rights. The cruiser tonnage that the British delegation sought was expected to meet the minimum Admiralty requirement of seventy vessels – fifteen 10,000 tonners and fifty-five 6,000 tonners.[58]

For the next two weeks cruiser discussions were held in abeyance as a British proposal to reduce the Washington treaty maxima for the largest capital ships became the centre of attention. However, at a meeting of the Technical Committee on 5 July, Admiral Jones circulated a note embodying the Coolidge Administration's position regarding cruiser limitation.[59] This stated categorically that for the duration of the Washington treaty – it was to expire in 1936 – the United States could not entertain a cruiser class tonnage exceeding 400,000 tons. Although Jones' note showed a willingness to contemplate an increase of 100,000 to 150,000 tons allotted for cruisers above that announced by Gibson on 20 June, it declared that the United States must have 'full liberty of action' to decide how to utilise this tonnage. The Americans wanted to construct twenty-five 10,000 tonners and reserve the remaining tonnage, some 150,000 tons, for light cruisers with eight-inch guns. The main impediment in the way of an Anglo-American naval agreement had now risen. It was not a matter of the British recognising the American claim to parity, rather it was whether the level of parity should be at a figure convenient to Britain or to the United States.

By the time that the second plenary session was held, on 14 July, the British and Americans were at opposite poles about deciding how best to tackle cruiser limitation. Bridgeman and Cecil assumed the stance that the decision regarding a maximum number of cruisers must precede that on the tonnage per class. The Baldwin government wanted the conference to differentiate between heavy and light cruisers, but to limit only the former in terms of the 5:5:3 ratio. Although the size and armament of light cruisers would be restricted, the number built would be flexible, so long as it did not exceed whatever tonnage per class was set by the conference. Numbers were crucial in Admiralty thinking, since its planning had to consider the global nature of British commitments. Britain had an 'absolute need' as far as cruisers were concerned, a need based on its own defensive requirements rather than on the naval power of others. It was in the light of the doctrine of absolute need that Bridgeman and Cecil negotiated. Once Britain's minimum cruiser strength of seventy vessels was acknowledged by the other Powers, the question of arriving at an overall cruiser tonnage would be relatively easy.

Gibson and Jones were adamant in insisting that an agreement on total cruiser tonnage had to be reached before any serious negotiation of numbers or armament could ensue. Since at least the Great War, American naval planners wanted a powerful cruiser fleet to form the nucleus of the United States Navy. The push at Washington in 1921 for the 10,000-ton cruiser with eight-inch guns was the most obvious manifestation of this desire. There was a legitimate worry amongst American leaders that during wartime the British could arm their merchantmen, significantly increasing their maritime potency. Since the United States could possibly be in an inferior position because of the large British merchant fleet,[60] the more powerful eight-inch gun offered American naval forces some insurance. Gibson and Jones approached the cruiser question on the premise that American naval strength was 'relative' to that of the other Powers. Therefore, a doctrine of relative need preoccupied the American delegates and led to their determination to get an agreement on total cruiser tonnage before beginning the laborious task of limiting numbers, displacement, and armament.

In this cruiser debate, Saito and Ishii trod warily between the British and American positions without compromising the Japanese point of view. On 20 June Saito had announced that his government wanted to limit cruiser construction by tonnage per class rather than by numbers.[61] Though this proposition was akin to that of the Americans, the Japanese were clear in a desire not to embark on new building. The uppermost American ceiling contained in Jones' note of 5 July merely represented an estimate of what Congress would likely sanction.[62] The Japanese proposal was more rational, suggesting that the upper limit for cruiser construction be determined by combining existing cruiser tonnages with those derived from authorised building programmes. Obviously this was a bargaining position. But the Japanese attitude hardened after the circulation of Jones' note. Since it was no secret that the Americans wished to extend the 5:5:3 capital ship ratio to lesser craft, the suggestion of 400,000 tons each for Britain and the United States meant only 240,000 tons for Japan. This brought immediate resistance from Saito and Ishii. A member of the Japanese delegation told Gibson that Japan would not consent to a limit for itself of less than 300,000 tons, and that the delegation would rather go home than agree to a 400,000 ton Anglo-American ceiling. On 6 July Ishii made a counter-proposal: if Britain and the United States each agreed to a 450,000 ton limit, then Japan would take 300,000 tons.[63] This meant that the cruiser ratio would be 5:5:3.3, a decided improvement for Japan over that permitted for capital ship construction. With this move the Japanese retained the middle ground in the negotiations; though still advocating limitation by tonnage per class, as the Americans wanted, the total tonnage envisaged inched nearer to that which the British sought. Until the second plenary session the Japanese position did not alter.

The second plenary session was convened at British insistence. As early as 8 July, in the Executive Committee, the British delegation had asked for a chance to state their case fully in public. American pressmen at Geneva had so distorted the British case concerning cruisers that both government and public opinion in the United States were becoming decidedly anti-British.[64] When the opportunity to put the British case was given to Bridgeman on 14 July, he explained why Baldwin's government advocated the doctrine of absolute need:

It is not parity with America that is troubling us. We have not raised any objection to that. Nor are we troubled by the proportion to which Japan should be entitled. It is our security with which we are concerned and our power in future to protect our sea communications against hostile raids of whose disastrous effects we had such bitter experience in the war.[65]

Bridgeman's defence of the British point of view, and his exposition of the difficulties in accepting a total tonnage package without prior knowledge of how it was to be utilised, was done in calm, dispassionate terms. It prompted Gibson to suggest a possible method of obviating a deadlock over cruisers. He confided in Bridgeman that if the British and Japanese could compromise on tonnages and numbers, the Americans would probably be able to adhere to it.[66] The implication in this was that the British and the Japanese were at opposite poles. If both of these extreme positions could be moderated, the main impediment in the way of cruiser limitation could be broken down.

Over the next few days Bridgeman, Cecil, Saito, and Ishii discussed the possibility of an Anglo-Japanese compromise. On 17 July an agreement was achieved which proposed a combined cruiser–destroyer tonnage – 500,000 tons each for Britain and the United States, and 325,000 tons for Japan – in which there would be 'a definite agreed percentage allocated to cruisers and destroyers'.[67] The key to this compromise as far as Bridgeman and Cecil were concerned was that 10,000-ton cruisers would be limited to twelve each for Britain and the United States, and eight for Japan, and that the number of light cruisers mounting eight-inch guns would be restricted. When these compromise proposals were put to the Americans, Gibson condemned them outright. The United States would not agree to any proposed treaty that would restrict American 'liberty of action' in arming light cruisers with eight-inch guns and that would assure Britain of 'cruiser supremacy for many years to come'.[68] For different reasons American misgivings were shared in Britain by a section of the Cabinet, led by Churchill, and by Beatty and the Admiralty. On 19 July Bridgeman was instructed to ask for a week's adjournment of the conference so that the British delegation could return to London for consultations.[69]

These consultations resulted in a British hard-line over cruisers. Baldwin, who was to sail for Canada on 21 July, wanted a decision to be reached before he left. On 20 July he presided over a Cabinet which agreed to adopt the compromise subject to certain Admiralty conditions which would have to be incorporated into it. These concerned aspects of British security.[70] Baldwin left as arranged and Chamberlain took his place at the head of the Cabinet. As soon as Baldwin was gone, Churchill began a concerted effort against the idea of granting the United States ton for ton parity in the form of a treaty.[71] He had nothing against the Americans building to equality with Britain if they wished, but there was no need to concede formally to such a development. A few influential ministers, including Birkenhead, the Indian secretary, and Joynson-Hicks, the home secretary, supported him.[72] This rear-guard action within the Cabinet resulted in a decision that the British delegation must seek a total cruiser–destroyer–submarine tonnage of 590,000 tons each for Britain and the United States, and 385,000 tons for Japan.[73] In effect the Cabinet merely tacked on the submarine tonnages, that had already been agreed, to the proposed Anglo-Japanese compromise. But the significance of this move was that the scheme that Bridgeman and Cecil were to take back to Geneva was a package-deal. The Cabinet wanted an Anglo-American–Japanese naval limitation agreement, but it did not want an agreement on destroyer and submarine limitation without one relating to cruisers.

At the Cabinet's insistence, Chamberlain and Salisbury made

statements in Parliament emphasising that Britain's particular geographical position and Imperial commitments meant that its naval requirements were dissimilar to those of the United States and Japan.[74] These statements were designed to put the British case, once and for all, in its proper perspective. The primary purpose was to clear the air about what precisely the Baldwin government wanted. Despite Bridgeman's public efforts on 14 July, a number of American journalists who opposed an Anglo-American naval agreement were continuing a deliberate distortion of British limitation policies. William Shearer, a newspaperman in the pay of several American steel and shipbuilding companies, was distinguishing himself in this respect.[75] Salisbury and Chamberlain reaffirmed the stance that the British delegates had taken at Geneva. Britain was not about to dictate to the United States and Japan what their light cruiser requirements were. In the same way the two Powers had to accept the British view of what British requirements were. After accepting it, the United States and Japan could build as many light cruisers as they wished, as long as the total tonnage did not exceed whatever would be agreed at Geneva and the armament on light cruisers remained at six inches maximum. Like Bridgeman had done, veiled reference was made to the potential danger to Imperial lines of communication in the Mediterranean: 'the sea routes on which Britain depends for her existence lie largely in narrow waters bordered by other States'. Britain had to reserve its right either to break or to enforce a maritime blockade; the diminution of British naval power, the spectre of which was raised by the failure of the United States to acknowledge the doctrine of absolute need, could imperil such a right.

Once the talks resumed at Geneva, it immediately became apparent that there was no chance of the British and Americans finding common ground on the cruiser question. Both the Baldwin Cabinet and the Coolidge Administration refused to budge on the matters of absolute need and total tonnage.[76] On 28 July the diplomats on the American delegation, led by Allen Dulles, a State Department legal adviser and an anglophile, tried to remove British fears about accepting a total tonnage figure before deciding on numbers and armament. Dulles proposed an additional clause that would guarantee each Power the right to seek a readjustment of the total tonnage allocated for cruisers if one or both of the others were seen to have broken the agreement.[77] But, repeating its determination not to retreat on its decision about a cruiser–destroyer–submarine package, the Baldwin Cabinet would have nothing to do with this.[78]

On 4 August the third and final plenary session was held to permit each delegation to make a final statement of its limitation policies.[79] The key remarks were those of Bridgeman and Gibson. Bridgeman pointed out that an attempt to bring about naval limitation by total tonnage alone would only increase competition; as they had in the past, each Power would build to the maxima permitted by the treaty. Bridgeman emphasised that limitation by type and class of vessel remained the only practical solution to the problem. Gibson countered with the doctrinaire American arguments. The United States wanted only to reduce naval armaments to a point where the national security of the Powers would not be impaired. This would best be done by reliance on limitation by tonnage per class, a scheme that would permit each Power to decide how best to utilise this for their own defensive purposes. Although there was no rancour visible at the third plenary session and the conference ended amicably, at least publicly,[80] the lack of agreement produced hard feelings in official circles on both sides of the Atlantic. The period of Anglo-American naval deadlock had been inaugurated.

4. BELLIGERENT VERSUS NEUTRAL RIGHTS, AUGUST–DECEMBER 1927

The issue of naval equality having now been squarely joined at Geneva, naval competition between the two countries will continue to be an important factor in their relations unless some means can be found of eliminating this 'blockade' difficulty.

Craigie, August 1927

British reaction to the naval deadlock

For the Baldwin government, the immediate result of the Coolidge conference was Cecil's decision to resign. Cecil's ministerial career had been distinguished by his reliance on the threat of resignation if policy did not develop in the way he thought it should. He had held ministerial rank for an aggregate of only seven years and, in that relatively short time, he had resigned twice and threatened resignation nine times.[1] Cecil was unable to sacrifice his personal convictions for what he believed to be political expediency. The great difficulty with him was his failure in the heat of the moment to appreciate fully the repercussions of resignation. In 1917, when he was a junior minister at the Foreign Office under Balfour, he felt that he had to resign over some minor point. This forced the normally patient foreign secretary to speak harshly to his cousin.[2] Balfour pointed out that if Cecil tendered his resignation, he, Balfour, would be forced to resign as well. Cecil's withdrawal would be interpreted as a censure of the government's foreign policy, which was Balfour's ministerial responsibility. Although reasoned advice prevailed in 1917, ten years later the basic problem remained: if Cecil was convinced that his cause was just, his quick temper, self-righteousness, and stubbornness precluded any compromise.

During Baldwin's second government, Cecil had announced his intention to resign a few times. The most notable occurred in 1926 when Chamberlain bested him in a quarrel about British policy and the restructuring of the League Council after Locarno.[3] In 1927 Cecil

77

concluded that the cruiser deadlock at Geneva had been aggravated by the Cabinet's decision not to relent over gun calibres. This brought his differences with his colleagues to a head.[4] His antipathy toward Chamberlain's League policy and his championing of disarmament in opposition to the service ministers and Churchill had isolated him from the rest of the Cabinet in crucial foreign and defence policy matters. For some time he had been at odds with his associates over domestic policy as well. He considered himself on the Cabinet's left wing when debating domestic questions, and the government's handling of the 1926 General Strike seems to have pushed him further leftward. By mid-1927 he was convinced that the Conservatives would lose the next general election because they had not come to grips with what he held to be pressing domestic problems – trade union policy, House of Lords reform, extension of the women's franchise, and poor law reform.

In announcing his intention to resign in a private letter to Chamberlain, who was still the acting prime minister in Baldwin's absence, Cecil pointed out that he had lacked the influence to dissuade the Cabinet from taking its hard line over cruisers.[5] This denoted the belief that he could perhaps bring more pressure to bear from the public platform, where he could discuss disarmament policy unhindered by the strictures of public office and Cabinet solidarity. To his friend, Lord Irwin, the viceroy of India, his words were blunter:

But what really moved me more than ought else was the fact that it became clear that in any definite controversy between Winston and myself on a Disarmament question, the Cabinet would decide in favour of Winston . . .[6]

But Cecil's difficulties were of his own making. He held views which, though theoretically sound, were in practice paradoxical: he wanted a practical expression of disarmament that would not diminish the power of the Royal Navy whilst he tried to cement closer Anglo-American relations. He believed that the Anglo-Japanese compromise of 17 July could serve as the basis for cruiser limitation,[7] despite the fact that Gibson found it unacceptable. After the British delegation returned to Geneva from the consultations at London, Cecil proposed that cruiser guns be limited to a calibre ranging between six and seven and one-half inches – the precise size was to be open to negotiation.[8] This was nonsense. Cecil was trying to reach a compromise with the Americans by inventing a new gun; both sides rejected his idea.

After warning his colleagues that he would be forced 'to reconsider' his position if the cruiser question could not be resolved,[9] he had no option but to resign once the conference ended in failure. The resignation process took almost a month to complete. The initial delay was caused by Baldwin, who did not return from Canada until the fourth week of August. Cecil's letter of resignation then became the main obstacle in the way of a speedy resolution to this problem. Since it was common practice to publish both a departing minister's letter of resignation and the prime minister's reply, Baldwin would not accept Cecil's original letter until some of its more extreme phraseology had been modified or removed. Hankey served as the Cabinet's agent in negotiating with Cecil over the contents of the letter – there were four drafts – and he met variously with Baldwin, Balfour, and Chamberlain to sound out Cabinet opinion on the matter.[10] On 29 August, after Baldwin had departed on his annual holiday in France, Chamberlain accepted a modified version of Cecil's letter, and the next day it and Baldwin's reply were published in the press.[11]

Cecil made it clear in private that he did not want his departure from the government to lend support to the American view of what had happened at Geneva.[12] But, despite this probably ingenuous assertion, an influential section of American opinion saw his action as proof that the American position over cruiser limitation had been the correct one. In early October Craigie circulated a memorandum which summarised differing assessments of the impact of Cecil's resignation in the United States.[13] Howard had reported on 12 September that Cecil's departure had 'not made any serious impression on public opinion here'. This sanguine appraisal ran counter to that of Willert, who had just finished giving his lectures at Williamstown. Willert reported that 'several financial gentlemen' he had met on his travels were now convinced that the Coolidge Administration's line at Geneva had been the correct one. The essential point was that these same Americans had thought, before Cecil resigned, that the British cruiser policies were probably justified. The American Department shared Willert's pessimism. Craigie pointed to shifts in influential American press opinion as an indicator of growing United States disillusionment with British naval policy. He concluded by noting that even Coolidge was becoming uncharacteristically uncompromising on the matter of arms limitation: '. . . the President, who had originally been reported as still hoping that an agreement might eventually be reached, now considers it a waste of time for him to talk of another Disarmament Conference since Lord Cecil is no longer in the Cabinet.'

On 2 August, two days before the final plenary session but after the fate of the talks had been sealed, Coolidge suddenly announced that he would not seek another term of office. Although he had been vacationing for most of the time that the conference sat at Geneva, the president had been in constant contact with Kellogg about the course of the negotiations. With the British hard-line over cruisers that precluded a compromise along the Dulles or other lines, Coolidge obviously realised that his attempt at achieving a coup in foreign policy would fail.[14] During the following months, the White House seemed less and less willing to resist the arguments of American navalists for the expansion of the United States cruiser fleet. Whilst Coolidge did not become perceptibly anti-British, he was forced by the failure of the naval limitation talks to endorse a strengthening of American naval forces. When the next year's naval appropriations came before him, calling for an increase in cruiser numbers, he did not veto them.

More important was the Foreign Office's growing awareness of the effect of the failure of the conference on Kellogg and the State Department. Because of Washington's hot, humid summer climate, Coolidge had made the trek to the relative comfort of South Dakota. As a consequence Kellogg had to remain in the capital to coordinate the Administration's handling of the negotiations. Washington's weather served to increase Kellogg's irritability and to shorten further his already short temper. The object of much of his displeasure was Howard,[15] a situation deriving as much from jealousy over the fact that Howard and the bulk of the Embassy staff were spending the summer at a temporary facility in the cool of Manchester, Massachusetts, as from the passions raised by the cruiser question.[16]

Just as during the blockade claims controversy, Kellogg's state of mind affected his diplomacy. He became petulant and niggling. This caused Chamberlain to complain about being 'harassed beyond endurance by the outrageous behaviour of the American delegation & press correspondents at Geneva & the stupidity & ignorance of old woman Kellogg at Washington'.[17] The already-tarnished reputation of Kellogg and the State Department in the eyes of the Foreign Office became more so as the conference progressed. It derived from

Kellogg, who lectured Howard and other Embassy staff as often as he could about the similarity of British and American naval require- ments. Howard received his last lecture the day before the final plenary session.[18]

Compounding the State Department's disfavour within the Foreign Office was the obvious lack of coordination between the American diplomats and naval officers. It was no secret that Kellogg was responsible for the lines which Gibson and Jones took at Geneva. Despite this responsibility, Kellogg was ignorant of what precisely Gibson and Jones were doing. As late as 14 July, the day of the second plenary session and the ninth day of intense debate over cruisers, Howard reported that Kellogg 'was much surprised at Admiral Jones' proposal for 25 10,000 ton cruisers which he had never heard of'.[19] Chamberlain supposed that the Navy Department might have purposely kept the State Department in the dark about specific American naval needs,[20] though this did not change the situation. More important than this was that Kellogg did not seem to know what exactly had transpired at Jones' 4 March meeting with Bridgeman, Beatty, and Field. Either the secretary of state was again misled by the sailors, or he misinterpreted a report of the meeting. Kellogg told Howard in the first week of July that as far as he knew the British would not oppose 'parity in any class of vessel'. He therefore found it surprising that Bridgeman and Cecil were blocking an agreement on cruiser limitation that was based on the concept of Anglo-American equality.[21] What emerged from this was Kellogg's belief that the Baldwin government was less than honest in its negotiations at the tripartite talks. It was somewhat surprising that when the conference ended without result, Kellogg saw Howard in an interview marked with calm and reason.[22] Obviously the Coolidge Administration did not want to add to its other foreign policy problems by upsetting Anglo-American relations any more than they had been already. Chamberlain expressed relief at the seeming reasonableness of official American opinion at this early stage:

The only hopeful signs are that Kellogg took it quietly & spoke in a wise & friendly spirit & that we are not losing our heads & have no intention of rushing into a new race of armaments.[23]

However, as the blockade claims controversy had amply demon- strated, the secretary of state was not the sole force behind the creation and implementation of American foreign policy. Once the Coolidge conference broke down, Howard became aware that some congressmen were beginning to assert a determination to maintain the 'rights of neutrals' against blockade in future war.[24] This news caused the American Department to worry about the political repercussions of an Anglo-American shouting match over belligerent versus neutral rights.[25] Departmental concern found expression in a lengthy memorandum by Craigie, which discussed the possibility of concluding an Anglo-American agreement regarding the conditions under which future blockades could be conducted.[26] Craigie's case for the possible British reconsideration of belligerent rights was based on two assumptions. First, he was convinced that domestic American agitation for naval equality with Britain would wither and die 'were it not that the problem of "blockade policy" lurks in the background'. From this he assumed that, with the conclusion of an Anglo-American agreement of belligerent rights, the possibility of continued Anglo-American naval competition would lessen, and that this in turn would ameliorate the political discord that had derived from the failure at Geneva. Through Craigie, the American Department advocated that an examination of this matter be undertaken to see if a basis for an approach to the United States on the issue of reducing belligerent rights could be made. Both Wellesley and Chamberlain concurred with the idea of an examination, but the foreign secretary indicated that it should be delayed for a couple of months.[27]

Complicating the Foreign Office's handling of the American question at this time was Herbert Hoover and his decided interest in the state of Anglo-American relations. In reporting on Coolidge's decision not to seek the presidency in 1928, Howard indicated that Hoover had the best chance of securing the Republican Party nomination: '[he] would have the support of the President and of large sections of the country.'[28] During the final stages of the Coolidge conference, Howard had met Kellogg and Hoover at a dinner party at the home of William Castle, the chief of the State Department's Western European Division.[29] Howard took the initiative of suggesting to Kellogg that it might be advantageous to educate British and American public opinion about 'the real absurdity of contemplating the possibility of war between the United States and the British Empire'. Howard suggested that the best way of doing this would be to concentrate on 'the economic and financial losses' that would occur, even if either side never fired a shot. Kellogg indicated that Hoover could best judge the probable effect of such an education campaign, and Hoover, who liked the idea, said he would think it over and let Howard know.

A few days later Howard and Hoover talked over lunch. Hoover felt that the best way to conduct the education campaign would be to have two papers prepared on the subject, one by an American and one by an Englishman. The papers could then be published together. Hoover did mention that it would be 'impossible to avoid certain political implications' from the publication of the papers. He referred specifically to the course that a probable Anglo-American war would take, and the rest of the conversation speculated on this matter. Both men concluded that the Royal Navy would attempt to blockade the United States whilst the American Navy would try to do the same against Britain. They surmised that this would mean that the United States would be precluded from trading with Europe and that Britain would be unable to rely on obtaining foodstuffs and raw materials from the western hemisphere. An integral part of Hoover's argument, and one that Howard accepted, was the idea that even though Canada would be forced to declare neutrality, the United States could not allow Anglo-Canadian trade links to continue. Significantly, nothing was said about the possibility of an Anglo-American clash in the Pacific, nor about what Japan would do in all of this.

The Howard–Hoover war talk caused the foreign secretary and his advisers 'considerable anxiety'. Chamberlain wrote immediately to Howard to point out that, although 'English opinion' was angry with the United States over the failure at Geneva, the idea of war was not even remotely considered.[30] Chamberlain strongly deprecated the notion of a trans-Atlantic public education campaign, suggesting that the whole thing had to be scrapped at once: 'a peace propaganda conducted on such lines as Hoover suggests would have the very contrary effect to that which is intended.' The ambassador also was instructed on one crucial point – the idea of Canadian neutrality in the event of an Anglo-American war was a chimera. Chamberlain emphasised that every part of the Empire was bound to aid every other part, no matter how small that aid might be, in the event of aggression by a Power or group of Powers. Although this view was difficult to reconcile with the Canadian insistence at the 1923 and 1926 Imperial conferences on the independence of Canadian foreign policy and the sole responsibility of the Canadian government to the Canadian parliament and people, the foreign secretary made it clear that he believed that 'neutrality is not compatible with either the theory or practice of Imperial unity'.[31]

Howard concurred with Chamberlain on why the idea of a public education campaign had to be dropped; but the ambassador went on record to express his fear that the Foreign Office was 'over-optimistic' about important sections of British opinion discounting the chances of an Anglo-American war.[32] Howard recounted that during the course of the Coolidge conference the members of the Embassy had talked about this matter in some depth. Because of the vulnerability of Canada and the West Indies, Howard had always subscribed to the theory that an Anglo-American war would be 'the most disastrous thing that could happen to us'. Surprisingly, Captain Stopford, the naval attaché, did not share this view. Stopford contended that, by combining with Japan, Britain could successfully fight the United States. Whilst admitting that Stopford's views might not be shared by the Admiralty, Howard declared that they indicated an ignorance of the political consequences of an Anglo-Japanese war alliance directed against the United States. If shared by a number of British military and naval officers, such views could wreak havoc with the theory and practice of Imperial unity: 'It would certainly be impossible to imagine anything more calculated to produce the secession of Canada and South Africa – to say nothing of Australia – than a war against the United States carried on *in alliance with Orientals.*' Though admitting that he shared Chamberlain's views about Imperial unity, Howard realistically pointed out that Canada would have no option but to declare its neutrality. Though this could never be admitted publicly, British ministers and their advisers had to recognise it in discussing their American policy.

At this juncture the Foreign Office believed that the most immediate danger to reasonably cordial Anglo-American relations resided with the press in both countries. Just after the conference began, Howard suggested that the lack of objectivity of the American press occurred because 'these U.S. Papers work themselves into a state of red hot indignation over the positive immorality of anyone who dares to have a different point of view from that held by them'.[33] By the time that the British delegation was recalled for consultation, Howard reckoned that the advocates of a large United States Navy had won out and that the chances for an agreement at Geneva were non-existent.[34] After the third plenary session American press attacks continued, though they switched from the specifics of naval limitation to the political nature of Baldwin's ministry. Howard noted that comment was beginning to focus on the 'alleged fact that His Majesty's Government are imbued with the spirit of Tory reaction'.[35] He indicated that stories were circulating to the effect that the question of Imperial security would not have been so important if Britain had had a more liberal government.[36] Howard also warned that all of the Baldwin government's actions relating to foreign policy – he referred specifically to India, China, and Egypt – would be interpreted as 'the sinister machinations of the Tories'. The Foreign Office concluded that little would be gained by attempting to salve American press irritation over the failure at Geneva; the British government had not compromised its principles during the tripartite talks and it would be silly to do so in the aftermath.[37] Craigie's views exemplify the official attitude:

There is nothing whatever to be feared from these sporadic complaints about 'Tory' firmness. American respect can only be won by such exhibitions of firmness in a just cause and no American friendship is worth having which is not based on a wholesome respect.

When the American delegation returned from Geneva, United States newspapers once more turned to the specifics of naval limitation. This stemmed from Jones, who held a press conference on the day that he arrived home.[38] Although press opinion did not universally endorse the idea of a rapid and extensive expansion of American naval forces, the effect of Jones' remarks was to focus public discussion on the role of sea power in American national policy. Over the next few months, the time preceding the reconvening of Congress, more and more American press comment examined the naval situation in general and Anglo-American relations in particular.[39] It reached its peak in November – on 5 November the Foreign Office was informed that Coolidge had approved a $40 million increase in naval appropriations and, it was estimated, that eight new cruisers would be constructed.[40] This was followed by the revived interest of American newspapers in the reasons underlying Cecil's resignation. During a House of Lords debate on the League and disarmament on 16 November, Cecil was provided with an opportunity to make a lengthy speech on why he believed that the Coolidge conference had failed. His remarks were less than kind to his former colleagues.[41] Howard indicated that the 'Big Navy press' in the United States had seized on Cecil's remarks as further proof that the American position at Geneva had been the correct one. When Bridgeman tried to lessen the impact of Cecil's words, the Foreign Office was told that the *Washington Post*, an 'organ of the big navy party', had dismissed the first lord's statement as 'bluff'.[42]

Agitation in the American press for an increase in United States naval strength was mounting,[43] and it was obviously having an effect on American politicians. In his annual message to Congress, Coolidge genuflected to this pressure by asserting that the state of the navy remained a principal consideration of his Administration. This presidential bluster did not seem to worry London. The Foreign Office recognised that just as political considerations had prompted Coolidge to call a naval conference, the same considerations had forced his endorsement of a moderate increase in naval spending and a public espousal of the importance of the navy.[44] However, the domestic American clamour for a navy second to none did have a profound effect on the attitudes of those who made British American policy at that juncture. Almost all of them came to believe in the ability of the 'Big Navy party' to influence American public opinion through the medium of the press and, thus, American legislators and the Administration. The term 'Big Navy party' had occasionally been used by Foreign Office members and British politicians to describe American navalists before the summer of 1927. But in the aftermath of the Coolidge conference, with the strain that the cruiser deadlock put on Anglo-American relations, the term saw regular use in the vocabulary of the second Baldwin government.[45]

The term, 'Big Navy party', was not defined precisely until early 1929, when the Australian government enquired about its use in circular despatches that were sent periodically to the Dominions.[46] In responding to this enquiry, the American Department stressed that the representative members of this group were 'not so much any definite body of individuals but rather the general body of public opinion that are in favour of naval expansion up to, and perhaps beyond, parity with Great Britain'.[47] 'Big Navyites' were decidedly anglophobic and could be found amongst retired admirals, 'advanced members of the Republican Party', and journalists. One journalist in particular, Frank Simonds, who had strong links with the United States Navy League, was identified as 'the most able and insidious worker for the Big Navy cause'.[48] The American Department could not pin-point precisely the industrial groups which supported naval expansion, but it did believe that steel, armament, and shipping interests had contributed to 'Big Navy' propaganda at the Coolidge conference and afterwards. Republican newspapers, led by the *Chicago Tribune* and the *New York Herald Tribune*, were seen as principal supporters of United States naval expansion, whilst Democratic ones were not. The Australians were also informed that 'Public speaking, broadcasting, distribution of circulars by the Navy League, cinematograph films', as well as 'Substantial sums . . . provided annually by Congress for Navy Department "publicity"' supplemented 'Big Navy' propaganda. Whilst the American Department assumed that every member of Coolidge's Cabinet approved of the theory of Anglo-American naval parity, it was disinclined to believe that the policy of American naval superiority found equal support.

Members of the Cabinet and the Foreign Office did recognise that there was a difference between the government's firmness in resisting the diminution of British naval strength and the British jingo press' determination to lambaste the American position on naval limitation. It would do British interests no good to encourage Beaverbrook, Rothermere, and those like them in deriding American official and press opinion.[49] As Vansittart reasoned: 'I think all anti-American articles are regrettable because they irritate and do no good, since fighting the US press with their own weapons is like arguing with a cabman . . .' By moving to contain an Anglo-American press war, British leaders would make their political tasks that much easier. If journalists on both sides of the Atlantic were confronted with official British reasonableness over naval limitation, a calmer atmosphere in which the naval deadlock could be more easily broken might develop.

Cabinet members tried to dampen the passions raised by the cruiser question with clear statements of British policy.[50] Their words were generally conciliatory, though Bridgeman, still smarting from his exchanges with Jones, tended to be critical of the American naval specialists. The efforts of these Cabinet members boiled down to a careful restatement of the policy that had been followed during the Coolidge conference: Britain was not bound to extend the Washington treaty capital ship ratio to lesser craft; the Baldwin government did not oppose Anglo-American naval equality, but the Coolidge Administration had to acknowledge that British naval needs differed substantially from American ones; and, last, that the Baldwin Cabinet could not agree to a tonnage ceiling for cruisers without prior knowledge of how it was to be distributed. Whilst official British reasonableness had the desired effect on responsible papers in Britain,[51] this was not the case with those in the United States.[52]

The conciliatory efforts of the Cabinet were mauled by the opposition parties which, for partisan reasons, decided to use the failure at Geneva as a means of making political capital at the expense of the Conservatives. The British local elections were scheduled for early November. The Labour Party led by MacDonald, and the bulk of the Liberals led by Lloyd George, did not actually criticise Conservative naval limitation policy.[53] Rather, opposition attacks centred on the general question of disarmament, a tactic that permitted criticism of the government without the worry of arguing against the hallowed institution of the Royal Navy. Opposition arguments concentrated on disarmament and security and the supposed failure of Chamberlain's foreign policy, based on the League and Locarno, to link the two.

MacDonald's criticism stemmed from his displeasure with the Conservatives over their rejection in 1925 of his brainchild, the Geneva Protocol.[54] In September 1927, at the annual meeting of the League Assembly, Chamberlain had stated that his government would refuse to participate in a reconsideration of the Protocol. The reason was the same as that given two and one-half years earlier: the weight of Britain's Imperial responsibilities dictated that it could not assume any new obligations. In the three weeks following Chamberlain's statement, the time coinciding with the run-up to the annual Labour Party conference, MacDonald railed against what he saw as the foreign secretary's inability to use Locarno as a means of resolving the disarmament question. Since the system of security that the Locarno triplice had established had failed to bring about disarmament to any great degree, MacDonald felt that another approach was needed. The Protocol was an alternative. Contending that the Protocol could still serve as 'a practical pledge of security and safety', he proclaimed that it was also the only suitable means by which a reduction of armaments could be brought about. MacDonald held that 'the problem of security was psychological rather than military' – a view opposed diametrically to the official views of the British, French, and German governments – and he attacked the Conservative record at the Coolidge conference on the grounds that the British case had been conducted with 'war methods rather than peace methods'.

In the midst of rebuilding Liberal strength, Lloyd George used the platform of the League of Nations Union to question Conservative sincerity over disarmament.[55] This was an astute move. Despite its constitutional declaration to remain non-partisan, the Union had become one of Chamberlain's principal critics. Union leaders felt that the foreign secretary's reliance on Locarno and his constant meetings with Briand and Stresemann, the so-called 'Geneva tea party', were weakening the League's influence.[56] Moreover, Gilbert Murray, an Oxford don and the Union's guiding light, had strong pacifist leanings and was tied closely to Cecil by political conviction and personal friendship.[57] Lloyd George employed the Union's worries in his attack on the Baldwin government, but he went further. He argued that because Conservative foreign policy really centred around Locarno, this policy meant ever-increasing expenditure on arms and men.[58] The old Liberal cry of 'retrenchment and reform' was revived. Lloyd George's words did not have an impact only in Britain. Borah wrote to him to get a copy of his League of Nations Union speech and to congratulate him for the trend in 'English politics'.[59]

Opposition criticism of Conservative disarmament and security policy reached its peak after the local elections had seen Labour make substantial gains at the expense of the other two parties. On 16 November Bridgeman announced that the government was going to build just one of three cruisers permitted in the 1927–28 naval programme.[60] This modification was being made because, immediately after the Coolidge conference ended, Churchill had begun a campaign within the Cabinet to convince his colleagues that such a reduction would not affect British cruiser superiority. But, despite this reduction, opposition attacks continued and, on 24 November, MacDonald introduced a motion of censure in the Commons which deplored:

the lack of preparation by the government and the military character of the British delegation which seriously contributed to the failure of the recent naval conference at Geneva, the slow progress made by the League of Nations Preparatory Commission . . . and the refusal of the Government to accept the principle of arbitration and promote a scheme of international security guaranteed by the League of Nations.[61]

In the ensuing debate MacDonald, Lloyd George, Bridgeman, and Chamberlain were the principal speakers. Both opposition party leaders repeated what they had been saying outside of Parliament for the preceding two months. It fell to Bridgeman to reply to Lloyd George's charges about increasing arms expenditures. With a barrage of figures the first lord exposed the barrenness of the Liberal leader's rhetoric. Bridgeman pointed out that the naval estimates secured by the Liberal government of 1913–14, when Lloyd George was the chancellor of the exchequer, had amounted to £48.73 million. Whilst acknowledging that the 1927 naval estimates were £58 million, Bridgeman pointed out that the value of money in 1927 differed from that of 1913–14 by about 75 per cent. For the Baldwin government to reach the level of 1913–14, 75 per cent more than £48.73 million would have to be spent. This would mean a sum approaching £85 million. The first lord also responded to Cecil's speech of 16 November, the only result of which was a bitter private dispute between the two former colleagues.[62]

In a speech which he thought was one of his best whilst foreign secretary,[63] Chamberlain responded to MacDonald's manifold charges. Its effectiveness can be gauged by the fact that MacDonald dropped his campaign for the Protocol right afterward, despite the opportunity he had to continue his attacks on Chamberlain's foreign policy in several by-election campaigns that were just beginning. Chamberlain stressed that the delegation sent to Geneva was 'the least military of all' and that a cursory examination of the men sent would show this. As well, any charge that alleged a lack of preparation on the part of Baldwin's government was misdirected. Chamberlain and his colleagues had made a genuine attempt at formulating a disarmament policy that they felt would both reduce naval expenditure and limit 'aggressive power'. There was substance to the charge that there had been no diplomatic preparation for the conference to see if there was a basis for agreement.[64] However, the Americans had called the conference. The Baldwin government had taken the stance that it was up to the Americans to initiate preparatory talks. They did not. Chamberlain did say that he had thought of approaching the American government on this matter though, in the end, he had refrained from doing so. He did not want the Coolidge Administration to think that Baldwin's government might use the idea of exploratory talks as a means of 'seeking to evade an acceptance of [Coolidge's] invitation'.

The foreign secretary then homed in on the general attack on his foreign policy and on the ancillary questions of disarmament and security. Because of the limitations of British power and the paramount concern of Imperial defence, the Baldwin government had decided early on that it was necessary to confine British commitments to specific areas of the globe. In this way Britain could involve itself selectively in only those regions where its interests were vital, and where British power could be brought to bear to defend them. Although he did not mention it, Locarno was the obvious lesson. The adoption of the Protocol would have meant the opposite of this: Britain would have been forced to assume a responsibility for global peace even if its own interests were not imperilled and its ability to enforce the Protocol was less than certain. The advocacy of a regional approach to security did not mean that the solutions to the problems of disarmament and security were mutually exclusive. The failure of the three principal naval Powers to reach a separate limitation agreement had not affected adversely the Preparatory Commission. That body was still deliberating and the Baldwin government was making every effort for it to succeed.

Although Bridgeman and Chamberlain stymied the MacDonald–Lloyd George assault, it did create an atmosphere in which a number of people in Britain took it upon themselves to use the public platform to comment on Anglo-American relations and the naval deadlock. It began in the House of Lords when Lord Wester Wemyss, who had been the first sea lord in 1918–19 and who was arrogantly anti-American, brought up the subject of belligerent rights in a particularly contentious manner.[65] Wemyss' spirited defence of blockade, implying that the United States posed the greatest danger to British maritime security, led even Hankey, who admitted that he shared the former first sea lord's views, to deprecate such talk as it would stimulate public discussion of the problems in Anglo-American relations at an inopportune time.[66] Wemyss' remarks were followed by those of Sir Auckland Geddes, Howard's predecessor at Washington, who expounded at length on the difficulties in the way of close Anglo-American relations. In this discussion the question of what would occur in a future war was a principal consideration.[67]

The most important of these commentaries occurred on 13 December, when Henry Wickham Steed, the proprietor and editor of the *Review of Reviews* and a former editor of *The Times*, spoke to a private gathering of over one hundred MPs.[68] Most of Wickham Steed's remarks concerned nascent American efforts, at that juncture still unofficial, to support a 'peace policy'. The goal of these efforts centred on what would happen if the League declared a nation to be a transgressor of peace. The American peace policy was designed to force both houses of Congress to pass a resolution calling on the United States government to participate in the ostracism of a

League-defined aggressor state. Quite unexpectedly, Wickham Steed suggested that it might be time for Britain to modify its doctrine of belligerent rights toward the United States. He held that this doctrine was 'entirely obsolete under modern conditions and with modern developments of communications'. Public discussion of Anglo-American relations, which was centring on the two emotive issues of naval strength and belligerent rights, had the potential of impairing official British responses to the American question.[69]

The Foreign Office and belligerent rights

The last thing the Baldwin government needed was a public debate on the state of Anglo-American relations. Prompted by Chamberlain and the Foreign Office, Baldwin had agreed to establish a CID sub-committee to examine whether Britain should surrender some of its maritime belligerent rights. The work of this sub-committee, which would undoubtedly be of the most sensitive nature, would not be helpful if an emotional public debate on cruiser strength and future blockade policy were to break out.

The immediate origin of the belligerent rights sub-committee lay with two worried communications from Howard in mid-September 1927.[70] The first reported a conversation the ambassador had had with Colonel Edward House, the late President Wilson's principal foreign policy adviser and still an influential American voice on international affairs. House recognised that British and American naval needs differed. He acknowledged that settlement of the cruiser question by a formula of mathematical parity would be impossible as a result. Nonetheless, he impressed on Howard his belief 'that there was only one possible source of war between our two countries and this was British interference with American neutral trade'. House was certain that both Republican and Democratic politicians were united in a determination not to permit neutral trading rights to be infringed upon by Britain in another war. House enquired about the possibility of an Anglo-American agreement on the freedom of the seas so that 'the danger of collision in the future' could be eliminated. Noting that he was answering for himself and not for his government, Howard agreed in principle with the idea of such an agreement, but he added that the opportune time had not yet arrived. House then asked if he should raise the subject with Coolidge. Howard requested that nothing be said to the president or any other American leader –

Borah's name was mentioned – until after Howard could consult personally with his government during his scheduled leave in Britain in 1928; House agreed. Howard confided in Tyrrell that although House lacked political clout, he was correct in that the notion of resisting interference with American maritime trade had bi-partisan support in the United States.

Howard's second letter was a persuasive endorsement of House's views. Colonel Pope-Hennessy, the British military attaché at Washington, had had a conversation with an influential American general, Preston Brown. Brown suggested that the real reason for the deadlock at Geneva derived from the failure of both the British and American delegations to tell the truth. The British needed a large fleet of small cruisers to enforce maritime blockade in future war; the Americans wanted large cruisers to break such a blockade. Brown, who was described as 'very friendly to England', was trying to impress on Pope-Hennessy that war between the United States and the British Empire was 'unthinkable'. This was certainly overstating the case – the American Navy had its violent anglophobes. On the strength of his conversation with House and the remarks of General Brown, Howard recommended that efforts to conclude an Anglo-American belligerent rights agreement should begin without delay.

In late August Chamberlain had moved to defer the American Department's recommendation that an examination of the possibility of an Anglo-American belligerent rights agreement be undertaken. Howard's letters forced the issue. Impressed by what Howard had reported, Chamberlain addressed a memorandum to Tyrrell which examined the disfavour with which the Americans viewed the doctrine of belligerent rights.[71] The crux of this examination was the belief that: 'Blockade is therefore the root of our difference with the US over naval limitation & is the one question which might lead to war between us. Unless they are belligerents, the US will never again submit to such a blockade as we enforced in the Great War.' Dismayed at the obvious inconsistency in American thinking – in a war in which the United States was not neutral, it would assuredly enforce belligerent rights – Chamberlain wanted to avoid adding the United States to any list of enemies in a future war. The United States could build a navy of equal strength to that of Britain if it was pressed. More important, the foreign secretary took the realistic view that 'it is not even necessary for the US to declare war to bring us to destruction. They have only to refuse us supplies & credits to deal us a fatal blow.' The price of continued American antipathy toward existing British policies of belligerent rights was too high.

Chamberlain suggested that the best way to begin preparing to examine the possibility of reaching agreement with the Americans would be to establish clearly the Foreign Office view. After this, an approach could be made to the Cabinet and the CID. Within three days Vansittart circulated a memorandum to his superiors which had been penned by Craigie.[72] In a covering note Vansittart outlined four reasons why the American Department believed difficulties with the United States would increase rather than decline. First, there was the avowed intention of a wide range of American leaders to secure some sort of naval equality with Britain. Second, the volume of American foreign trade, the major portion of which moved across the oceans, was 'advancing by leaps and bounds'. In an endeavour to protect this trade and to ensure the safety of American investments abroad, the United States government would unlikely acquiesce to the stringent application of British belligerent rights in the future. Third, Vansittart was convinced that 'the Anglo-Saxon element' in the United States was declining as a percentage of the population. He felt that German-Americans, 'the most efficient element', were beginning to dominate in numerous fields and that this would do British interests no good in the long run. Finally, he argued that the attempt to resolve differences with the United States would be hindered by 'the alarming and deplorable growth of anti-American feeling' within Britain.

Underscored by the serious talk on both sides of the Atlantic about the possibility and course of an Anglo-American war, these four factors made an examination of belligerent rights imperative. The American Department emphasised that secrecy was crucial. Vansittart recommended that Howard not discuss the matter with any Americans, whether in government or not.[73] If the Administration heard rumours that Howard had talked to people outside of government, the chance of an agreement might be jeopardised. If the press in either country learned that Baldwin's government was reconsidering a reevaluation of belligerent rights, the problems surrounding the conclusion of any agreement would be made that much harder. Public knowledge that the British were considering to retreat somewhat on future blockade policy might tie the hands of the Coolidge or a successor Administration, either Republican or Democrat, preclude the chance for an agreement, and weaken any

British bargaining position. Vansittart closed with two recommendations. He suggested that when the time came to broach the matter to
the Americans a middle echelon member of the State Department be
sought out; Olds, he thought, would best fit the bill. He then indicated
that the initial British overture should be made by someone of lesser
rank than Howard.

In his memorandum, Craigie argued that the problem was not one
simply of defending the doctrine of belligerent rights from those who
wanted to promote the theory of the freedom of the seas. He opined
that it was just as much an American interest to come to terms with
Britain since, in time, the United States might be forced to apply
blockade. Thus, Craigie dealt at length with the specific problems
raised by belligerent versus neutral rights – the determination of lists
of contraband, the doctrine of continuous voyage, and so on – and
analysed each in terms of established British practice, American
objections, and the possibility of agreement. This amounted to a
compelling case for an enquiry into whether an Anglo-American
belligerent rights agreement should be concluded. Craigie admitted
that all of this depended on whether American authorities would be
prepared to sit down with their British counterparts. For a number of
reasons they might be unwilling; but, if they were agreeable, Craigie's
analysis showed that Anglo-American differences were 'not necessarily insurmountable'. Craigie was not blind to the fact that
opposition to an agreement would not reside solely in the United
States. Two arguments against a proposed agreement would surface
in Britain. Naval leaders would argue that they required a free hand
in defending the Empire and keeping sea-borne lines of communication open. A more diverse group could be relied upon to contend that
any belligerent rights agreement would be both legal and multilateral
and, as such, it could not be resolved suitably by bilateral
negotiations. This second group would almost certainly ask that the
question be turned over to the League.

The most important part of Craigie's submission was the list of
reasons why the American Department thought that Anglo-
American agreement on belligerent rights was imperative. It was
assumed that it would be impossible for Britain to apply effective
future blockades without the cooperation of the United States. The
United States was an exporter of goods and capital, whilst most
potential British enemies were importers. It would be easier and more
practical to cut off supplies before they left their source rather than as

they approached their destination. From this premise it was argued that it would be more profitable to conclude an agreement with the Americans in peacetime. In such circumstances American leaders would be able to consider their options, which might include support of some kind of belligerent rights, without a sense of urgency and the pressures brought to bear by an aroused public opinion. It was obvious that in the event of a war in which the United States was a neutral and Britain was a belligerent, American leaders would be anxious to defend neutral rights. Last, and most crucial, it was held that the negotiation of an Anglo-American belligerent rights agreement 'would have an arresting influence on the further development of the American navy, for the wind would to some extent be taken out of the sails of the "big navalists"'.

Craigie made three recommendations for proposed action. To ensure that an approach could be made to the Americans before the 1928 presidential election campaign began in earnest, the CID should examine whether it would be advisable to modify the traditional doctrine of belligerent rights. Once this enquiry was completed, assuming there were limits to which the British government could compromise, the Coolidge Administration could be approached 'discreetly and informally' about discussing an agreement. If such an approach was not rejected, the government could then consider setting up formal talks.

Craigie's memorandum became the subject of high-level discussion within the Foreign Office. Chamberlain felt the weakness in Craigie's brief, which British opponents of a compromise would grasp at immediately, hinged on the reasons why the Americans failed to break the British blockade imposed during the Great War.[74] The opponents of a compromise would probably say something like: 'Yet we *did* establish & maintain [a blockade] with ever growing stringency. True the U.S. *could* have made it impossible but they *did not*.' Craigie replied that the conditions in 1914–17 were unique.[75] In the first place, the German decision to impose 'a rigorous submarine blockade' against Britain and its allies had antagonised the Wilson Administration and a sizeable portion of American public opinion.[76] The sinking of American ships and the loss of American lives as a result of the German submarine offensive hurt the Central Powers' cause in the neutral United States. Craigie reckoned that it would be folly to count on enemy blunders in future wars to force the United States into Britain's camp. Of more significance was Craigie's observation that United States naval strength between 1914–17 had been much less than that enjoyed by Britain. The American Department was convinced that this situation would not arise again. Therefore, the future application of British belligerent rights had best not be based on the idea of an American inability to defend their concept of the freedom of the seas.

This argument was persuasive. The day after he received it, the foreign secretary approached the Cabinet about the need to examine whether it would be to Britain's advantage to surrender some of its longstanding belligerent rights *vis-à-vis* the United States. With his submission, he enclosed Howard's letters of 15 and 22 September, and Craigie's 17 October memorandum.[77] Chamberlain made it clear that both Howard and the Foreign Office had concluded independently that the failure of the Coolidge conference really lay with the vexed question of belligerent versus neutral rights. Whilst not minimising the difficulties that touched on the idea of compromising on Britain's traditional means of conducting naval warfare, the foreign secretary and his advisers were convinced that some sort of arrangement with the Americans had to be examined.[78] Chamberlain did not mince his words: 'It cannot be denied that the present difference on this subject between the United States and ourselves is the only matter which makes war between our two nations conceivable.' He relied heavily on the arguments Craigie had proffered the day before. The Cabinet had to understand that Britain's position in the world had changed since 1918, and that the change had not been to Britain's advantage. There could be no reliance on the unique circumstances of the past to ensure that the application of belligerent rights could be undertaken with impunity in the future. Chamberlain urged study of the matter as soon as practicable.

A number of Foreign Office memoranda relating to the American question and belligerent rights were also circulated to the Cabinet in the next few weeks.[79] They emphasised that political aspects of the American question had catapulted it into the first rank of British foreign policy problems, and that both Howard and BLINY shared the opinion that the failure of the Coolidge conference had done much to aid anglophobic groups in the United States in their attacks on Britain. Thompson was direct:

The failure at Geneva has certainly done nothing to improve Anglo-American relations; on the contrary, it has strengthened enormously those elements in the United States who are unfriendly to Britain and whose object it is to 'show the world' conclusively that while the 19th Century may have belonged to Britain, the 20th Century undoubtedly belongs to the United States.

The message to the Cabinet was that changing circumstances required an alteration to existing policy.

This barrage of memoranda derived from the emergence of opposition within the government to any agreement with the Americans. As Craigie had predicted, the objections were based on strategic and legal considerations. As soon as he became aware that Chamberlain was going to push for an examination of belligerent rights, Hankey wrote to dissuade him.[80] The Cabinet secretary outlined the strategic reasons why the Royal Navy's ability to defend British interests should remain unfettered by such things as a belligerent rights agreement. His brief encompassed the standard arguments about Imperial defence and the protection of sea-borne lines of communication. He tried to demonstrate that all that would result from an approach to the Americans would be the rejection of any negotiated settlement, the further embittering of Anglo-American relations as a result, and the renewal of naval competition.

Hankey harkened back to the abortive Declaration of London of 1909 as an object lesson in the futility of limiting belligerent rights.[81] A conference met at London in 1908–9 to create an international prize court that could act as an appellate tribunal above national prize courts. These individual courts ruled on whether impounded neutral vessels were guilty or innocent of carrying contraband to enemy states, on the disposition of captured cargoes, and so on. It was pointed out to Chamberlain that a reaction by influential sections of British opinion had prevented ratification of the declaration in 1909. Hankey suggested that an even greater opposition to limiting belligerent rights would arise in 1927. The critics of an accommodation with the United States would have the lessons of the Great War to bolster their opposition.

A more plausible argument against the surrender of any belligerent rights actually came from within the Foreign Office. Hurst attacked not only Craigie's perception of the problem, but he also took Hankey to task for not stating fully 'the case against the *proposal*'.[82] Hurst concurred with the observation that Central Power blunders had helped push the Americans into the Allied war coalition. He also acknowledged that there should be no reliance on this happening again. But he argued that for a single Power to enforce policies of blockade, two criteria were essential: naval superiority and conformity 'to admitted principles of international law'. Hurst surmised that the proposed agreement with the Americans would touch only the second criterion, whilst the first would decide whether belligerent rights were applied by or against Britain.

Hurst was critical of drawing the Declaration of London into the debate since, like Craigie, he believed that it was really unimportant in deciding if the Americans should be approached. Besides, Hankey had incorrectly assessed the document. Its genesis resided with Hankey's predecessor at the CID, Lord Sydenham. The idea of meeting with other Powers to create an international prize court had been approved by the government of the day and its advisers in the relevant ministries, including the Admiralty. Moreover, Hankey had ignored why the British government had wanted an international prize court – to preserve neutral trading rights. In 1907 British leaders looked back on almost a century of preeminent British sea power, the use of which had been to defend free trade: 'the whole situation [in 1908–9] was controlled by the belief that Great Britain stood to gain by the total abolition, or, if that were impossible, the restriction, of the right to seize contraband of war.' This was precisely the weakness in Hankey's case: he assumed that Britain would always support unrestrained belligerent rights. But if United States naval strength ever exceeded Britain's, something Hankey could not or would not believe, it would be incumbent on British leaders to endorse neutral trading rights. Hurst argued against an accommodation with the Americans because it would restrict future British options, whether Britain was imposing or protesting policies of belligerent rights.

Hurst then turned to the American Department's arguments. He felt Craigie had erred in assuming that the conditions concerning neutrality that had existed in 1914–18 would reemerge in the future. Hurst argued that this would not be so because of the League: 'If the League were universal, there would be no neutrals.' He showed that in terms of naval strength the United States was the only country of consequence that stood outside the League. This raised the question about the sort of situations in which Britain would seek to impose a future maritime blockade. Hurst was certain that this would happen only when the League went to war with a Covenant-breaker. Thus the application of British belligerent rights would be taken in conjunction with the rest of the League. Although the burdens of enforcing a maritime League blockade would fall to the Royal Navy, Hurst emphasised that British efforts at sea would be supplemented by ones on land, since the other League members would be bound by the Covenant to enforce economic sanctions against any transgressor of peace.[83] In Hurst's estimation the only states that would consider breaking a League blockade would be the Covenant-breaker and the United States. But existing principles of international law would be on the side of the League, so Hurst saw no reason to supplement these with a separate Anglo-American agreement. He reckoned that League strength was increasing, and he anticipated that its influence in international affairs would gain accordingly.[84]

In a desire to show his even-handedness, Chamberlain circulated both Hankey and Hurst's memoranda to the Cabinet.[85] Despite the strategic and legal arguments to the contrary, Chamberlain would not shelve the idea of examining belligerent rights. He shared the belief of his American specialists that the naval deadlock and the failure of the Coolidge conference stemmed from American worries about British blockade policy. In a covering memorandum to the Cabinet that accompanied the two dissenting points of view, Chamberlain repeated his belief that an enquiry into the advisability of approaching the United States was essential. He consulted both Baldwin and Balfour, the latter finding Craigie's 25 October memorandum particularly impressive.[86] The foreign secretary also kept Hankey fully informed, though the Cabinet secretary implored Chamberlain not to assume a partisan stance before any enquiry met.[87] On 23 November, the day before the Commons debate on MacDonald's motion of censure, the Cabinet agreed to 'institute an enquiry into the subject of Belligerent Rights at Sea'.[88] Baldwin was to decide who should conduct the enquiry and its terms of reference.

The members of the CID belligerent rights sub-committee were drawn from the Cabinet and upper levels of the civil service.[89] Recognising both the importance and sensitive nature of the enquiry, Baldwin tried to persuade Balfour to be its chairman. When his first choice begged off because of infirmity, Baldwin turned successfully to Salisbury, already loaded down with the work of the disarmament sub-committee. The selection of a chairman who would have the respect of both sides in this question was crucial. Because of the partisan interests of their ministries, Chamberlain and Bridgeman were chosen as a matter of course. As Cecil's replacement,

Cushendun was chosen because he had inherited the Cabinet responsibility for League and disarmament questions. Three lesser ministers in terms of foreign and defence policy were also asked to serve: Douglas Hogg, later Lord Hailsham, then the attorney-general; Viscount Peel, the first commissioner of works; and Philip Cunliffe-Lister, the president of the Board of Trade. Hogg's choice was obvious, since someone with legal knowledge and responsibility would be needed to sign the eventual report. Peel was nominated because he was a friend and protégé of the prime minister. Cunliffe-Lister became a member as his department was responsible for trade and ancillary questions. Although his name was added as a matter of form, and although Hankey kept him fully informed and supplied with the sub-committee's memoranda, Balfour attended just one meeting.

Seven senior civil servants were designated to sit on the sub-committee. Five were selected as 'expert assessors' whose role was to advise, ask questions of any witness, and submit memoranda whenever they felt inclined. These assessors were to be prohibited from signing the eventual report.[90] Charles Madden, the first sea lord, who succeeded Beatty on 1 August 1927, advised on all aspects of the naval question. After persuading Baldwin that he had 'made a considerable study of the question, and [had] the experience of the war', Hankey was given a place. He realised that Baldwin had made him an assessor because the prime minister did not want to overload the sub-committee with full members opposed to an agreement with the United States.[91] Hurst and Tyrrell represented the Foreign Office. Originally Hurst was to be the sole Foreign Office assessor, but Chamberlain, realising that Hurst, Hankey, and Madden opposed a deal with the Americans, pressed for Tyrrell's inclusion.[92] On Hurst's strong recommendation, Maurice Gwyer, the procurator-general and treasury solicitor, was added after the sub-committee's first meeting.[93] He administered the British prize courts, a fact that Hurst reckoned made him indispensable. It was also pointed out that Gwyer's legal knowledge could be relied on in the event that Hurst was absent, as he often was because of League business. The last two civil servants – the head of the American Department, Vansittart, and later Craigie, and the principal assistant secretary to the Admiralty, Alex Flint – never had an official designation, as their role was to provide additional support for their political chiefs.

The terms of reference for the enquiry concerned the question of belligerent rights as raised in the three memoranda on the subject that had been circulated to the Cabinet.[94] In essence this amounted to a consideration of whether it would be advisable to reduce British belligerent rights *vis-à-vis* the United States in the hope that this would lessen naval tensions between the two countries. Once these tensions were reduced, so the argument went, the naval deadlock might be broken. The sub-committee had to decide whether a limitation on Britain's traditional means of self-defence was worth the price of breaking the deadlock and ameliorating Anglo-American differences.

The equivalent of the American 'Big Navy party' within the British government viewed the desire of Chamberlain and the Foreign Office to dare to consider the possibility of compromising on British belligerent rights as less than patriotic. For the majority of these men, their assessment of the situation was more visceral than cerebral. Pound's reaction was typical. He wrote to his friend, Admiral Sir Roger Keyes, the commander-in-chief of the Mediterranean fleet:

The cry has been taken up in full blast by Austen Chamberlain, Tyrrell, Craigie (Foreign Office) and Locker Lampson [the parliamentary under-secretary]. Make a note of one thing in that wonderful memory of yours and that is that Locker Lampson ought to be hung as a traitor. I have never read anything like his papers – cold feet – cold feet.[95]

Pound also deprecated the analytical abilities of the Embassy at Washington. He remarked to Beatty that 'Esme Howard who is always on the "run" whenever an American opens his mouth has now been joined by a Major [sic] Pope-Hennessy.'[96] Hardliners at the Admiralty, led by Barry Domvile, the director of Naval Intelligence, felt that Stopford was failing to get the naval point of view across to Howard and the other diplomats; by mid-November Domvile had engineered Stopford's recall.[97]

British navalists also focused their scorn on Bridgeman and Madden. Bridgeman's agreement to the construction of only one of the three authorised cruisers brought a rebuke from Beatty, as did Madden's inability to bolster the first lord's resistance: 'Bridgeman is weak as putty & Madden carries no guns and they simply accepted the need for one cruiser with a mild protest.'[98] British navalist dissatisfaction about the measures proposed to restore good Anglo-American relations did not abate after Baldwin set up the belligerent rights sub-committee.

Hankey, however, originated a more inspired rear-guard action against the supporters of an accommodation with the Americans as he approached the problem more coolly than his Admiralty colleagues. By mid-December he became convinced that the Foreign Office, through Tyrrell, was conducting a clandestine propaganda campaign in favour of reducing belligerent rights.[99] He suspected Foreign Office members to be in league with *The Times*, whose principal shareholder was John Astor, an American. The final bit of evidence, so he thought, was Wickham Steed's speech to those hundred MPs.[100] Wickham Steed repeated arguments about the need to accommodate the Americans that Tyrrell had mentioned previously to Hankey. The evidence, of course, points in the other direction – the Foreign Office did not want press comment on Anglo-American relations.[101] Nonetheless Hankey decided that the pro-belligerent rights agreement arguments had to be countered: 'I decided, very reluctantly (for I hate these methods), that I must start my own propaganda.' For one who hated 'these methods', Hankey relished in his anti-Foreign Office whispering campaign. The range of individuals that he told about the CID enquiry was wide but, ignoring that in most cases he hypocritically breached the rule of confidentiality and impartiality he implored others to obey – Chamberlain, for instance – the effect of his agitation is uncertain. It did not, as some claim,[102] ensure the defeat of an Anglo-American agreement before the belligerent rights sub-committee even met. However, the efforts of Hankey and the British navalists, in combination with the hardening of American opinion and the attacks of the British opposition parties, did make Foreign Office handling of the American question that much more difficult for the remainder of the second Baldwin government.

5 . THE PACT TO RENOUNCE WAR, JANUARY–JULY 1928

I can form some opinion as to what France or Germany or Italy may be likely to do in this or that contingency. Except in a narrow field the course which will be taken by the United States is a riddle to which no one – not even themselves – can give an answer.

Chamberlain, July 1928

On 6 April 1927, the tenth anniversary of the American entry into the Great War, Aristide Briand announced to the press that his government was willing to conclude an agreement with the United States that would renounce war 'as an instrument of national policy' in Franco-American relations.[1] The Coolidge Administration did not receive formal notification of Briand's proposal until late June 1927, when the American ambassador at Paris, Myron Herrick, brought the suggested text for a renunciatory pact to Washington during his annual holiday.[2] There was no official American reply until 28 December 1927, when Kellogg informed Paul Claudel, the French ambassador at Washington, that the Coolidge Administration could not entertain the idea of a bilateral Franco-American renunciatory pact.[3]

Kellogg followed this with an interesting diplomatic counter. The existing Franco-American arbitration treaty, concluded in 1908 under the guidance of the then American secretary of state, Elihu Root, was about to lapse. Kellogg tied together the two ideas of international arbitration and a political instrument to renounce the resort to war in international politics. He indicated that the Coolidge Administration would not be averse to the notion of a multilateral renunciatory pact, and that such an agreement, as far as France and the United States were concerned, could be supplementary to a new Franco-American arbitration treaty. Kellogg also proposed a new approach to arbitration by indicating a desire not to exempt from a new treaty those questions relating to vital interests, independence, and national honour. These three areas had been at the core of Root's success in 1908 but, because of changing circumstances, Kellogg thought that all that needed to be exempted in 1928 were disputes relating to the domestic jurisdiction of the signatories, to third parties, and to the Monroe doctrine and the League Covenant.[4] Kellogg had reversed the tables on Briand.

The next two months witnessed a Franco-American dialogue on the proposed renunciatory pact which left its fate very much in doubt.[5] Briand wanted France and the United States to sign the pact first and, after this, other Powers could be invited to accede to it. More important, the French wanted the pact to apply just to wars of aggression. Such a proviso was necessary as France had mutual defence treaty obligations it could not and would not abandon. Foremost in Briand's mind were Locarno and the arrangements that had been made with the Little Entente. Kellogg wanted to consult the other Powers before agreeing to renounce war. If France and the United States signed an agreement, the Franco-American formula might not be acceptable to the other Powers, they might not sign as a result, and the whole project could prove abortive. Kellogg argued that the suggestion to renounce only aggressive war was too radical a departure from the original French proposal.

Whilst the dialogue over how best to renounce war was in progress, the French and Americans resolved one outstanding difference. Based on the Kellogg formula, a new Franco-American arbitration treaty was signed at Washington on 6 February.[6] With this problem out of the way, Kellogg concentrated on the renunciatory pact. On 27 February the French government was informed that the Coolidge Administration, whilst endorsing the concept of renouncing war, still thought that the best method of preserving international peace by this means would be to use the original French proposals as the basis of a multilateral arrangement.[7] The Coolidge Administration could not support the French contention that if the pact became multilateral, the original formula would have to be qualified by exempting defensive war. The basis for the rejection of this French contention, about which Kellogg was very explicit, was an inability to understand how renouncing war would violate obligations that France had assumed under the Covenant or be at variance with the League's purpose.

Before Briand could reply formally and privately to this, Kellogg placed his case before the American public in an address to the Council on Foreign Relations on 15 March.[8] Although Kellogg dealt with both the arbitration treaty and the renunciatory proposals, the thrust of his remarks concerned the latter. He expounded on why renouncing only aggressive war was so disconcerting:

It seems to me that any attempt to define the word 'aggressor' and by exceptions and qualifications to stipulate when nations are justified in going to war with one another, would greatly weaken the effect of any treaty such as that under consideration and virtually destroy its positive value as a guaranty of peace.

He could not understand why France was opposed to the notion of a multilateral treaty, with all of the obligations that would entail, if, at the same time, it was willing to conclude a bilateral arrangement under which those same obligations would be assumed. As far as Kellogg was concerned, multilateralism did not run counter to the League Covenant. He alluded to a resolution of the fourth League Assembly which left to national legislatures the decision about what degree their governments were bound to undertake obligations assumed under the Covenant.[9] This seemed to be a devastating piece of logic, the more so since Kellogg had used a public platform to outline American policy.

Less than two weeks after this speech, Briand agreed grudgingly that proposals for a multilateral renunciatory pact should be submitted formally to the British, German, Italian, and Japanese governments.[10] But he made it plain that he disagreed with Kellogg on a number of points, especially the non-exemption of defensive war. On 13 April, under Kellogg's authority, a circular note was despatched to the four Powers.[11] It included all of the Franco-American correspondence dating from June 1927, as well as the American draft multilateral pact. One week later, since Paris and Washington could not agree on a common draft for the proposed pact, the four Powers received an alternative French draft based on Briand's final letter to Kellogg.[12]

The difference between the two drafts derived from Briand's determination not to restrict unduly French freedom of action. The Briand draft sought to qualify France's support of a multilateral instrument by specific reference to four conditions necessary for French agreement. Briand recommended that the pact should be truly universal in order not to tie the hands of the original signatories. He wanted the pact to come into force only after it had been universally endorsed or, if that was impossible, after a special arrangement was devised to circumvent any difficulties that might arise if one or more Powers failed to ratify. Briand next sought an assurance that if a signatory subsequently went to war in clear violation of the pact, the other signatories would be released automatically from their avowed obligations towards the pact-breaker.[13] The third condition reaffirmed the French desire to exempt defensive wars. The fourth devolved from the third. Briand wished to ensure that the pact would not call into question existing French obligations assumed under the Covenant, Locarno, and other treaties between France and other Powers – this last, an obvious reference to the Little Entente. It fell to Chamberlain and his advisers and colleagues to evaluate these conflicting drafts, devise a policy to protect British interests, and avoid injecting poison into either Anglo-French or Anglo-American relations.

For two reasons, once it was apparent that the renunciatory pact was not going to die, Foreign Office members advised that it would be folly for the British government to turn down any approach on this issue.[14] Cecil and the League of Nations Union had become bewitched by the notion of renouncing recourse to war in international politics. Soon after the failure of the Coolidge conference, when Cecil was lamenting about the Baldwin government's coolness toward disarmament, he told Gilbert Murray that 'I feel it is not at all unlikely that we shall have to take up a more or less hostile attitude toward the Government.'[15] By early January 1928 Chamberlain was enmeshed in his dispute with Gilbert Murray about the anti-Conservative bias in the Union's public activities.[16] Prior to Kellogg's speech to the Council on Foreign Relations, Cecil and the Union busied themselves in organising a bloc of influential opinion 'to press the Prime Minister not to reject the proposal off-hand'.[17] Although this project came to nothing, Cecil did publish articles in influential journals and give speeches on important public platforms, both of which impressed on the Foreign Office his ability to prevail on public opinion in both Britain and the United States.[18]

The second factor which mitigated against an outright British rejection was more important; such an act might add further to Anglo-American discord. To deprecate the notion of renouncing war was not a simple matter of offending just Kellogg. Howard was reporting that vast sections of American public opinion, particularly in the traditionally isolationist Middle West, felt 'that the United States ought to do something besides [give] lip-service to the cause of peace'.[19] It was also apparent that Borah was going out of his way to support Kellogg, and that the Senate Foreign Relations Committee was endorsing its chairman's actions.[20] Thompson put the Foreign Office view best:

I am no advocate of what may be described as 'toadying' to the United States . . . but nevertheless to me it is an unpalatable but none the less convincing fact that we have some difficult years ahead of us *vis-à-vis* that country. It seems to me that if we can with dignity and without sacrificing any essential interest keep on their right side we should do so.[21]

With a view to impressing on British and international opinion the sincerity with which the Foreign Office greeted the renunciatory proposals, Craigie and Willert met with Harold Williams, the foreign editor of *The Times*.[22] Though suggesting that it might be best if *The Times* gave 'cautious support' to the project, Craigie and Willert adopted an air of optimism. They confided in Williams that, assuming the pact was made multilateral, Briand's letter of 26 March seemed to offer adequate protection for any signatory with prior treaty commitments.[23] Craigie then argued that if the pact's provisions could be squared with existing British treaty obligations, the Baldwin government should give the project 'a warm welcome'. His rationale was entirely political, since such a welcome would do Anglo-American relations nothing but good.[24]

Despite Foreign Office willingness to support the idea of a multilateral renunciatory pact, its members were under no illusion that the threat of war would be eliminated. Kellogg did not share this view. In December he told Howard that the value of the proposal was that it might 'prove a real step in advance in the education of public opinion of the world for the promotion of peaceful settlement of disputes'.[25] By the time of his speech to the Council on Foreign Relations, he seemed to feel that a declaration renouncing any recourse to arms would actually prevent the outbreak of future war. The change in Kellogg worried even State Department officials:

For weeks the press has chorused approval of [Kellogg's] exchange of notes with Briand on outlawing war . . . actually it is futile . . . The political trick has been turned and now we should take a well deserved rest. *The funny thing is that Olds and the Secretary seem to take it all with profound seriousness* . . .[26]

The best indication of the Foreign Office's poor assessment of the proposed pact's ability to prevent war lies with Chamberlain. In mid-February he wrote to Howard expressing doubt about the value of a treaty that lacked machinery to enforce its provisions.[27] But the basis of Chamberlain's criticism was Kellogg's refusal to exempt defensive war whilst admitting that no signatory would be forced to repudiate its right of self-defence. Exasperated at this inconsistency, the foreign secretary observed: 'Why does [Kellogg] insist on signing a treaty which says what he does not mean and reject words which say exactly what he does mean and admits to you that he means.' Two months later, when it was clear that the proposal would be circulated to the four major Powers, Chamberlain's opinion had not altered. As he candidly told the Japanese ambassador at London: 'I could not myself attach to it quite the same importance as it appeared to have in the eyes of some people, since it seemed to me to be a rather platonic declaration accompanied by considerable mental reservations.'[28]

With the circulation of the American draft treaty, the British began serious analysis of renouncing war.[29] Hurst began the process with a perceptive minute that centred on the need to maintain British diplomatic strength in Europe:

At the present time the peace of Europe depends more upon the maintenance of cordial relations between Great Britain, France and Germany than on anything else, and acceptance by the British government of this American draft treaty in a way which would make France consider that Great Britain intended to leave her in the lurch would be harmful to British interests.[30]

Since Kellogg's handling of the diplomacy of this matter had obviously upset both government and public opinion in France, Hurst opined that the unconditional acceptance of Kellogg's draft by Baldwin's government could jeopardise Anglo-French relations, weaken the Locarno triplice, and reduce Britain's ability to influence European events. Hurst suggested that the Foreign Office should tiptoe warily between the conflicting French and American positions without alienating either Paris or Washington.

Hurst's minute dealt with the precise wording of Kellogg's proposals and with Briand's conditions which had to be met before the French would support the American plan.[31] Hurst pointed out that Article I of Kellogg's draft contained two disparate elements. It called on the signatories to the treaty to condemn the 'recourse to war for the solution of international controversies', whilst binding them to renounce war 'as an instrument of national policy'. In a legal sense, Hurst reckoned, these two critical phrases were dissimilar. The first was an expression of opinion; the second obliged the signatories not to go to war with one another. Hurst also observed that Kellogg's proposals would prohibit the 'pursuance of a policy announced to all the world that a state will reply to certain acts by a resort to war'. An unqualified acceptance of Kellogg's draft would preclude both the American use of the United States Army and Navy to enforce the Monroe doctrine, and any British attempt to employ armed force to defend Egypt.[32] Hurst felt that if a signatory to the pact attempted to support an ally which was invaded by a third Power, that signatory could be held to be in breach of its obligations not to use 'war as an instrument of national policy'. Thus, despite Kellogg's protests to the contrary, his proposals struck at the heart of the notion of collective security, a notion which was at once the basis of the League Covenant and the *raison d'être* of Locarno.

Hurst then turned to Briand's conditions for French adherence to the American draft: the exemption of wars of self-defence; the provision for an escape clause that would permit the signatories to be released automatically from their obligations towards a pact-breaker; and the need for universal acceptance of the pact before it came into effect. In Hurst's opinion the first reservation was probably unnecessary because Article I made no specific mention of renouncing wars of self-defence. He also argued that the third reservation was dispensable, though only if Kellogg could be persuaded to invite Belgium to be amongst the original signatories. This would mean that all of the Locarno Powers would be parties to the pact from the outset. Hurst did recommend that the second French reservation – severing obligations toward a pact-breaker – be incorporated into Kellogg's draft. This would buttress all of Britain's international commitments[33] because if a signatory to the pact resorted to aggressive war, Britain would be released from its obligations to the pact-breaker and ties with other signatory Powers would be strengthened.

With ingenious logic, Hurst demonstrated that the second French reservation really made the first 'superfluous'. If, for instance, Germany attacked France after the conclusion of the pact, Britain would be forced by Locarno to intervene against Germany. However, the Anglo-French effort would have to be considered defensive since Germany invaded France. The key here was that as soon as French sovereignty was violated, the Powers signatory to the renunciatory pact would be released from their obligations *vis-à-vis* Germany. Hurst contended that this would both free Britain from the worry of being condemned with Germany and unite the rest of the signatories against Germany. Hurst believed that the phraseology of the second French reservation should, if possible, be more explicit.

Hurst concluded by evaluating certain political questions in terms of the Kellogg proposals. Whilst he discussed Franco-Italian differences in the Balkans and the problem of the Soviet Union signing the pact, the most important matter concerned the possibility of Kellogg's draft precluding both the American enforcement of the Monroe doctrine by military means and the British use of armed force to defend Egypt. Although Kellogg had never mentioned the Monroe doctrine with regard to the renunciatory pact, Hurst was percipient enough to recognise that the Coolidge Administration would certainly move to reserve this basic tenet of American foreign policy.[34] Hence it would be incumbent on the Baldwin government to reserve British rights to intervene in Egypt, rights which Hurst characterised as 'precisely similar' to those enjoyed by the Americans in Central and South America. He believed that there were only two ways of doing this. If the Americans decided to amend the draft to reserve the Monroe doctrine, this reservation would have to be worded so as 'to safeguard Great Britain's policy with regard to Egypt'. If the Americans refused to broaden such a reservation, the British would have to conclude 'a separate arrangement' with the other signatories. Hurst suggested that the Americans would probably not oppose a broad reservation, but if they did, the idea of the pact would be seen as sham designed only to bolster Republican electoral fortunes.

Two days later the Foreign Office received Kellogg's reaction to the French draft treaty.[35] Kellogg found fault with the three French attempts to qualify their acceptance of his proposals. He saw no reason to make specific reference to wars of self-defence, since 'self-defence . . . was the inherent right of every country, and so understood by all'. He deprecated the notion of universality because the treaty would be unduly delayed from coming into force. Last, but most important, he thought that the formula for releasing signatories from their obligations towards a pact-breaker was too restrictive. Kellogg favoured the release of obligations 'with reference to any Power which might become involved in war, whether in contravention of the treaty or not'.

Hurst quarrelled immediately with Kellogg's attempt to circumvent the French scheme for releasing signatory Powers from their obligations toward a pact-breaker.[36] If accepted, Kellogg's counter would alter the announced intention of the pact: to have Powers renounce war 'as an instrument of national policy in their relations with one another'. Kellogg was suggesting that a country would be condemned for fighting a defensive war, and that a group of countries, united by a treaty of mutual guarantee or some other defensive arrangement, would also be ostracised because they moved to resist an aggressor. Hurst's earlier assessment of Kellogg's proposals was entirely correct; they struck at the basis of the League and Locarno – collective security.

The American Department became suspicious of Kellogg's diplomacy at this time. It seemed as if the secretary of state was seeing rather a lot of Howard, which demonstrated that Kellogg recognised the importance of Britain's acceptance of the pact.[37] However, it also seemed that Kellogg was striving to isolate France and put Britain firmly in the American camp. This caused Thompson and a few senior Foreign Office members to reaffirm Hurst's *caveat* about the necessity of not offending France.[38] Britain's stake in Europe had to be protected at all costs.

On 28 April Kellogg tried to clarify the American position in a speech before the American International Law Association at Washington.[39] He stressed that because self-defence was the right of every country, his renunciatory pact required no special mention of it. More to the point, Kellogg argued that the pact would strengthen both the League and Locarno. He indicated that any Power which violated Locarno would *ipso facto* violate the renunciatory pact; the same would be true in the event that existing treaties of guarantee were called into operation – he made mention of the Franco-Polish treaty of October 1925 which had been concluded as supplementary to the main Locarno treaty.

Kellogg then made an abrupt retreat on two crucial points. On the matter of universality, he noted that it would benefit international peace to have the pact signed by the six major Powers as soon as possible. He was certain that other countries would then adhere. But he appeared much less adamant than he had before, leaving a diplomatic door ajar for some sort of compromise to squeeze through. More important was his implication that the Powers signatory to the pact would be released from their obligations toward any of their number which resorted to aggressive war, and that those Powers which were obliged to confront the pact-breaker would not be held to be in violation of the pact. There were practical political reasons for this seeming about-face. Although he made it plain that he was unwilling to be more explicit when the time came to set the final form of the pact, Kellogg took this public stance to acknowedge that

Briand's concerns were justified. By this speech he sought to preempt a Franco-American stalemate which would cause the pact to fail. There is also evidence that Kellogg worried privately about Chamberlain intervening between Paris and Washington to capture some of the glory for Britain.[40] Perhaps most critical was the apparent ebb of enthusiasm for his proposals in the United States, a situation which BLINY reported in great detail.[41] Nonetheless, the net effect of Kellogg's effort to allay French anxieties – that were shared by the British – was to permit Chamberlain and his associates to concentrate on their reply to the American note of 13 April.

On 3 May Chamberlain provided the Cabinet with a Foreign Office evaluation of Kellogg's draft pact.[42] This paper discussed the intention of the renunciatory proposals, their relation to the League Covenant and Locarno, and so on. Chamberlain's memorandum impressed on the Cabinet that one new factor had arisen to make the British acceptance of Kellogg's plan that more urgent: the German government had already accepted the American draft. Indeed, the Germans had scored a 'diplomatic success' by being the first to reply favourably.[43] The Cabinet authorised Chamberlain to have the Foreign Office draft a reply to Kellogg, which Chamberlain asked Hurst to prepare.[44] In order to keep Anglo-French relations on an even keel, Hurst first met with Henri Fromageot, the legal adviser to the French Foreign Office, to make certain that the British reply would be acceptable to the French government. After this, Chamberlain, Tyrrell, and Hurst sat down with de Fleuriau, the French ambassador at London, and Fromageot to discuss what the two legal experts had covered. With the air cleared, Hurst wrote the British reply.

On 16 May, after two Cabinets had met to make and to approve alterations to Hurst's draft, the British reply was telegraphed to Howard; he was to give it to Kellogg on 19 May, the same day that Chamberlain would hand Houghton a copy.[45] Kellogg was informed that the British government saw little difference between the American and French drafts, and that his speech to the International Law Association corroborated this view. Reference was made to the three principal French concerns: self-defence, the need for an escape clause to permit the signatories to deal with a pact-breaker, and universality. Chamberlain acknowledged that these concerns were shared equally by the British government, but that Kellogg's speech had clarified the situation. The only observation in the British note was that perhaps there were other Powers which ought to be included to mollify the French, who wanted to make certain that their Eastern European allies would become parties to the agreement.[46] This had the additional value of getting Belgium into the pact from the outset and, thereby, ensuring that all of the Locarno Powers would be included in the arrangement. The British note did point out that the government in London could not sign the pact for the Empire as a whole. To assure Imperial unity, a *sine qua non* for the Baldwin government to sign, the Dominions and India would each have to be invited separately to accede to the proposals.

The most important point in the British reply, however, was made in the tenth paragraph. It made no bones about the fact that there were 'certain regions of the world the welfare and integrity of which constitute a special and vital interest for [British] peace and safety'. Although specific regions were not listed – it was thought that a general statement would cover all possible contingencies – there was no doubt that reference was being made to Egypt and the Suez Canal. Kellogg was reminded that the British government had gone to great lengths to inform the rest of the world that there were parts of the globe which it considered strategically important, where interference by any Power or group of Powers would be resisted.[47] Since Hurst had drafted this note, it is not surprising to find that the equation of the Monroe doctrine with these special British rights appeared in paragraph ten. Kellogg could be under no illusion that in reserving its right to go to war to defend those regions of 'special and vital interest', the British government considered that it was adopting a code of conduct that had been practised by the United States for over a century. Not unnaturally, paragraph ten immediately became known as the 'British Monroe doctrine'.

Some British critics of the Baldwin government, particularly Cecil and his supporters, felt that the note of 19 May raised unnecessary difficulties.[48] Cecil was particularly irked about the decision to make reference to self-defence, and about the inclusion of the British Monroe doctrine. He claimed that the renunciatory proposals did not preclude the conduct of defensive war, and he remonstrated against the Baldwin government's 'rather obscurely worded objection to the effect that, in certain quarters of the globe, they must be allowed to resist any change of territorial conditions'. He categorised the attempts by both the British and French governments to clarify the American draft as 'raising difficulties', though he failed to mention that Kellogg had recognised that the Anglo-French concerns were justified and had moved to allay their suspicions with his 28 April speech. With undoubted petulance, Cecil complained that the Baldwin government had not only replied in 'a somewhat grudging spirit', but that it had delayed that reply.[49]

More responsible government critics found little to fault in the note of 19 May. Just when the Cabinet had been putting the final touches on the draft note, both Houses of Parliament discussed the question of renouncing war. In the Commons this happened on 10 May, during the debate on the Foreign Office estimates.[50] Both MacDonald and Lloyd George joined with Chamberlain to give their support to the idea behind the proposed pact. Lloyd George was effusive in his praise of the American plan, and he strongly urged the Baldwin government to accept it. After the publication of the British reply, the Liberal leader did not find any reason to quarrel publicly with its contents. MacDonald took a more circumspect line; indeed, he repeated the cautious approach that he had used in a recent article that had been published in the United States.[51] Whilst lauding Kellogg's efforts, MacDonald raised the question of deciding on 'sanctions and ways of dealing with matters that now cause war'. In essence he was arguing that while war ought to be renounced, some sort of arrangement must be made to ensure international peace and security. It appeared as if MacDonald was once again trying to exhume the Geneva Protocol. Fletcher, of BLINY, in reporting on the appearance of MacDonald's article, noted: 'Of course, this insistence upon realities does find expression in some quarters of this country, but most often it is found in the opposite camp to Mr MacDonald's friends.'[52] Like Lloyd George, MacDonald did not go on the record against the contents of the British note of 19 May.

The House of Lords discussed the renunciatory pact the day before the British reply was telegraphed to Howard.[53] The Marquess of Reading, the British ambassador at Washington in 1918–19, had moved a resolution that welcomed Kellogg's proposals and that asked the British government to accept the principles contained in the draft treaty. Cushendun spoke on behalf of the government; he commended the efforts of Briand and Kellogg, whilst deftly avoiding any mention of the points to be made in the note that was about to be sent to Washington. A variety of peers, including Cecil, the Archbishop of Canterbury, and Lord Parmoor, who had been responsible for League affairs during the first Labour government, favoured renouncing recourse to war in international affairs. The Lords consequently adopted Reading's resolution, an event which created in the United States a favourable impression of British attitudes toward this question.[54] After 19 May, only Cecil argued against the Cabinet's policy.

For Chamberlain and the Foreign Office, however, the reaction of official American opinion was decisive.[55] On 22 May Houghton wrote to Chamberlain that there would be no problem whatsoever about meeting the request for separate invitations to the Dominions and India.[56] This was not the case with the Cabinet's decision to reserve the British Monroe doctrine from the strictures of the proposed pact. On 24 May Chamberlain and Houghton dined privately;[57] in conversation which followed their meal, the foreign secretary explained the stance taken in the note of 19 May. The American ambassador regarded this talk to be of such importance that, in order to spend more time with Chamberlain, he cancelled an appearance he was to make at a party at the Swedish Legation.

Chamberlain prefaced his remarks by explaining why his foreign policy was based on close Anglo-French relations. He did this because he knew of 'the suspicions which [Houghton] entertains of French policy and his dislike of our very close co-operation with France'.[58] Chamberlain outlined the European situation confronting him when he took the Foreign Office in November 1924: France living in fear of a revitalised Germany and a recalcitrant Germany resisting the limitations imposed on it by the Treaty of Versailles. The combination of these two factors had the potential of disrupting European peace. Soon after he came to the Foreign Office, Chamberlain concluded that the only way to resolve Europe's problems was to remove France's fears whilst restoring Germany's confidence in itself and the postwar settlement. Houghton was told that Chamberlain had decided how to do this within two months of becoming foreign secretary. The key was France. French confidence in Britain had first to be won back, and then the project to guarantee the eastern border of France, which had died when the United States failed to ratify Versailles, had to be reborn. Only when all of this was accomplished could the Anglo-French alliance be transformed into an Anglo-Franco-German guarantee. When Stresemann suggested such a guarantee in January 1925, the possibility of combining all of the steps at once offered itself. Locarno was the result. There could be no doubt, Chamberlain argued, that the European situation had improved markedly since then because of close Anglo-French relations.[59]

The foreign secretary then turned to the British note of 19 May. He told Houghton that he wanted to make certain that Kellogg would give the note 'a fair and even friendly consideration'. When he tried to impress on the American ambassador the idea that the Baldwin government was sincere in wanting to work with the Coolidge Administration on the renunciatory pact, Houghton took the stance that the British note suggested that 'we accept, *but*'. Chamberlain disagreed. As far as he was concerned the note said 'We accepted *because*'. He was candid in his explanation. Standing by itself, the American draft of 13 April had raised a number of unanswered questions; however, Kellogg's speech of 28 April had relieved almost all British anxieties. 'I insisted', said Chamberlain, 'that every interpretation which I attached to our acceptance was explicit in Mr Kellogg's speech or, in the single case of the Monroe doctrine, implicit in the history of America for one hundred years.'

The rest of the conversation dealt with paragraph ten of the British note. Houghton agreed that the British position with respect to the Suez Canal was analogous to that of the Americans and the Panama Canal. What he found disquieting was the British reluctance to specify Suez and its environs as a region of 'special and vital interest'. As a result of this British action, there was now the chance that the French, the Italians, and the Japanese might each decide to reserve their rights in 'special spheres'. Chamberlain remarked that as far as the Foreign Office was aware, the Japanese reply to Kellogg's circular note would make no mention of reserving Japan's rights in particular regions, for instance, in Manchuria.[60] The foreign secretary felt that if this information proved to be correct on the receipt of the Japanese reply – which it did – that reply would be less than honest. The British note was obviously held up to be a paragon of veracity and candour.

Chamberlain explained what had motivated the Baldwin Cabinet to include the British Monroe doctrine: 'All that we desired was that no other great Power should establish itself upon our route to India or on our Indian frontier.' He enumerated the regions in their order of importance: Egypt, the Persian Gulf, and Afghanistan. With regard to the latter, Chamberlain emphasised that the British had not bothered to occupy all of the area to which they were entitled, and that they would not do so unless the threat of invasion arose. When Houghton queried why the Cabinet had bothered to include paragraph ten at all – what were they afraid of? – Chamberlain stressed that it had nothing to do with the state of Anglo-American relations. What was true in the Anglo-American case, however, was not so in other British relationships.[61] The Baldwin Cabinet had no idea how many or which governments would eventually sign the renunciatory pact, thus British interests had to be protected with a blanket statement. The foreign secretary argued that paragraph ten had the added advantage of being broad enough to safeguard American interests as well. Without such a statement there was the risk of future condemnation – for both Britain and the United States – if a doctrine of defence was later invoked and found to be exempt from the pact by only a mental reservation. Chamberlain stated that he was motivated by a desire to ensure that both the British and American Monroe doctrines were somehow enshrined in the renunciatory pact. Though he favoured a separate document containing reservations to be appended to the final draft so as to leave the original as unaltered as possible, Chamberlain was willing to let Kellogg decide how best to achieve this.[62]

Within a week Kellogg's assessment of the British note was in the hands of the Foreign Office.[63] The only comments of substance were on paragraph ten. Howard had tried to explain that the 'United States position in Central America was much like ours in countries near Suez'. When the ambassador enquired about how the American government would react if one of the Central American states allowed a non-American Power to lease one of its ports, Kellogg replied 'we can risk that. We do not believe that it will ever happen.' Howard concluded that Kellogg was implying that Britain should abandon its Monroe doctrine and be willing to take the risk that no Power would interfere along the western land and maritime approaches to India.

The Foreign Office found Kellogg's views disquieting.[64] Whilst the American position in Central America might well be secure, Britain's in Egypt, the Persian Gulf, and Afghanistan was not necessarily so. Wellesley put the problem in a nut-shell with his comment that: 'It is all very well to speak of measures short of war but you cannot in all cases ostracise an offending state commercially, financially, and economically without the use of force, i.e. an act of war.' Thompson was inclined to think that Kellogg's willingness not to include wars of self-defence in the pact could provide Britain with a suitable excuse for going to war to maintain its hegemony in Suez, its environs, and eastwards. He argued that an attack on Egypt could be construed as an attack on Britain, and to resist such an attack would be an act of self-defence.

When Chamberlain, his senior advisers, and the American Department were evaluating Kellogg's reaction to the British note of 19 May, the News Department received a comprehensive analysis of the major American newspapers' views on the renunciatory pact.[65] BLINY reported that press comment was 'unusually divided' on the question of renouncing war, an indication that American public opinion was undecided. Moreover, although a great many Americans appeared willing to support Kellogg, there was uncertainty about whether the Senate would ratify a pact which formally renounced the recourse to war. The key to any final decision on the part of United States politicians resided with their perception of the reaction of American public opinion. BLINY felt that 'the course of the negotiations' would sway American public opinion one way or the other.

The Foreign Office was greatly impressed by BLINY's analysis.[66] How the British government conducted itself during the ensuing renunciatory pact diplomacy would be crucial to the state of future Anglo-American relations. This view was given added weight in an important telegram from Howard.[67] He reported that Kellogg's reply to the five Powers would be ready for despatch by the second week of June, that the Americans would opt for a 'simple renunciation of war', and that the preamble to the pact would be revised to include those reservations which had been championed by the other Powers. The ambassador did point out that the mention of the right to defend special areas by the resort to arms was unlikely. Each of the other Powers had important regions to consider – France's rights in Siam were noted – but none of them had bothered to reserve categorically their rights in any of them. Howard cautioned that Britain might find itself isolated from the five Powers unless some device could be found which would not only preserve the British Monroe doctrine, but would be acceptable to the others.

The net effect of Chamberlain's talk with Houghton, Howard's two critical reports from Washington, and BLINY's analysis of recent American press opinion was to make the British prepare carefully for their reply to Kellogg's anticipated new note.[68] On 12 June Craigie wrote to R. I. Campbell, now the first secretary at the Washington Embassy, to inform him that the renunciatory pact diplomacy was entering 'a new phase'.[69] To aid London in its deliberations, Craigie requested that a detailed summary of American press comment be compiled after the new American note to the Powers was circulated and published. The Foreign Office wanted to know the position that each newspaper took on the second Kellogg note, the political bent of each paper, and whether or not each paper spoke for a particular group within American public opinion. Craigie suggested that Campbell might think it best to have BLINY carry out this task – which he did[70] – but he made it clear that the Foreign Office did not want eastern newspapers to dominate the summary:

What we need is, so to speak, a bird's eye view of comment and/or the policy of the American press on this subject, together with any observations you may wish to add as to the extent to which this comment is representative of, or likely to influence, public opinion in the different sections of the country.

The Foreign Office was already hard at work trying to discover some device which would have the double merit of protecting the British Monroe doctrine whilst being acceptable to the other Powers. Craigie, Hurst, and the heads of the Eastern and Egyptian Departments – respectively, Thomas Spring-Rice, the third Baron Monteagle, and John Murray – began to confer regularly with Chamberlain, Tyrrell, and Wellesley on this matter. Their discussion was based on a memorandum by Craigie setting out the precise problems which it was anticipated Kellogg's note would raise.[71] Tyrrell, Wellesley, Craigie, and Murray first discussed the special regions question on 8 June. Because Howard's second telegram of 30 May had only repeated speculation that there would be no reference to paragraph ten of the British note, it was decided to have secret enquiries made about the precise nature of Kellogg's new proposals.[72] Henry Chilton, the counsellor at the Embassy at Washington who was in charge because Howard was in Britain on leave, had met Kellogg at a weekend house party. Chilton reported that the new American note would avoid any mention of special rights.[73] Chilton indicated that Kellogg was in an optimistic mood, especially with regard to being able to meet those Anglo-French concerns about the League and Locarno. Craigie found little solace in this with respect to the British Monroe doctrine, and he remarked that 'we must hope that [Kellogg] has discovered some formulae which will satisfy everyone'.[74]

Hurst had been toying with the idea of not bothering to say anything about special regions in subsequent correspondence with the Americans. In a reversal of the position he had taken in April, he surmised that the British position in Egypt, the Persian Gulf, and Afghanistan might not be analogous to that of the United States in Central America.[75] Murray had told Hurst that, as long as the Royal Navy was preeminent in the Mediterranean, Britain would have little difficulty with other Powers interfering in Egypt. This exposed the incongruity of the British and American Monroe doctrines. The Americans did not have to worry about threats to their hegemony in an area populated by weak states, that lay virtually on their doorstep. This was not so for the British and their sphere of influence in Egypt and immediately east of Suez. That region was far from Britain, and a number of potentially hostile Powers, including two of the first rank, stood astride the lengthy lines of Imperial communication that ran across the Mediterranean. Unforeseen events such as those that might derive from the trend toward international disarmament could make the future defence of the western approaches to India more difficult.

Hurst reckoned that to strengthen Britain's position in this area, it might be advantageous if the Baldwin government sought to place a broad interpretation on the proposed pact. In essence, this would amount to a claim that the renunciatory proposals were a guarantee of the international *status quo*. A broad interpretation could cover every other signatory's rights in special regions and, if the other signatories would agree to it, there would be no need to press for the British Monroe doctrine to be an integral part of the final draft of the pact. Hurst briefly considered the tangled question of whether it would be wise for the British government to oppose the notion of the Egyptians signing the Kellogg pact. He thought such a notion should be resisted. If the British were forced 'to prevent the Egyptian Government doing something which we dislike, e.g. passing unwise Assembly laws or ordering 500 tanks from Italy', the British might be held to be violating an agreement which they had assumed in concert with the Egyptians. After all, Kellogg proposed that the signatories to the pact renounce the use of war in their relations with one another.

Although Craigie and Murray could see possible benefits accruing from Egyptian adherence to the renunciatory pact, Craigie opposed the suggestion to give a broad interpretation to the proposals.[76] Craigie contended at first that the Americans would never agree to the guarantee of the existing international *status quo*. The only practical alternative was to press the other Powers to accept the British Monroe doctrine. On 9 June Craigie's hand was strengthened with the receipt of a telegram from Dormer, the British *chargé d'affaires* at Tokyo.[77] Dormer suggested that the Japanese had not reserved their rights in special regions out of deference to American and Chinese opinion. He also pointed out that a number of Japanese saw the British position in Egypt and the Japanese position in Manchuria to be akin. Two days later Dormer reported that the Japanese vice-minister of foreign affairs told him that Japan's special rights in Manchuria were not mentioned in the reply to Kellogg's first note because the Japanese government felt its right to intervene there was covered by the provision relating to self-defence.[78] As a result of Dormer's telegrams, the Foreign Office felt that there was no option but to press for the inclusion of the British Monroe doctrine in the final draft of the pact. Craigie, Murray, and Monteagle were joined by their colleagues in the Northern and Far Eastern Departments – the former monitored Soviet affairs – to devise a means of protecting British rights in Egypt, the Persian Gulf, and Afghanistan.[79]

The second American draft was sent to the interested governments – now numbering fourteen – on 23 June and, as expected, it made no mention of the right to defend special regions by the resort to arms.[80] Indeed, Kellogg had conceded little in his reply to the Powers. All that he did was to resubmit the original draft of 13 April with a revised preamble, which attempted to meet the strong Anglo-French protest about the need for the pact's signatories to be released from their obligations toward a pact-breaker. To ameliorate the worries that had been expressed about the proposed pact compromising the right of self-defence and existing obligations that had been assumed under the League Covenant, Locarno, and other treaties of guarantee, Kellogg referred to the points he had raised in his speech to the International Law Association. He attempted to do the same with respect to the release provisions but, despite his best intentions, the interpretation of this aspect of the pact still remained obscure.

The British moved quickly to come to terms with what they knew were the final American proposals. Kellogg's ambiguity over the release of obligations was the immediate Foreign Office concern. Although the preamble had made it clear that signatories to the pact would be released from their obligations toward a pact-breaker, Article I did not. As Hurst pointed out in an earlier minute, Article I obliged the signatories to renounce the use of war; the phrases in the preamble were no more than expressions of opinion. Thus, it was uncertain whether Kellogg meant to put a wide or a narrow interpretation on those instances where signatories, which were also League members, would be released from their obligations toward a pact-breaker, whether a member of the League or not.[81] At Chamberlain's request, Craigie, R. H. Campbell, Wellesley, and Malkin, who was substituting for Hurst because of the latter's attendance at a special League meeting at Geneva, met with the foreign secretary to discuss the problem.[82] Two decisions were reached at this meeting. First, Hurst would have to be consulted so that, in turn, he could discuss the question with his French and German colleagues. Second, the Washington Embassy would have to discover what interpretation Kellogg put on the release provisions. It was felt, however, that the Washington Embassy's enquiry should be delayed until after Hurst could report; what he had to say might preclude an approach to Kellogg.

Malkin telegraphed the Foreign Office's assessment of the problem to Hurst:

Wider interpretation (a) covers warlike action under Article 16 [of the Covenant] against a signatory who has attacked a non-signatory Member of the League, and (b) allows us, without losing benefits of treaty, to defend any country in which we have special interests (not being a signatory) against attack by signatory. It is not clear that it (c) allows us to defend such countries against attack by non-signatory, since no signatory would have gone to war before we did. It might also debar us from (d) assisting a Power which had, without violating Kellogg treaty, gone to war under gap in Covenant or (e) from intervening in a war between two non-signatory and non-League Powers. It would (f) only allow us to take warlike action under Article 16 against a non-signatory if such action were not regarded as 'seeking to promote our national interests by resort to war'.

Narrower interpretation would not cover (a) or (b), but does cover (c), (d), (e), and (f).[83]

Hurst immediately replied that Friedrich Gaus, the legal adviser to the German Foreign Office, was not at Geneva.[84] Fromageot was, however, and Hurst indicated that he would hold conversations with his French opposite as soon as possible. Three days later Hurst wired to say that, whilst his discussions with Fromageot had been useful, it would still be necessary to consult with Gaus.[85] Hurst had had a telephone conversation with his German colleague that morning, and Gaus had interpreted Kellogg's revised draft to mean that any League action against a transgressor of peace, particularly if it was justified under Article 16 of the Covenant, would not be in violation of the renunciatory provisions. This was an endorsement of the wider interpretation, but neither Hurst nor Fromageot was convinced that it was correct; there had to be further consultation. The difficulty was that Gaus could not leave Berlin because of domestic political matters. After some deliberation,[86] it was decided that Hurst should accompany Fromageot to Berlin to discuss the release of obligations question with Gaus. Great care was taken to ensure the secrecy of the Hurst–Fromageot mission;[87] the three principal Locarno Powers did not want their caution to be interpreted as an anti-American cabal.

The Berlin talks resulted in a consensus of opinion amongst the three legal advisers about how to interpret Kellogg's revised draft.[88] It is interesting that even before the talks began, there was agreement that it would be impolitic to reject Kellogg's latest overture. Rejection would not only damage the relations of the three Powers with the United States, it would almost certainly cause an unfavourable reaction amongst their separate public opinions. There was no doubt that this opinion had come to favour the idea of renouncing the use of war in international relations.[89] Nonetheless, the point of the Berlin talks was for the British, French, and German governments 'to find the interpretation of the text most consistent with their interests, and to place that interpretation on record as their understanding of its terms and as the basis on which they became a party to it'. After two days of discussion the legal experts agreed that the Gaus interpretation was the only one which they could accept. The three embodied the fruit of their talks in a joint note which, though it would remain secret, would form the basis of their separate replies to Kellogg.[90] Hurst informed Chamberlain that the loopholes in the proposed pact were now plugged, permitting Baldwin's government to accept the second American draft. In an important aside, Hurst informed the Foreign Office that neither the French nor the Germans saw anything wrong with the British determination to exempt the enforcement of the British Monroe doctrine from the provisions of the proposed pact.

Since Hurst had had to delay his advice on the second American draft, the Foreign Office decided that the Washington Embassy's enquiry into Kellogg's interpretation of the release provisions could not wait. Chilton was ordered to conduct the enquiry.[91] Accompanied by Broderick, Chilton met with Kellogg and Theodore Marriner, the head of the Western European Division of the State Department, twice on 5 July.[92] The chief difficulty concerned Kellogg's interpretation of how the pact would apply to a situation where a signatory, whether a League member or not, attacked a member of the League which was not a signatory. The British interpretation, was not hidden from Kellogg, asserted that any attack on a League member, whether it had signed the pact or not, was *ipso facto* an attack on all League members; it had to be resisted. Thus, those League members which were signatories had the right to go to war against the transgressors of peace without being denied the benefits of the pact. Chilton reported that Kellogg did not agree:

Secretary of State replied in substance that to agree to your interpretation would be to allow members of the League of Nations to be a law unto themselves. His treaty would be nothing but an endorsement of the League covenant [sic] and would be attacked as such in the Senate which would probably refuse to ratify it.

Kellogg also attempted a bit of diplomatic blackmail when he told Chilton that 'further alterations or definitions' might create an unfavourable reaction in the Senate. Chilton interpreted this as deriving less from Kellogg's worry about the Senate and more from the sniping that the Democrats might undertake against his foreign policy in the upcoming American elections. Kellogg did concede somewhat to British worries by noting that he would not be opposed to getting as many signatories to the pact as possible, but only after the original fifteen Powers had signed.

Despite its gloomy appreciation of how Kellogg's mind was working, Chilton's report was welcomed by the Foreign Office. With this and Hurst's report of the Berlin talks, the official British reply to Kellogg could be devised. The Foreign Office did recognise that, in including the Gaus interpretation, great care would have to be taken to ensure that it was phrased so as not to raise Kellogg's ire.[93] But the American secretary of state's willingness to enlarge the number of signatories beyond the original fifteen was encouraging. The greater the number of signatories, the less the chance that Britain and its League allies would quarrel with the United States over the application of Article 16. 'In other words', Craigie perceptively observed, 'all of the six hypotheses of the "Malkin" telegram of June 26 would then be covered, without recourse being had to the Gaus interpretation.'

Chamberlain placed the matter of deciding on the final form of the reply to Kellogg before the Cabinet. The Cabinet was not ignorant of the course of pact diplomacy, since the foreign secretary had kept his colleagues fully apprised of the events that had followed the receipt of the second American draft. Under Craigie's direction a comprehensive Foreign Office memorandum had been prepared and circulated to explain the problem of the British Monroe doctrine and the absence of any reference to it in Kellogg's final note.[94] Hurst's work at Geneva and Berlin was also reported.[95] Thus, once Hurst had returned to London and the Washington Embassy's enquiry into Kellogg's attitude was complete, the Cabinet was ready to move. As the basis of discussion, it used a draft reply prepared by Hurst and followed Chamberlain's lead almost without question in approving it.[96] The final note was actually quite short. The British government welcomed the explanations that Kellogg had given on 23 June, seeing in the revised preamble suitable safeguards to release signatories from their obligations toward a pact-breaker. However, the Cabinet would not budge over the two most critical points. In a carefully worded paragraph which summarised the Gaus interpretation, the note asserted that the renunciatory provisions would in no way restrict British action which might have to be taken under the authority of the League or Locarno. Whilst willing not to force the issue of having the British Monroe doctrine placed in the final draft of the pact, the Cabinet reaffirmed that the renunciation of war would in no way place strictures on the right to defend 'certain regions of which the welfare and integrity constitute a special and vital interest to our peace and safety'.

The only dissent came from Balfour. Because of ill health he could not attend these Cabinets, so he prepared a memorandum to impress his views on his colleagues. He argued that their reply should concur enthusiastically with Kellogg's proposals, this to avoid needless bickering over details and support good Anglo-American relations.[97] After some discussion, the Cabinet followed this advice to the extent of adding 'a sentence of "gush" which it was thought would respond to the sentiments of a large number of people here and flatter American vanity'.[98] Beyond that, the Cabinet endorsed the views of Chamberlain and the Foreign Office.

BLINY's first detailed summary of American press comment had been received as the Cabinet was in the final stages of these deliberations;[99] its findings supported resistance to major alterations to the draft reply. Based on a large cross-section of American press comment which spanned the period from January to June 1928, BLINY's work suggested that the renunciatory pact was not exactly a burning issue. Fletcher opined that the Middle West was the bastion of Kellogg's support, whilst the East and South saw little value in his proposals. The Far West, though warmer to the idea of renouncing war, was 'not thinking very much about it'. There was nothing to be lost by insisting on the right to use armed force to resolve certain difficulties in Europe, or to defend Egypt and the western approaches to India. Chamberlain remained firm in this resolve not to sacrifice legitimate elements of British and Imperial defence on the altar of improved Anglo-American relations.[100]

Because of the need to consult the Dominions, the British note was not given to the Americans until 18 July. Kellogg's pleasure was expressed to Chilton the next day.[101] The receipt of further reports from BLINY confirmed that the Cabinet's strong line had been correct.[102] The renunciatory pact was about to become a reality, and the Baldwin government's decision to adhere to it with reservations had been accomplished without arousing antipathy on either side of the Atlantic.

6. ARBITRATION, BELLIGERENT RIGHTS, AND DISARMAMENT, JANUARY–JULY 1928

I do not pretend to set myself up as a judge of the value of belligerent rights but I do say that what we are not in a position to enforce is of no value at all, and becomes merely a source of danger . . . So long as we maintain our rights so long will the Americans build. It is surely more important to put a stop to the race in armaments than to maintain belligerent rights which we can never enforce.

Wellesley, March 1928

There is no doubt that the possibilities presented by a pact to renounce war captured public attention in Britain, the United States, and other countries for most of 1928. But the negotiation of the pact, with all of the work it entailed for the diplomats, really served to divert the public and the press in Britain and the United States from the more critical political differences that separated the two countries. Whilst the form of the renunciatory pact was taking shape in that series of published notes, the Baldwin government devoted itself behind the scenes to resolving the two main problems in Anglo-American relations: preventing the diminution of belligerent rights below a point consistent with Imperial security and further naval limitation.

The renewal of the Anglo-American arbitration treaty

The process began with the renewal of the Anglo-American arbitration treaty. The day after Claudel received the Coolidge Administration's first note respecting the idea of a Franco-American renunciatory pact, Howard met with Kellogg.[1] Kellogg read the note that had been given to Claudel, the one that linked arbitration with the renunciation of war and which indicated an American preference for a multilateral renunciatory pact. Kellogg indicated that he would propose a new arbitration treaty to those Powers whose Root treaties were to expire in 1928. This would include Britain. Howard was then

128

instructed on why the questions relating to honour, vital interests, and so on were not to be excluded from any new arbitration treaty to which the United States became party:

Mr Kellogg explained to me that he as a lawyer had never been able to understand the real value of these words. It was clear that whatever Latin countries might do Anglo-Saxon countries would never consent to bind themselves to submit matters belonging to the domestic sphere such as taxes, tariffs, immigration etc. to arbitration unless some treaty right was involved which would make such questions justiciable and therefore arbitrable. . . So nations when having recourse to arbitration must prove breach of international law or breach of treaty, which was a contract.

A crucial part of Kellogg's presentation concerned the role of the Senate in establishing an arbitration tribunal, and in determining that tribunal's parameters of operation. Senate leaders had told Kellogg that these matters would have to be assessed as if they were a separate treaty. Thus, the advice and consent of the Senate would have to be sought before the United States government could agree to enter into arbitration with another Power. In order to impress on Howard the goodness of American intentions, Kellogg held up two diplomatic carrots. He said that the Coolidge Administration would sign any treaty that would abolish the submarine; he also indicated that his government would seek to ratify a long-standing convention that sought to prohibit the use of poison gas in wartime.

The American Department approached with caution Howard's interview with Kellogg. Although Vansittart took the line that any comments of substance would have to wait until the text of the proposed new treaty was received, he did pose one question about the Kellogg formula: 'Is it or is it not an "all in" proposal?'[2] All-in arbitration meant that everything except questions relating to domestic affairs and disputes with third parties would be covered by treaty. Kellogg's intention to seek to delete any mention of national honour and the like seemed to indicate an all-in proposal. However, Vansittart was concerned because a few newspaper reports were suggesting that the Americans were going to reserve their rights respecting the Monroe doctrine. The British government would have to give serious consideration to how belligerent rights would be covered in any new arrangement with the Americans, especially if Kellogg was genuinely seeking all-in arbitration.

Two days later Vansittart advised his superiors that the problem might become 'fairly pressing'.[3] Evidence was mounting that the

Coolidge Administration would reserve American rights over the Monroe doctrine and a few other matters, notably Oriental immigration. Vansittart suggested that the British government should consider reservations of its own, particularly regarding belligerent rights. He pointed to the blockade claims controversy as an object lesson. In 1926 the Cabinet had decided to resist any attempt to arbitrate the claims because there was no, way that this vital British interest should be the subject of an arbitral award.[4] No matter how just the cause, a decision could go against Britain. But the Coolidge conference had broken up on the rocks of belligerent rights. The American Department felt that the two options concerning belligerent rights which were available to the Baldwin government would only aggravate the situation. A decision to reserve those rights would upset the Americans, damaging Anglo-American relations further. A decision not to reserve would seriously compromise the British ability to enforce a future blockade. The latter, in addition, would open with a vengeance a problem which had been avoided successfully during the blockade claims controversy. Vansittart strongly recommended that the belligerent rights sub-committee meet as soon as possible.

The senior members of the Foreign Office could not agree amongst themselves about Vansittart's assessment of the problem. Wellesley and Hurst, in possession of copies of the Briand–Kellogg correspondence which had been given secretly to the British by both the French and the Americans, debated the implications of Kellogg's arbitration proposal.[5] Wellesley saw the attempt to tie arbitration to the renunciatory pact as 'a very astute move on the part of the Americans which promises to place us in an exceedingly difficult position'. Whilst Wellesley agreed with Vansittart about the poor reception a British reservation of belligerent rights would have in the United States, he also felt that there was no option but to reserve those rights unless an Anglo-American agreement on them could be reached before the conclusion of a new arbitration treaty. Wellesley endorsed Vansittart's recommendation about the CID enquiry beginning as soon as possible, but he worried about the advisability of reserving other British vital interests. He suggested that a profitable course might be the discovery of 'some formula that will cover naval rights without specifically mentioning them'. The beauty of a general reservation was that it could thus cover a whole range of contingencies.

Hurst thought that both Vansittart and Wellesley were over-estimating the 'inconvenience' of Kellogg's proposal. There existed the chance that the French might not take Kellogg up on his offer. On the other hand a League Security Commission, an appendage of the Disarmament Preparatory Commission, was to meet at Geneva in February. It was scheduled to discuss matters relating to vital interests, national honour, independence, and third parties. Perhaps the Security Commission findings would provide a means for rejecting what Kellogg had proposed. But the crux of Hurst's minute was to take Vansittart and Wellesley to task for their misappreciation of the legality of British blockade practices. Hurst emphasised that there had been nothing illegal in the application of belligerent rights by the Royal Navy during the Great War. Vansittart and Wellesley worried too much about what an international arbitration tribunal would do. Hurst's position was that the practices in a future war would be similar to those of the Great War. The reason that the Americans did not press for an arbitration respecting the legality of the British blockade between 1914 and 1917 – which they could easily have done because of British dependence on American supplies – was because the blockade was indisputably legal.

Chamberlain came down on the side of Vansittart and Wellesley.[6] He wrote immediately to Hankey to ask that the belligerent rights sub-committee meet as soon as possible;[7] the first meeting was arranged for 11 January. Hankey privately condemned the Foreign Office reaction to Kellogg's proposal, suggesting that the foreign secretary was 'panicking unnecessarily'.[8] Nonetheless, the committee met as arranged, though Chamberlain took the chair as Salisbury was indisposed.

The first sub-committee meeting was of consequence because there emerged two factions: those who thought there should be some agreement with the Americans; and those who believed that there would be nothing to gain and, perhaps, everything to lose in an accommodation. Chamberlain emerged as the principal spokesman for the first group, whilst Hankey became the voice of the second.[9] In the debate which occurred during that meeting, arguments that came to dominate the discussion of British American policy for the remainder of the second Baldwin government were laid down. It amounted to a quarrel between those who felt British interests were best served by limited commitments in various parts of the world where those interests might be endangered and those who wished to retreat within the Empire, eschewing as many international commitments as possible. Chamberlain's interventionist foreign policy, the foreign policy of the second Baldwin government, had led to friction with the United States. In order to protect this policy, at the hub of which stood the League, Locarno, and European security, Chamberlain and his supporters argued for an Anglo-American belligerent rights agreement. This would not only defuse immediate diplomatic difficulties, it would also ensure that the probability of future clashes with the United States on this question would be reduced markedly. The imperialists would have nothing to do with this proposition. The Empire was the basis of British global power and to place strictures on Imperial defence was akin to madness. For those who clustered around Hankey, resistance to the arguments of Chamberlain and his supporters was imperative.

Chamberlain opened the discussion by noting that the Briand–Kellogg exchange had made the work of the sub-committee more urgent. He repeated the concern that had been expressed by Vansittart and Wellesley about the need to protect the doctrine of belligerent rights by political means. Kellogg's proposed arbitration treaty with France, which would soon be presented *mutatis mutandis* to Britain, had brought matters to a head. The foreign secretary suggested that the work of the committee was twofold: to enquire into whether or not it would serve British interests to seek an agreement with the Americans; and, depending on that answer, to determine what such an agreement should entail. Chamberlain pointed out that he did not want to see any diminution of British belligerent rights.[10] Indeed, he stressed that it was 'in our interest to keep belligerent rights as high as possible, since the exercise of our sea power was, and always had been, of vital interest in our greatest struggles'. But there was no doubt that British and American interests coincided as far as belligerent rights were concerned. Britain and the United States were the world's preeminent naval Powers. They both lacked land forces of consequence. Chamberlain concluded that if the United States ever went to war, its navy would certainly be employed to enforce belligerent rights. Hence, it was to Britain's advantage to convince the United States about the utility of setting those rights as high as possible. Not only would this remove the biggest bone of contention between the two countries, which was presently embittering their relations, it would both diminish the chances of future disagreement and preclude the possibility of any American call to arbitrate.

Chamberlain was convinced that if 'Great Britain and the United States were in agreement on the subject, they would carry the rest of the world with them'.

Hankey would have nothing to do with this assessment of the situation. When a minor disagreement arose between Hogg and Peel about whether or not the increasing size of the United States Navy would make a belligerent rights agreement much more easy, Hankey was provided with the opportunity to attack Chamberlain. He interjected that there was no reason to suppose that a belligerent rights agreement would see the end of 'Big Navy' propaganda in the United States. Besides, he felt that it did not matter one way or the other. There was no indication that the Americans would oppose a British application of belligerent rights in the future. He agreed with the view that the war effort before April 1917 would have been weakened if the Americans had prevented the export of goods and capital to Britain. But the Americans had not done so, and Hankey saw no reason to assume that they would in the future.

Chamberlain cautioned that Hankey's line of thought ignored the very real risk of American embargoes against Britain. The Cabinet secretary countered that bargaining with the Americans meant the chance of being forced into a position where too much might be given away. This would be far worse than if there was no agreement whatsoever. Again, Chamberlain interrupted. He repeated what had transpired in the Howard–Hoover war talk.[11] If the United States decided to enforce neutral rights in the future, and an Anglo-American war broke out as a consequence, Britain would be placed in an unenviable position: Canada would be forced into neutrality; western hemispheric trade with Britain and Europe would be prevented; strategic British possessions in the West Indies would be occupied by American forces;[12] and the prospects of Britain's success would be clouded by 'a war of naval, financial, and economic attrition'. This failed to persuade Hankey. He repeated that he could not accept that the Americans would resist a British maritime blockade just because they had the ability to do so.

The rest of the meeting touched on a number of points pertaining to the general question of blockade and American reaction to them. Almost every member of the sub-committee spoke, but again Chamberlain and Hankey dominated the discussion. A key exchange occurred over what the Americans would do if a League-sponsored blockade was imposed against some transgressor of peace and justified under Article 16 of the Covenant. Supported by Hurst, Chamberlain reckoned that a League blockade, especially if it was implemented under the provisions of Article 16, would be condemned by both American government and public opinion. Both men thought, however, that a League blockade would probably be successful. Hankey argued this point with Hurst. Hurst, with his strong League proclivities, argued that the United States would be unable to disregard the universal condemnation of a transgressor of peace that would result from the imposition of Article 16. Hankey, who had little use for the international organisation, felt that the United States would have to be approached before a League blockade could be effective. Chamberlain immediately saw the inconsistency in Hankey's position: why did he think that a League blockade would fail without American concurrence, whilst one imposed unilaterally by Britain would not? Chamberlain pointed out that Hankey's comment about the need for American agreement was precisely the reason why an approach to the United States over belligerent rights was necessary. After an inconclusive discussion of the ability of the Royal Navy to enforce 'a "close" as opposed to a "long distance" blockade', that is, one adjacent to the enemy coast as opposed to one on the high seas, the meeting ended.

Although three members of the sub-committee were unable to attend the first meeting – Salisbury, Balfour, and Cunliffe-Lister – the other five took very definite positions on the question of seeking some sort of agreement with the Americans. Chamberlain, Cushendun, and Hogg felt that some sort of approach should be made; Bridgeman and Peel opposed this. The expert assessors were also divided. Tyrrell supported Chamberlain; Hankey and Madden wanted nothing to do with an agreement. With his League convictions, Hurst stood somewhere between; he did not endorse the concept of a bilateral agreement with the United States but, at the same time, he did not see the value of a unilateral British blockade now that the League was in existence.

Cushendun was a solitary figure in the sub-committee. Where Chamberlain and Hankey and their supporters were arguing about how high to keep belligerent rights, Cushendun favoured their reduction to the lowest level possible. Soon after he replaced Cecil in the Cabinet, Cushendun – then Ronald McNeill – wrote Chamberlain about the problems of British disarmament policy.[13] The naval question was naturally paramount. Cushendun thought that the abandonment or, at the very least, the modification of the doctrine of belligerent rights was necessary for Britain's future. He believed that the successful blockade against the Central Powers during the Great War had occurred through a set of unique circumstances; he saw the eight-inch versus the six-inch gun controversy at the Coolidge conference as a question of the freedom of the seas versus belligerent rights; and he was convinced that a failure to come to terms with the Americans would result in the continuation of naval deadlock and an escalation of cruiser construction. More than Chamberlain and the Foreign Office, Cushendun became the arch-enemy of Hankey and the navalists within the second Baldwin government.[14]

The second meeting of the sub-committee occurred on 6 February and, in the interim, the Foreign Office decided to sit back and observe the Franco-American handling of the arbitration treaty-renunciatory pact diplomacy. This derived from Vansittart, who advised a cautious approach.[15] He argued that the essential point at that juncture was the arbitration proposals rather than the renunciatory pact, and he advised that there should be no official British reaction until after Briand and Kellogg had sorted out their differences. Caution was also encouraged by reports indicating that the idea of a multilateral pact was being well-received by important governments.[16]

On 6 February the new Franco-American arbitration treaty, based on the Kellogg rather than the Root formula, was signed at Washington.[17] The conclusion of this treaty created problems for Chamberlain and his advisers. Since Kellogg had told Howard that the Coolidge Administration would seek to negotiate new, identical arbitration treaties with those Powers whose Root treaties would expire in 1928, the British were confronted with a major political problem. The new Franco-American arrangement saw the rights of the United States Senate entrenched in its provisions. Before a dispute could go to arbitration, it had to be transformed into a special treaty that defined the issue at hand. The new agreement, like the old one, acknowledged the Senate's constitutional right to advise and consent to any treaties that the United States government contemplated signing. If it was so disposed, the Senate could block an attempt by the Coolidge or a future administration to enter into arbitration. The French had tried to circumvent the Senate by including reference to the Hague Convention of 1907, but this had failed.[18] Kellogg did succeed in reserving from arbitration those matters relating to the application of the Monroe doctrine, something the Root treaties had not done. For their part, the French were able to exempt questions relating to the League. The British problem with the Franco-American treaty was the inclusion of 'vital interests, honour, and integrity' amongst those matters that were arbitrable. Vansittart recognised as early as 18 January that this could make subsequent negotiations with France and the United States – both the Anglo-French and Anglo-American arbitration treaties lapsed in 1928 – much more difficult, particularly over belligerent rights.[19]

By the third week of January the Foreign Office had actually received a copy of the proposed new Anglo-American arbitration treaty, which was *mutatis mutandis* the same as the Franco-American one. Though the draft was circulated immediately to the Cabinet, it was assumed that Paris and Washington would take a while to complete their negotiations.[20] This hiatus would give Baldwin's government an opportunity to formulate carefully its response to the 'vital interest' question. It came as a surprise, therefore, when the British Embassy at Paris discovered on 1 February that the new Franco-American treaty was 'practically "*à point*"'.[21]

The belligerent rights sub-committee held its second meeting in the wake of these developments.[22] Salisbury began the discussion by observing that two questions had to be faced: 'firstly, should our policy be governed by our needs as a belligerent, and, secondly, was this an opportune time to approach the United States on the subject?' With only Cushendun dissenting, the sub-committee agreed that the enquiry had to be approached from Britain's needs as a belligerent. The timing of the approach to the Americans was the issue that dominated the second meeting. Except Cushendun, no one wished to seek an agreement unless the minimum rights to be determined by the sub-committee could be assured. Chamberlain felt that the sooner an approach was made, the better; his adversaries disagreed.

Chamberlain made much out of the fact that the Franco-American arbitration treaty was to be signed the day the sub-committee was meeting. He argued that the sub-committee's work was urgent because 'reservations which would have protected us in disputes regarding belligerent rights were now in doubt'. He suggested a two-part strategy that might protect British belligerent rights. First, by means of informal conversations before formal Anglo-French discussions began about the new arbitration treaty, Briand should be instructed on British views about arbitrable subjects. Chamberlain believed this could best be accomplished if Hurst talked to Fromageot.[23] Second, and more important, was the approach to the Americans. To avoid the sort of problems that had contributed to the failure of the Coolidge conference – inadequate diplomatic preparation, along with a plethora of press comment that had poisoned public opinion on both sides of the Atlantic[24] – the Americans had to be sought out secretly and informally. To impress on his colleagues the soundness of this part of his proposed strategy, the foreign secretary pointed to the successful resolution of the blockade claims controversy. He pointed out that a few members of the State Department had seemed sympathetic to the British point of view at that time; they were still serving. Chamberlain then repeated Vansittart's earlier suggestion about broaching the subject of an Anglo-American belligerent rights agreement to the middle echelon of the State Department.[25]

At this juncture the contentious question of when was the opportune time to approach the Americans arose. Chamberlain stressed that unless the Americans were sounded out soon, the opportunity to do so again would probably not reoccur for eighteen months to two years. By early July 1928 the American presidential-congressional election campaign would begin; it would last until November. This would be followed by a period of uncertainty in American foreign policy, whilst the new Administration would be forming and setting its objectives. In any event an approach would have to be put off until after March 1929, when the new president would be inaugurated. Chamberlain noted that a British general election would have to be called sometime in late 1928 or early 1929; this, too, would delay making an approach to the Americans. The foreign secretary thought that one other factor favoured an early sounding of the Coolidge Administration, and this was the president himself. Despite Coolidge's disappointment over the failure of the naval limitation talks at Geneva, Chamberlain urged the sub-committee to consider the feasibility of exploiting the president's desire to leave office with some monument to international peace that would bear his name at least in part. The foreign secretary ended his remarks by observing that if an early approach was thought to be practicable, it should be made after the conclusion of the 1928 congressional debate on naval appropriations in a month's time.[26]

Bridgeman and Hankey responded immediately with admonitions about early soundings of the Americans. Bridgeman argued that the question of a belligerent rights agreement should be raised when the negotiations for a new Anglo-American arbitration treaty began. Alluding to private remarks by Craigie, Hankey suggested that it would be best to wait until after the American elections.[27] Somewhat disingenuously, Chamberlain responded that he was not attempting to determine whether it was advantageous to approach the Americans now or later; rather, he merely wanted to impress on the sub-committee the need to be 'prepared to take advantage of any occasion that might arise'. His introductory remarks suggested, however, that he felt that the opportunity to canvass official American opinion would present itself in the interim between the end of the naval appropriations debate and the beginning of the election campaign. Madden and Chamberlain were reduced in the end to repeating their standard departmental viewpoints. Madden stated that the Admiralty did not want a belligerent rights agreement because 'the next unlimited war' would probably not break out for fifty or one hundred years. It was impossible, therefore, to predict how such a war would be fought. The Admiralty took the line that it would be to Britain's advantage to enter such a war with the highest belligerent rights and, if the tides of war went against Britain, those rights could then be lowered by agreement. Chamberlain responded that 'it was wiser to try to reach agreement now than to trust to circumstances and day to day diplomatic skill as [Britain] did in 1914–1917'.

The significance of the second meeting, apart from the decision that the enquiry should be conducted from the point of view of British belligerent needs, was the deeper division of the sub-committee and the first indication of the in-fighting that was developing between Chamberlain and his advisers and the navalists. As chairman, Salisbury assumed strict impartiality in the discussions; he demonstrated his calm and reason after a particular discordant outburst by Cushendun. Cushendun had suggested that British hegemony on the seas had passed with the Great War and that the only hope for the future was to consider seeking an international agreement that would put belligerent rights as low as possible. Salisbury defused a potentially explosive exchange between Cushendun and the navalists by sympathising with the chancellor's views whilst pointing out that the consensus of the sub-committee was to keep belligerent rights as high as possible. Cunliffe-Lister embraced the arguments of those who did not want an accommodation with the Americans, thus splitting the sub-committee evenly: Bridgeman, Peel, and Cunliffe-Lister versus Chamberlain, Cushendun, and Hogg.

There also emerged the first indication of a campaign by the navalists to discredit the basis of Foreign Office arguments favouring an Anglo-American belligerent rights agreement. Prior to the second meeting, Howard's argument that the United States would 'never again' permit Britain or any other Power to interfere with American neutral rights had been circulated.[28] The central strand of this argument was that the Americans now realised that they had the ability both to break a British blockade and to imperil British war effort by withholding supplies of goods and capital. Responding to this, Hankey circulated a paper euphemistically entitled 'A Rejoinder to Sir Esmé Howard'.[29] Although ostensibly a comment on Howards views, it amounted to an attack on the ambassador's ability to interpret correctly what was happening in the United States. Hankey argued that the Americans had been at odds with British policies of belligerent rights for over seventy years, since the Crimean War. 'Never again' had been the cry of American anglophobes during the Great War, yet nothing had come of it. More important, the Americans had been fully aware between 1914 and 1917 that they could easily have disrupted Britain's war effort if they really wanted. They had not because the British cause was just, and they would not in future for the same reason. Thus, Hankey stressed that what Howard was saying was not only not new, it was proven to be incorrect based on the lessons of the Great War. Hankey repeated what he had said at the sub-committee's first meeting: just because the Americans could resist a British blockade did not mean that they would.

Two days after the second meeting of the belligerent rights sub-committee, the Cabinet's preliminary consideration of Kellogg's proposals for a new Anglo-American arbitration treaty set in train a series of events which removed temporarily the urgency of this aspect of the American question.[30] The Cabinet decided that the Dominions had to be consulted about the American proposals; it took a month for the Foreign Office, in tandem with the Dominions Office, to prepare a suitable despatch. Great care was taken at the insistence of Craigie, now the head of the American Department, to mention nothing about the Baldwin government's enquiry into belligerent rights. The worry was expressed that this information, if somehow leaked to the Americans, could compromise any subsequent British diplomatic

initiative to resolve the belligerent rights question.[31] Two days before
the Dominions were informed about the new arbitration proposals,
Howard was instructed to inform Kellogg that the Cabinet was
considering the draft treaty and consulting the Dominions.[32] Though
an obvious delaying tactic, the Americans could not complain.
Houghton had asked Chamberlain on 5 July 1927, in an informal talk,
if the British government would be willing to renew the 1908 Root
treaty.[33] Chamberlain replied that it probably would, and the
American ambassador seemed to imply that a formal notice of
renewal would be made in due course. It was, therefore, somewhat of
a shock when Kellogg proposed an entirely new arbitration
agreement six months later.

The Anglo-French disarmament compromise

The Anglo-American arbitration treaty did not reemerge as a major
British diplomatic problem until the autumn of 1928. In the ensuing
period the questions of the renunciatory pact and disarmament, with
the problem of belligerent rights always lurking in the background,
preoccupied Chamberlain, his Foreign Office advisers, and his
Cabinet colleagues. But it was the attempt to resolve the disarmament question, by seeking a compromise with the French, that
precipitated the crisis in Anglo-American relations which preoccupied the second Baldwin government during the winter of 1928–29.

In March 1928, when Kellogg was preparing the diplomatic
ground for the circulation of the first draft of the renunciatory pact,
the Disarmament Preparatory Commission was on the verge of
collapse.[34] A year earlier, in April 1927, the third session of the
Commission produced a draft convention for the limitation of
armaments which did not represent a united point of view. It was
based on the two draft conventions that had been submitted by the
British and the French.[35] The president of the Commission, Jonkheer
Loudon of the Netherlands, had described the document as a means
by which the Commission

had marked the points on which unanimity was obtained with or without
reservations, placed side by side the texts on which agreement had not yet
been established, and noted the statements and proposals on which
unanimity was not reached but which the delegates who made them expressly
wished to keep until the second reading.

The second reading was to occur at a later session, and Loudon suggested that Commission members who were at odds with one another should consult privately to remove their points of difference. If such consultations were to occur in the interim between sessions, valuable time would not be wasted debating these points when the Commission met and, perhaps, the production of a suitable draft convention would be facilitated.

At the fourth session of the Commission, held in late November and early December 1927, there was still great divergence of opinion amongst the participant delegations. It was obvious that consultations had not occurred. The major obstacle was an Anglo-French inability to agree on how naval limitation should be handled – it was more and more the tendency to see arms limitation as the Preparatory Commission's goal. The differences in the British and French points of view had emerged when the separate draft conventions were tabled at the third session.[36] The British, who despite the cruiser deadlock and failure of the Coolidge conference were still supported by the Americans, contended that it would be most practicable to limit warships by tonnage per class. The French pressed for one overall tonnage for each Power, which could build as many vessels of as many types as it wished as long as the total tonnage did not exceed its allotted individual ceiling. The fourth session of the Commission ended without any naval limitation agreement.

The March 1928 meeting of the League Council came two weeks before the scheduled fifth session of the Preparatory Commission. At this meeting, at the request of Cushendun and those Cabinet members who were involved with British disarmament policy, Chamberlain suggested to the French that a compromise on arms limitation might be beneficial.[37] On 9 March Chamberlain met privately with Briand to discuss the questions of air, military, and naval disarmament.[38] Lamenting that the British and French positions respecting military and naval issues were 'diametrically opposed', Chamberlain argued that it was essential that some sort of Anglo-French compromise be struck. For some time the French had been pressing for the exclusion of trained reserves in determining the strength of military forces. This was opposed by Germany, which by the Treaty of Versailles was limited to an army of only 100,000 men and was prohibited from conscripting, and a few other countries, including Britain and the Soviet Union. Chamberlain suggested that British opposition in the matter of trained reserves could vanish if the French would agree to naval limitation by tonnage per class. Briand expressed interest in Chamberlain's offer and, in asking for a list of British proposals, said 'that he would put them to the French Naval authorities and use all of his influence to obtain their acceptance'. The basis for a compromise now existed.

In the ensuing discussion, Briand stressed that he had continually told French naval officials that an Anglo-French war was 'out of the question'. He told Chamberlain candidly that France's principal naval concern was the ambitions of Italy. He even went so far as to suggest that French worries about Italy mirrored British worries about the United States. Briand suggested a basis for the proposed compromise:

In each case our Oversea responsibilities were much greater and our sea communications much longer. It would be to our mutual advantage, when the proper time came, jointly to press that those factors should form the basis of assessment of cruiser strength which States could justifiably claim.

Chamberlain has been criticised for not rejecting this 'lines of communication' thesis out of hand.[39] However, his detractors ignore that this was a French bargaining position, that it would have to be examined by competent British authorities, and that it would then be a matter for in-depth discussion at a later date.

After seeing Briand, Chamberlain met with Cushendun, Alexander Cadogan, a Foreign Office member seconded as Chamberlain's League assistant, and Vice-Admiral Howard Kelly, the Admiralty representative on the British Delegation to the Preparatory Commission.[40] The four concurred in the belief that Briand's suggestion was a basis for further Anglo-French discussions which could be recommended to the Admiralty and, later, the Cabinet. The four also agreed that it might be best if the compromise was achieved before the second reading of the draft disarmament convention which would occur later in 1928. Kelly was designated to compose a letter encapsulating the British proposals which Chamberlain could give to Briand. It follows that the British proposals which Chamberlain handed to Briand on 10 March had the stamp of Admiralty approval.[41] There were two essential points about these British proposals: first, they contemplated the limitation of submarines of all classes; and, second, they showed no intention to limit cruisers below 7,000 tons.

The British motives for offering the compromise to the French have become an issue of controversy because of its subsequent effect on Anglo-American relations. The second Baldwin government's ideological enemies, both past and present, have labelled the compromise as everything from 'an unfortunate piece of diplomacy' to 'a bizarre diplomatic *démarche*'.[42] The most prominent opponent of the Baldwin ministry, and Chamberlain's principal critic, has laid the blame for the offer of a deal squarely on the foreign secretary's shoulders, even going so far as to charge that 'Chamberlain's motives must remain a matter for speculation'.[43] There is no need to speculate.

The British reasons for the offer of a disarmament compromise with the French can be seen in the record of the 12 March 1928 meeting of the Cabinet Committee on Policy for the Reduction and Limitation of Armaments.[44] This body, the direct descendant of Cecil's old Cabinet committee on disarmament, had been restructured after the Coolidge conference.[45] Salisbury was selected as chairman and he was joined by Cushendun, Hogg, and the three service ministers. When the committee met to discuss Chamberlain's report of his meeting with Briand, Salisbury expressed concern about the compromise stimulating a recrudescence of the Anglo-American cruiser controversy. He counselled that it might be of advantage not to mention cruiser limitation until after the American elections had been held. Chamberlain replied that the Preparatory Commission was about to meet again. Although it was almost certain that a second reading would be postponed, the settlement of Anglo-French differences could not wait another eight months. There were indications that if an attempt was not soon made to break the Anglo-French deadlock, Britain might become isolated in the disarmament debate. He defended the approach to Briand by remarking that he was 'only anxious to secure that, in putting forward these proposals, we should not stand alone, but should have at least the support of France'. British interests could only benefit by making the Commission work, and to attempt this in collaboration with the French would strengthen Locarno.

For the British, especially Chamberlain, the worry of being isolated in the naval limitation question was very real, the more so if Britain was on one side by itself, and France and the United States were on the other. The first indication of possible British isolation came at the fourth session of the Preparatory Commission, when Kelly met with Admiral Salaun, the chief of the French Naval Staff.[46] Kelly was told that Italy was France's principal concern, though, in future, Germany might also present problems. Salaun emphasised that the French were not concerned with British naval ambitions but, like the

British, they had to defend their seaborne lines of communication to their Empire. The conclusion drawn from Salaun's remarks was that the French were looking to make a naval deal with someone; the difficulty was that this might not be the British. Two days after Chamberlain spoke to Salisbury's disarmament committee, to underscore the chance of British isolation, Kelly reported from Geneva that the French were also talking to the Americans about a disarmament compromise.[47]

The diplomacy which resulted in the Anglo-French compromise was unlike that which led to the renunciatory pact. The compromise did not raise many political and legal problems, and its negotiation, which by-passed the lower levels of the Foreign Office, was conducted by a few Cabinet ministers and their advisers. These men were aware that their work could affect the state of Anglo-American relations[48] but, from the British point of view, the political atmosphere in which the compromise was reached was not one in which these relations were seen to be worsening. At the third meeting of the belligerent rights sub-committee, held on 30 March, the decision was reached to send Craigie on a double-purpose secret mission to the United States.[49] He was to brief Howard fully on the enquiry being made into belligerent rights,[50] whilst making informal soundings of the official American attitude toward the negotiation of a belligerent rights agreement. The purpose of Craigie's mission was to be disguised by a long-planned visit to his wife's family in Georgia. His subsequent reports demonstrated that key State Department members saw the belligerent rights question as less pressing at that juncture.[51] This was thought to be the result of the renunciatory pact emerging as the dominant issue in Kellogg's foreign policy. American officials were 'unable even to consider seriously a set of circumstances which presupposes [the] existence of a state of war'. Since the annual congressional debate over naval appropriations had been accompanied by a perceptible lack of public support for the 'Big Navy party',[52] the time was opportune for an attempt at an Anglo-American compromise. Adding to the British desire to deal through the French was the fact that the proposals presented to Briand affirmed the principle of naval limitation by tonnage per class; in this, the British and Americans were at one.

The compromise took almost four months to conclude, a situation deriving from the French. In March they were canvassing both the British and Americans but, by mid-May, it was clear that Britain was a better French ally. French discomfiture with Kellogg's proposals to restrict the use of armed force in international politics was the telling point.[53] Anglo-French solidarity over the need to reserve both wars of self-defence and the enforcement of the League Covenant and Locarno from the renunciatory provisions preempted close Franco-American ties over disarmament. The British note of 19 May served to bring Britain and France closer together. It was no coincidence that five days after the British reply to Kellogg was made public, the British Embassy at Paris was informed that there would be 'no difficulty' in the matter of a compromise 'if only it could be discussed in a general manner and not as between experts'.[54] The French obviously wanted the agreement to be reached by civilian authorities and, accordingly, Chamberlain met with Briand at Paris on 2 June on his way to the League Council at Geneva.

The final phase of the negotiation began at that 2 June meeting and lasted until the end of July.[55] The first part was conducted by the diplomats, as Chamberlain met variously with Briand and Joseph Paul-Boncour, the principal French delegate to the Preparatory Commission.[56] The focus of their attention was the naval rather than the military aspect of the compromise, and the main impediment in the way of speedy agreement was cruiser limitation. Briand and Paul-Boncour were frank in wanting to arrange a system of naval limitation that would give France superiority over Italy. The French suggested that the way to do this was to determine cruiser numbers by the length of the lines of communication to be defended. Through Madden, the Admiralty criticised the French scheme because distance was just one of four factors that determined the number of vessels needed to defend sea lanes.[57] The other three were whether a line was 'vital', the volume of trade passing along it, and its geographical position.

The Admiralty also surmised that the French definition of 'lines of communication' lay open to two interpretations: did it mean sea routes over which all of a country's maritime commerce passed, that is, to both colonial possessions and foreign ports, or did it mean just those between colonial possessions and the mother country? The Admiralty felt that the first interpretation was the correct one but, by endorsing it, France would gain no advantage over Italy. The second would be objectionable to both Italy and the United States. The Cabinet endorsed Madden's view that without knowing the specific French interpretation, no decision could be made about employing the French proposal as the basis for cruiser limitation.[58] By mid-June it seemed as if there might not be common ground for a compromise.

This changed in informal discussions Kelly was having with his French opposite in the Preparatory Commission, Captain Deleuze. At the same time Chamberlain was talking with Briand and Paul-Boncour, Kelly met with Deleuze. Without the apparent authority of his superiors, Deleuze proposed that the compromise limit only those cruisers below 10,000 tons armed with guns of a calibre more than six inches.[59] He suggested that the success of this proposal would derive from Britain accepting parity with the United States in the limited cruiser class, and from France doing the same with Italy. In contrast, each Power would be free to build as many of the more lightly-armed cruisers as it felt necessary. The implication was that Britain and Italy, each with large reserves of armable merchantmen, would not bother to initiate large-scale construction of the unlimited cruiser class. Deleuze did concede that submarines would have to be limited by tonnage per class.

The Foreign Office learnt of the Kelly–Deleuze conversations on 23 June, and when it did it assumed that the Deleuze formula had been proffered with the authority of the French government. However, the French government claimed that its naval expert had adumbrated the plan on his own and, on 27 June, Cushendun, at Geneva on disarmament business, reported that Kelly had ascertained that Paris would not endorse what Deleuze had proposed.[60] But the members of Baldwin's Cabinet who were responsible for foreign and disarmament policies wanted a compromise with France to prevent British isolation in the Preparatory Commission.[61] Cushendun's report from Geneva suggested that the French were divided over whether to seek an accommodation on the basis of Deleuze's formula.[62] It was felt in London that the chance to secure an Anglo-French compromise should not be allowed to slip away.

Kelly had met with the French, Italian, and Japanese naval representatives to the Preparatory Commission on 27 and 28 June in separate talks.[63] The Japanese representative 'grasped the virtues' of a scheme to limit cruisers with guns greater than six inches – Kelly did not specifically mention the Deleuze formula – whilst his Italian counterpart said that Italy would only accept limitation by a total tonnage. In meeting with Deleuze, Kelly found that the French were prepared to use the compromise outlined on 5 June provided that two conditions were met: first, the maximum light cruiser displacement would have to be raised from 7,500 to 8,000 tons; and, second, an allowance would have to be made to permit the transfer of tonnages to both higher and lower categories of vessel, though the amount transferable could be limited to a percentage of the total agreed tonnage per class. This change in the official French attitude was marked by an invitation to Kelly to stop at Paris to meet with officials at the Ministry of Marine.

With the consent of the Admiralty, Kelly stopped at Paris on his way back to London.[64] He met with Admiral Violette, the new chief of the French Naval Staff, who disclosed that the Council of National Defence, the French equivalent of the CID, would meet in two days' time. At that time the Ministry of Marine would urge strongly that naval limitation be arranged by four categories of vessel: capital ships, aircraft carriers, surface vessels below 10,000 tons with guns greater than six inches, and ocean-going submarines, that is, those over 600 tons. Violette indicated that the size of the submarine to be limited was open to negotiation. This was immediately contrasted with the existing French plan that had been advanced at the third session of the Preparatory Commission in March 1927; but Kelly was certain that the new scheme would be the only one examined by the Council of National Defence. Since he believed that fire-power was more important than the size of vessel and that limitation by calibre of weapon was 'preferable', Violette argued that the only cruisers that should be subject to limitation were those of less than 10,000 tons with more than six-inch guns. Kelly recognised that the Americans would view the Deleuze–Violette plan with disdain, though he remarked that 'it is difficult to repress amused surprise at seeing all the old British proposals, flatly rejected by the French for years, now put forward by their Chief of Naval Staff'. Kelly impressed on his superiors that the French wanted the Americans to be consulted about the compromise prior to it being placed before the Preparatory Commission. Consultation was an essential prerequisite for success, and Violette stressed that the refined plan, though its Anglo-French origin would not be disputed, should be circulated by the British because 'it would be receding too much from [France's] existing proposal'.

On 20 July the British Embassy at Paris received a note from the French Foreign Office formally proposing the compromise.[65] Reference was made to the Kelly–Violette discussion and to the belief that Anglo-French cooperation was fundamental to any eventual disarmament agreement. There were three main points in the French note. First, there had to be provision made for the limitation of ocean-going submarines 'by fixing the same maximum tonnage for all of the great naval Powers, the advantages of such a system being to avoid the possibility of engaging on delicate discussions concerning the relative needs and importance of different navies'. The French also wanted this system of limitation to apply to the cruiser class to be limited by the compromise. Second, the governments of Italy, Japan, and the United States, the three other principal maritime Powers, had to be informed of the new proposals for naval limitation. Third, in an attempt to forge a new political bond between France and Britain, the French note made an unexpected proposal: whether the compromise succeeded or not, Britain and France should 'concert either to ensure success by other means or to adopt a common policy so as to deal with the difficulties which would inevitably arise from a check to the work of the Preparatory Commission'.

Salisbury's disarmament committee met on 24 July to examine the French note; its decision to accept the compromise was placed immediately before the Cabinet.[66] The only question of importance that Salisbury's committee had to consider was the proposal for parity in ocean-going submarines and cruisers amongst the five Powers. This amounted to a trade-off between those Powers which were prepared to build large submarine fleets and those willing to construct a great many heavy cruisers. The Admiralty made it plain in Salisbury's committee that it was prepared to take the risk involved in agreeing to this trade-off. The problem, of course, would be the American attitude. The compromise tended to favour the British and French – a not unnatural situation considering the nature of the agreement – but the point of the deal was to break the deadlock within the Preparatory Commission that stemmed from the Anglo-French inability to agree on how to effect naval limitation. Moreover, both the British and the French recognised that what they proposed would not be the final word on the matter. The French desire to inform the other Powers about the lines of the compromise before the Preparatory Commission next met, with which the Salisbury committee concurred, demonstrated a belief that other viewpoints would have to be assessed before securing an international arms limitation agreement. With the Salisbury committee, the Admiralty, and the Foreign Office firmly behind the compromise, the Cabinet could only endorse it.[67]

On 27 July Chamberlain instructed the Paris Embassy to inform Briand that the British government accepted the Deleuze formula for naval limitation, subject to the conditions regarding submarine and cruiser parity outlined in the 20 July French note.[68] To alleviate Violette's worry about France appearing to recede too much from its 'existing proposal', Chamberlain agreed to acquaint Italy, Japan, and the United States with the compromise. For political reasons, the decision was made to omit reference to the supplementary agreement on trained reserves. Since the fate of the naval aspect of the compromise was uncertain, it would not help to complicate the situation more than need be. However, Chamberlain did not reply to Briand's proposal to use the compromise as a means of forging stronger Anglo-French political ties. The Baldwin government saw no need to encourage an Anglo-French political alliance; such a course would play havoc with Locarno. On 28 July Crewe gave Briand the formal British reply,[69] and the Anglo-French disarmament compromise was a reality. Two days later the British Embassies at Rome, Tokyo, and Washington were informed that Britain and France had achieved a compromise on naval limitation; they were to inform their host governments of the nature of the deal and to invite the observations of those governments on the proposals.[70] Thus, by the end of July 1928, a difficult time in Anglo-American relations seemed to be drawing to a close. Arbitration, the renunciatory pact, and naval limitation each appeared to be withdrawing from the first rank of foreign policy problems.

7. THE CRISIS IN ANGLO-AMERICAN RELATIONS, AUGUST–NOVEMBER 1928

Americans are notoriously hasty and impetuous in their judgements and the actual advantages which they derive from good relations with Great Britain are patent only to a relatively small and thoughtful minority. Any United States Government is liable to allow feelings of temporary animosity or disappointment to obscure its considered judgement, and to lose sight in times of stress of the more solid and permanent interest of its own country.

Craigie, November 1928

On 30 July, the day that the three naval Powers were informed of the Anglo-French compromise, the House of Commons discussed aspects of British foreign policy. On the verge of a severe illness,[1] Chamberlain was pressured about the supposed failure of the Preparatory Commission; to enhance the government's disarmament record he disclosed the existence of the compromise, indicating that the proposals were being despatched to the principal naval Powers and could not be elaborated at that time.[2] Despite the excuse of ill health, Chamberlain erred in making this statement. He had not had clearance from the Cabinet and, because of time-zone differences, the other Powers would not see the proposals for some hours. On 31 July the foreign secretary collapsed because of his poor condition[3] and Cushendun took his place. This did not occur before that unfortunate Commons' statement set in train the events that created the crisis in Anglo-American relations which preoccupied Baldwin's government during the winter of 1928–29.

The rejection of the disarmament compromise

Immediately upon being notified of the compromise Kellogg, whilst restrained by Coolidge to make no commitments to the British about arms limitation, asked the American Embassy at London for clarification.[4] He wanted to be certain that the proposal's intent was to place no limits on the number of surface vessels, that is, cruisers and destroyers, with guns of six inches or less, or on submarines displacing less than 600 tons. Atherton, the *chargé d'affaires*, then met with Lindsay.[5] The importance of this meeting did not derive from Atherton being told that it was proposed that the three classes of vessel mentioned by Kellogg would be unlimited. Rather, it came from Lindsay's disclosure, that whilst the compromise itself concerned naval limitation, the French decision to agree to that limitation by tonnage per class meant that the British would not now oppose the exemption of trained reserves in determining military strength. To reduce American opposition, Lindsay suggested falsely that the British concession over trained reserves had been granted late in the negotiation.

Confused about the lines of the agreement, Atherton returned to the Foreign Office a few days later. He met with Craigie, impressing on him that 'the terms of the Anglo-French understanding had come like a bombshell to Washington and, indeed, to the United States generally'.[6] Atherton had to be certain that the compromise sought only to limit the cruiser class that the United States saw as the backbone of its fleet, whilst that required by Britain would remain unlimited. Ignoring what Lindsay had told him earlier, he asked if there was substance to rumours that Britain and France had made a supplementary agreement in the matter of trained reserves. Craigie replied truthfully that the purpose of the compromise was to eliminate Anglo-French differences within the Preparatory Commission. He added that he regretted the possibility of Americans reading into this agreement more than proposals designed to circumvent the block in disarmament discussions. But, because Lindsay's meeting with Atherton had occurred on the weekend and its record was in the Western Department files, Craigie was unaware that the American *chargé* had been informed of the concession over trained reserves. Believing that a disclosure of such importance had to come from someone with more authority, he skirted the second half of Atherton's enquiry. However, when he discovered later that day that Atherton had been told of this, Craigie recommended that the Americans receive 'the fullest possible details on this point'.

The decision was then made to inform the Americans fully about the purpose and nature of the compromise. Theodore Marriner, the head of the State Department's Western European Division and the official responsible for American disarmament policy, was visiting London for a few days. Cushendun asked him to call at the Foreign

Office to discuss the compromise; he did so on 9 August accompanied by Atherton, and met with Cushendun and Craigie.[7] The two senior officials covered much the same ground that had been gone over earlier, but two important points did emerge in the ensuing conversation. Marriner suggested that his government would require more time than the 3 September deadline, the anticipated date of the next session of the Preparatory Commission, to study the proposals. Those American officials who would deal normally with this matter, Secretary Wilbur, Admiral Jones, and Admiral Long, were each on their annual vacations. The danger existed that the Anglo-French scheme might be rejected out of hand because of inadequate time for study. Whilst Marriner made it plain that his government would reject the idea of limiting only those cruisers with guns greater than six inches, he implied that this might not be the case with the other classes of vessel. Cushendun replied that the Americans could have as much time as they needed for study, since the date of the next session of the Commission had been pushed into the future.

The second important point raised in this conversation was Marriner's suggestion that the Preparatory Commission might not be the best place to debate cruiser limitation. More fruitful discussion might occur during preliminary talks that would have to happen before the anticipated second Washington conference, scheduled for January 1931. Replying to a query by Cushendun, Marriner noted that Kellogg might not be averse to an informal discussion of the compromise when he came to Paris to sign the renunciatory pact. It was then assumed that Kellogg would travel to London after the signature ceremony.

On the day of the Cushendun–Marriner talks, the Embassy at Washington was sent a lengthy telegram outlining the background to the compromise and explaining the British withdrawal of opposition to the exemption of trained reserves in determining military strength.[8] Chilton received instructions to read the telegram to Kellogg, and, when he did, Kellogg asked for a copy of the message – which also mentioned that the 3 September deadline could be ignored – saying that the official American reply could not be given until after his return from Europe.[9] By mid-August the Americans had been fully apprised of all aspects of the origins and nature of the compromise; the British could only sit back and wait to see if the Americans would accept it.

Prior to Kellogg's departure for Paris, official American opinion did not express any anxiety about the Anglo-French agreement. Kellogg interpreted the move as a strategy designed to make the Preparatory Commission work whilst advancing simultaneously both British and French disarmament interests. He said as much to Coolidge on 3 August, though adding that he did not believe that the Preparatory Commission would endorse the compromise.[10] He also observed correctly that the British probably held the compromise to be the first step in a new round of naval negotiations. It was incumbent on the Navy Department, therefore, to plan carefully for the next session of the Commission.

By the time that the renunciatory pact was signed at Paris on 27 August, the official American attitude was perceived to have hardened. On 17 August Chilton had wired to say that Kellogg would likely spend two days each in Britain and Ireland after the signature ceremony.[11] Within a few days, however, it became clear that Kellogg would not be coming to Britain.[12] Claiming that he had insufficient time for two separate visits, he decided to travel only to Ireland. This had deep political significance. Long an element of discomfiture in Anglo-American relations, the Irish question had ceased to be important after the creation of the Irish Free State in 1921.[13] But to the British, particularly the Conservative Party, who were still sensitive over the matter of Irish independence, it was obvious that Kellogg was participating in a diplomatic snub.[14] Adding to this, on the same day that the renunciatory pact was signed by the representatives of the original fifteen Powers, Reginald Hoare, the acting British high commissioner at Cairo, reported that the Americans were about to invite the Egyptians to accede to the pact.[15] Though the Foreign Office had assumed that such an invitation would eventually be offered, it was not expected so soon. The American and Egyptian Departments consequently had to scramble to prepare Egypt's acceptance to the invitation, the key to which was London's refusal to define the precise regions where the British Monroe doctrine applied.[16] It was clear that the Coolidge Administration, displeased with the British attempt to get around the cruiser deadlock by aligning with the French, was creating difficulties for Britain in matters unrelated to the compromise.

An indication of why the official American attitude to the compromise hardened can be seen in a despatch that crossed Thompson's desk on 9 August.[17] This showed that the usual pre-budget publicity on behalf of a large American navy had started already. 'We must expect "big navy" propaganda', Thompson cautioned, 'to wax and grow as the month of December and the reassembly of Congress approaches.' The premature announcement of the compromise provided anglophobic American navalists with a hook on which to hang their arguments for a large navy. Throughout August, sections of the American press speculated about the 'real' nature of the compromise, probable secret clauses supplemental to it, and so on.[18] An air of suspicion was engendered. One of the reasons Cushendun had wanted to see Marriner was to dispel 'a certain amount of misapprehension in Washington as to the exact scope and purpose of the Anglo-French proposals'. The same motive lay behind the message that Chilton was ordered to read to Kellogg. The fact that the British had told all they could by mid-August meant that, when they tried to explain after this, they bored their listeners with the same story.

The growing distrustfulness of American officials at Washington was compounded when the American Embassy at London began to adopt an anti-British attitude. Thompson first detected this in late August when he lunched with F. Lammot Belin, the first secretary, and a few other American diplomats.[19] Thompson reported that these men 'made no attempt to conceal their entire lack of sympathy with the so-called agreement with France'. Belin kept mentioning the poor reception of the compromise in the United States. When an unsigned article that was particularly hostile to the Chamberlain Foreign Office and the Baldwin government appeared in the *Daily Telegraph*, which was owned by Lord Burnham, a political enemy of Baldwin, the American and Far Eastern Departments suspected that it was inspired by the American Embassy.[20] The article, which Willert discovered was written by a man named Gerothwohl, who was held to be 'a correspondent of importance by the U.S. Embassy', touched on a number of subjects in Anglo-American relations ranging from naval limitation to China. Though Willert was unsure that the Americans had fed Gerothwohl, Lindsay supported the view of the American and Far Eastern Departments:

In all this, the main point of the American indictment is the Anglo-French Compromise on Disarmament, and I take the rest on Mexico, Egypt, China, etc. as mere trimmings, to make us feel more uncomfortable. And indeed the Compromise does present an open flank to American criticism.[21]

Before official American comment on the compromise was received, the Foreign Office realised that the Americans would reject it. Houghton, returning to London from his annual holiday in the first week of September, saw Lindsay.[22] Though the ambassador portrayed himself as sympathetic to the British attempt to break the disarmament deadlock, he left the impression that his subordinates at the Embassy and 'the leading American press men in London' were deeply suspicious. On 13 September Chilton reported that 'the president is much annoyed over [the] agreement and [the] State Department are having considerable difficulty in preventing him from replying strongly without more mature consideration'.[23] Three days later Chilton added to this disturbing image of an enraged White House with a distressing report about the attitude of the State Department.[24] Castle had mentioned to Broderick that he did not believe the British had been completely frank in their disclosure about the purpose and nature of the compromise. Emphasis was placed on the decision to say nothing about the concession over trained reserves in the original communication announcing the existence of the compromise. Broderick surmised that Castle and his colleagues were at one with Coolidge and Kellogg on this point. Official American pique with Britain now seemed to have been transformed into outright hostility.

At this time Congressional agitation by the supporters of the 'Big Navy party' was beginning to emerge in direct opposition to the endeavours of the American 'peace movement'. The main reason for the early beginning of the annual 'Big Navy' propaganda for increased naval appropriations was the obvious success of the renunciatory pact diplomacy. By early September the Washington Embassy observed that the Anglo-French compromise was strengthening the hands of Americans who opposed disarmament and sought greater United States cruiser strength.[25] The actions of the 'Big Navy party' compelled Borah to see Kellogg several times to assure him that the renunciatory pact would be ratified by the Senate.[26] Borah also demonstrated his penchant for independence in foreign policy by suggesting that the Anglo-American naval problem could be resolved easily by an international conference to codify maritime law.[27] He went as far as proposing a Senate resolution calling on Coolidge to convene such a conference.

The confusion surrounding the compromise that was being fostered by the 'Big Navy' press – especially the Hearst chain[28] – did much to poison Anglo-American relations. But the antipathy of these newspapers was only to be expected. More damning indictments came from organs traditionally anti-Republican and anti-navalist. A case in point was the *New York World*, presided over by Walter Lippmann, which had not only opposed the Coolidge Administration over most policy questions, but had even been moderately pro-British. On 25 August the *World* published a report that Chamberlain had sent Briand a letter during the latter stage of the negotiations proposing 'the pooling of [the] British and French navies and co-operation in the Atlantic and Pacific'.[29] Though untrue and denied immediately, the source of the charge, rather than the charge itself, added considerably to the worsening of Anglo-American relations. Thus, a key assumption of the Chamberlain Foreign Office that had resulted from the blockade claims controversy – that division over foreign policy was endemic in the United States and could be relied upon to aid British interests – was shown to be incorrect. The Administration, the State Department, American diplomats, navalists in Congress, and a large section of the American press were united, if not in agreement on a specific response to a perceived British threat, at least in condemning British naval ambitions that found expression in the compromise with the French.

Adding to these difficulties were the reactions of the other Powers. The Germans, though not informed about the compromise's specific proposals, guessed correctly that the British had yielded to the French over trained reserves. German concern about the compromise centred on its political aspects.[30] The Italians were wary in their analysis, and Italo-American talks were held after Kellogg discovered that Mussolini was not happy with the possible advantages France might gain at Italy's expense. The Italians and Americans were assured, as a result of these consultations, that neither would stand alone in rejecting the compromise.[31] Only the Japanese looked favourably on the Anglo-French scheme, and this was because that portion dealing with cruisers offered Tokyo a way around the problem, encountered at the Coolidge conference, of extending the Washington treaty ratio to include lesser craft. Though Dormer cautioned that the Japanese were not sanguine about the official American reaction, formal Japanese acceptance of the plan was given to the British Embassy at Tokyo on 29 September.[32] This was to no avail; the Americans on 28 September, and the Italians on 6 October, rejected the compromise.[33] The Anglo-French effort to break the deadlock in the Preparatory Commission had come to nought.

Since early August both the British and French Foreign Offices had been adamant in resisting the publication of their correspondence regarding the compromise. They did not want the matter brought into the American election campaign. Hoover, who had secured the Republican Party's presidential nomination, demonstrated early that he had no fear of embarking on a partisan approach to foreign policy.[34] The political risks of publication were too great, though some influential sections of the British government, notably the Admiralty, were pressing for publication as a means of showing how uncompromising the Americans were.[35] Nonetheless, the Foreign Office led a successful opposition against publication throughout August and most of September.[36]

A revelation by the *New York American*, a Hearst newspaper, one week before the official United States rejection of the compromise forced the issue. The *American* had acquired and published a secret French document pertaining to the compromise which had been sent from the Foreign Office at Paris to the French Embassies at Rome, Tokyo, and Washington.[37] This fired a new round of speculation in the United States, forcing the British and French governments to communicate confidentially to their Italian, Japanese, and American counterparts the letters which formalised the deal.[38] This was done to stave off possible displeasure at Rome, Tokyo, and Washington – the three governments had not received any copies of the Anglo-French correspondence prior to this, thus, the *American*'s acquisition of one document was significant. As far as creating further suspicions of Anglo-French intentions in the public mind, the damage was done.

The British position softened when the Cabinet, apparently over Cushendun's opposition, decided that the publication of the relevant correspondence should occur, but only after the American comments on the proposals were received.[39] It was subsequently decided to withhold publication until after the Italian and Japanese replies were also in. Tyrrell, now the ambassador at Paris, moved to impress on Cushendun the need to publish.[40] He reported that the French Foreign Office now supported the idea of publication as a means of salving American irritation over the cruiser question. Tyrrell added that the appearance of candour by the Conservative government would do it nothing but good in the upcoming British general election, particularly against the Labour Party.[41] More to the point, as a francophile, Tyrrell warned that continued resistance to publish might help those in Britain and abroad who attacked the Baldwin government's foreign policy, at the basis of which stood 'close co-operation with the French'. However, even as Tyrrell's entreaties favouring publication were being sent, the essential papers concerning the compromise were being gathered.[42] After considerable Cabinet discussion, the British White Paper on the disarmament compromise appeared at the end of October, simultaneously with a French Blue Book on the same topic.[43] But even this caused trouble for the British. In a unique move, the decision was made to publish only parts of the relevant documents, probably to protect ciphers, more probably to put the British case in the best light. It made no difference; the Americans were unimpressed with the edited papers.

The Foreign Office under attack

The Coolidge Administration's rejection of the compromise, coupled with the unfavourable reaction of American public opinion, gave those members of the second Baldwin government who disagreed with the Foreign Office's handling of the American question an opportunity to challenge its dominance in determining British American policy. As a result the preeminence of the Foreign Office was temporarily eclipsed, and this coincided with a significant decline in Anglo-American relations.

Chief amongst those who quarrelled with the Foreign Office handling of the American question was Bridgeman. In early September, once it was clear that Chamberlain would be away for some time, Bridgeman wrote to Baldwin about the problems that would confront the Foreign Office whilst the foreign secretary was absent.[44] The focus of his attention was Cushendun – 'it is never satisfactory to have a deputy long in such a post' – who was still the principal adversary of the British navalists within the belligerent rights sub-committee. Although he made no concrete suggestions about how to resolve the problems facing the Foreign Office, Bridgeman implied that the Cabinet should take the lead in those areas where foreign policy problems were going to be most acute; he listed amongst these the American reaction to the disarmament compromise. Thus, it is not surprising that Bridgeman pushed vigorously for the publication of the relevant correspondence. In his submission to the Cabinet, the first lord made no bones about the fact that the Admiralty felt it was time for the Baldwin government to adopt a hard-line toward the Americans.[45] By implication the more flexible Foreign Office approach, that it was necessary to sound out the Americans on substantive foreign policy issues, was held to be barren.

The Admiralty agitation for a hard-line was endorsed strongly by Hankey, who outlined his arguments supporting Bridgeman in an exchange with Tom Jones.[46] Jones contended that the fundamental flaw in the British approach to their relations with Americans was the failure to perceive the United States as a major threat to Britain's international position. Hankey responded with the argument that he had used in the belligerent rights sub-committee in early 1928 – just because the United States could oppose Britain in a war, either as a belligerent or, if a neutral, by withholding financial assistance, did not mean that it would do so. The time for concern about American sensitivities was past:

We have been practising your policy for 10 years, and it has been a failure. We played up to America over the Covenant of the League, abandonment of the Japanese Alliance, Washington Treaties . . . always making concessions and always being told that the next step would change their attitude. Yet they are, as the result, more overbearing and suspicious against us than anyone else.

For Hankey, the American rejection of the disarmament compromise left the British with just one option. They had to ignore the United States in determining Imperial defence and, in a radical departure for a critic of Locarno, Hankey suggested that close Anglo-French ties in the context of that treaty had to be maintained. He now reckoned that a greater threat to British security resided with European as opposed to American problems, thus, the compromise should be retained as a means of keeping the European situation in balance.[47] To garner support for a hard-line towards the United States, Hankey began to canvas important members of the Cabinet with his ideas.[48]

The American rejection of the compromise persuaded Eustace Percy to involve himself in the Cabinet discussion of British American policy for the first time. In mid-October, when the Cabinet was debating the lines that the formal British reply to the American rejection of the compromise should take, Percy entered the fray with a memorandum arguing for British withdrawal from the Preparatory Commission.[49] He concluded that the Commission represented 'a positive menace' to both the peace of the world and the Empire. What was required by Britain was a more independent attitude toward the question of naval disarmament; it would not enhance international peace and security to have British naval requirements determined by the needs of other Powers, particularly the United States. There was bitterness in Percy's submission, deriving from his strong belief in trans-Atlantic Anglo-Saxon ties.[50] Thus he held the anglophobic attacks of the American navalists and others to be the worst perfidy. He declared that the American rejection of the compromise provided a diplomatic hook on which the opportunity for independence in disarmament policy could be hung. But a speedy reply was crucial, hence, a British response to the American rejection had to be formulated before the next session of the Preparatory Commission, which was scheduled for January. For the consideration of his colleagues, Percy included a draft reply to the Americans which would lay the ground for British withdrawal from the Commission. The essential part of the draft was the claim that the Baldwin government had made a contribution toward the solution of the problem of naval limitation, but rejection by both the American and Italian governments now meant that there was no basis for further discussion within the Commission.

This memorandum made such an impact on Salisbury that he invited Percy to attend the next meeting of the committee on policy for the reduction and limitation of armaments; it met on 2 November.[51] The purpose of the meeting was to decide on the line that Cushendun should take at the next session of the Preparatory Commission; there were three proposed courses of action. The Foreign Office position, contained in a paper by R. H. Campbell, was that the most profitable course would derive from 'negotiation through the normal diplomatic channels'. Salisbury offered the second proposal, which amounted to a policy of 'wait and see', because he surmised that American displeasure with Britain would soon dissipate and allow an opportunity for agreement with America to present itself again. The third proposed course was Percy's.

The initial debate in the committee occurred amongst Salisbury, Bridgeman, Cushendun, and Percy. Salisbury reckoned that time was on Britain's side. By waiting out the storm of unfavourable American reaction to the compromise, the British would witness the reemergence of conditions conducive to the settlement of the cruiser question. Bridgeman argued that the Americans had misunderstood the agreement with France. He recommended that a note be prepared to explain precisely what was proposed, especially that portion dealing with cruisers. At the Coolidge conference the Americans had sought twenty-three 10,000-ton cruisers; the

Anglo-French compromise would permit them to retain that number. Bridgeman indicated that the Admiralty did not want to put forward new naval limitation proposals. Aspects of the compromise had potential and, in league with the French, the British might get them adopted.

Cushendun opposed a further explanation of the compromise, labelling it 'premature'. The committee had been assembled to decide, first, whether it would be of benefit to come to terms with the Americans, and, second, what the British position should be at the next session of the Preparatory Commission. The acting foreign secretary quarrelled with the suggestion that the Americans did not understand the compromise; the problem was that they did. The difficulty was not one simply of how many 10,000-ton cruisers the United States should or should not be entitled. It was, rather, one of how many the Royal Navy should have in addition to the smaller, more lightly armed ones. Cushendun put the American case succinctly: 'In effect, they said, therefore, that if we required small cruisers we could only build them at the expense of the 10,000 ton cruisers.' It was the cruiser controversy of the summer of 1927 all over again. But, as far as Cushendun was concerned, the American note rejecting the compromise was not in the least truculent, nor did it bar the way to future discussions. The question posed by Percy's memorandum was fundamental: should Britain opt out of the Preparatory Commission? Cushendun counselled against such a move, advising that British policy should be one of making the Commission work. As a step in this direction, he recommended that 'normal diplomatic channels' be employed to have the representatives of the five principal naval Powers meet informally to discuss naval limitation.

Percy was emphatic in insisting that he had no intention of breaking off 'all discussions with the United States in regard to Naval Armaments'. He felt that some sort of accommodation with the United States would have to be arranged, but that this should not occur under the auspices of the Preparatory Commission. Like Cushendun, he was sure that the Coolidge Administration had not misunderstood the compromise; thus, it would be senseless to despatch a note which implied that Washington had missed the point of the Anglo-French proposals. Percy believed that the Baldwin government had to determine first how much room there was for a naval agreement with the United States. Only after this decision could effective policy be pursued. If an Anglo-American naval accord was not thought impolitic, the British could move to conclude it within the limits determined by Salisbury's committee. If, on the other hand, such an agreement was reckoned to be undesirable, 'then the best course would be to state the issue clearly and allow public opinion to form its own conclusions on the subject'. Percy's impression was that British disarmament problems revolved around the cruiser question rather than the matter of arranging naval limitation by either tonnage per class or one universal tonnage. The cruiser question was solely of Anglo-American interest, thus, he felt this was where British energies should be directed. There was no need to employ the Preparatory Commission in resolving this bilateral problem.

Hogg, now Lord Hailsham after his elevation to the lord chancellorship, broke in to comment that a reply to the American rejection was essential, but that it had to be despatched soon or there would be no reason to send one. He suggested that this reply should encompass two points. First, the American claim that the compromise sought to limit only the cruiser class unwanted by the United States should be challenged. It should be stated that the Anglo-French proposals represented only a basis for discussion within the Preparatory Commission, and that there was no prohibition either on the number of vessels per category that each Power could claim or on having the compromise extended to include other classes of vessel. Second, since the purpose of the compromise was to propose a possible line of agreement on points which threatened the Commission with collapse, it had to be emphasised that there was nothing hard and fast about the Anglo-French scheme. The Amercans had to be assured that the British government was open to other plans, whether their purpose was to refine the compromise or not.

Hailsham went further by asserting that Britain would only lose by failing to attend the next meeting of the Preparatory Commission. By showing up, the British delegation could do much to repair the situation: the history of the Anglo-French discussions could be recounted; the compromise could be more fully explained; it could be impressed on other Commission members, and public opinion generally, that Britain had tried to get disarmament discussions moving again, and that it was now willing to view the suggestions of others in 'the most accommodating spirit'. Of course, this was a public stance, designed to garner sympathy for the British situation.

Behind the scenes, Hailsham recommended, the British delegates would do nothing to initiate a way around the impasse. The other delegations could be told that the British would follow the lead of the Commission in any proposals it put forward – an improbable turn of events given the division between the French and the Germans, the French and the Italians, and so on. Hailsham assured Salisbury's committee that by following this course of action at the next session of the Commission, 'we should appear before the world as having done all that lay in our power, as being willing to co-operate in any further efforts, and as being in no way responsible for any breakdown which might occur'.

Salisbury and Percy saw merit in Hailsham's suggestions about both the reply to the American rejection and the strategy proposed for the next session of the Commission. Salisbury did point out that if the Foreign Office drafted a note to the Americans along the lines of Hailsham's remarks, the committee would be better able to judge the value of Percy's proposals. Other than to say that the Foreign Office should put as many of Percy's points in the draft note to the Americans as it could, Bridgeman remained silent. Salisbury, Percy, and Bridgeman appeared to be at least temporarily of the same opinion.

This isolated Cushendun. Whilst agreeing with what Hailsham had said about the note to the Americans, he opposed Bridgeman's suggestion to incorporate points raised by Percy. The Foreign Office experts, notably R. H. Campbell, objected to many of these, hence, the committee would have to take the responsibility for their inclusion. Cushendun did take issue with Hailsham's proposed strategy for the next session of the Commission. There was the danger of this policy leading to British isolation on disarmament, as happened prior to the negotiation of the compromise. He expressed particular concern about the emergence of a Franco-American combination which might attract the Italians.

Hailsham responded by maintaining that the French would not desert the British out of fear of losing what they had gained in the matter of trained reserves. Percy concurred, adding that he thought Cushendun was assuming incorrectly that the British delegation to the Commission would declare the compromise to be 'dead'; this was not necessarily so. The committee then concluded that 'the Foreign Office [should] draft a reply to the United States on the lines suggested by Lord Hailsham, and embodying as many of the points in

Lord Eustace Percy's draft as they considered advisable'. This, together with the strategy to be used at the next session of the Commission, would be examined at the following meeting of the committee.

The committee met a week later.[52] Two draft notes to the Americans were placed before it: one from the Foreign Office and, to underline the determination of some members not to give the Foreign Office a free hand in the matter, one from Percy. The subsequent debate over which draft was preferable centred on the wisdom of mentioning whether one or two cruiser classes should be limited. The Foreign Office draft, written by R. H. Campbell and defended by Cushendun, made no mention of this; Percy's did. Cushendun reported that, in the Foreign Office's opinion, to raise this contentious issue so soon after the American rejection of the compromise would only help the American 'Big Navy party'. He realised that Percy sought to appeal to 'the saner and more pacific American opinion', but the result of his efforts would see only the whipping up of anglophobia in the United States. Percy admitted that he possessed 'an open mind' about whether the matter should be mentioned and, if it was, how much should be said. He had included the reference to instruct British public opinion on the cruiser question. But the American note rejecting the compromise had discussed this point; unless the British reply alluded to it in some way, there was the chance that the raising of this particular question of cruiser categories might be precluded in the future. Bridgeman sided naturally with Percy, as the Admiralty believed that it would be better to meet American objections head on. In the end, Cushendun was reduced to arguing that 'a dignified silence' was the best course of action.

As in the previous meeting, Hailsham offered comments in an attempt to reconcile the divergent points of view. He thought that Salisbury's committee was concerned with two different sets of reaction to the cruiser question that would develop out of adopting either the Foreign Office or Percy's draft: the impact on American public opinion and the impact on British public opinion. Since Percy's draft would do much to educate the latter, this was a persuasive reason for mentioning categories. However, what Cushendun had said about the negative influence such mention would have in the United States could not be dismissed. There was nothing to gain by adding to the discord in Anglo-American relations. As a

consequence, Hailsham recommended that the British reply emphasise that there was no 'useful purpose' in discussing the question of
cruiser categories at that time; but, to leave the door open for future
Anglo-American discussions, the reply could state that a solution to
the problem was not thought to be impossible. The committee
accepted Hailsham's recommendation, a situation which meant that
Foreign Office advice about how best to handle the American
question was ignored.

After considering a few minor points about the draft reply, the
committee turned to the strategy to be employed at the next session of
the Commission. The debate led to a number of suggested courses
of action being proffered, a circumstance that caused Salisbury to
request those who had made suggestions to draw them up as
memoranda for consideration at the next meeting. Over Percy's
objections, the committee did decide that Britain should continue to
seek some sort of arms limitation agreement through the medium of
the Preparatory Commission. Although this was what Cushendun
had implored his colleagues to accept, it did not amount to a Foreign
Office victory. The original Foreign Office recommendation had been
to employ 'normal diplomatic channels', that is, informal discussions
amongst the representatives of the five principal naval Powers, to get
some preliminary agreement on naval limitation. Salisbury's committee would have none of this. All that it suggested was 'that the
British Representative should endeavour, without taking any undue
initiative in the matter, to dissuade the Preparatory Commission from
bringing its labours to an untimely end'.

Although naval limitation remained the most pressing problem
during the crisis in Anglo-American relations, a situation that led to a
diminution of Foreign Office power in determining British American
policy, two other questions emerged in the autumn of 1928 to erode
further the influence of the Foreign Office. The first was the
reemergence of the Anglo-American arbitration treaty as a foreign
policy of the first rank; the second developed out of a perceived
American threat to Canada that resulted in a restructuring of the
belligerent rights sub-committee. In May 1928, ostensibly because of
Dominion tardiness in replying to the British circular despatch
concerning the new arbitration treaty, the British and American
governments agreed that there would be no harm in letting the
existing treaty lapse. It was anticipated that a new agreement would
be signed by early 1929, therefore, nothing would be lost by not

having a treaty for a period of six to eight months – the Root treaty was to expire in June 1928.[53]

The Foreign Office, chiefly Hurst and the American Department, had been responsible for evaluating Kellogg's overtures for a new arbitration arrangement and in making recommendations to Chamberlain and the Cabinet. The difficulties surrounding the announcement of the Anglo-French disarmament compromise changed all of this. The first indication of arbitration reemerging as a major problem came with a report from Chilton that the State Department had decided to offer to conclude Kellogg's arbitration treaty with the Egyptian government.[54] It was recognised that Cairo would secure American recognition of Egypt as 'an entirely independent country'. But this was really of secondary importance. Chilton felt, and his views were seconded by the American and Egyptian Departments, that the offer of the arbitration treaty to Egypt was part of a general American strategy to lessen British global power.[55] Moreover, the immediate American gain to be realised from this was thought to be to preclude any British attempts to exempt the enforcement of the British Monroe doctrine from the new Anglo-American arbitration treaty.[56] Thompson saw the hand of the enraged State Department in this piece of diplomacy, and his views typified those prevalent not only in the American Department, but in the Foreign Office generally:

We in this country are, I believe, too prone to assume that the United States Government desire nothing better than to work in cooperation with us . . . I believe that the State Department look upon us as rivals politically, commercially, and economically, and as competitors who may seriously menace the growth of America's export trade, now becoming a vital necessity to the national well-being.

The difficulty was that the Foreign Office wanted to meet this American problem with circumspection, to concede a point here to gain an advantage there. This was not the view of others, like Hankey, who were deeply suspicious of the powerful role that the United States Senate would be accorded in the proposed treaty.[57]

Early in the fourth week of October, it became known that the Senate Department was impatient with the British delay in negotiating the new treaty. This expression of annoyance was not communicated through normal diplomatic channels, rather it appeared in the press.[58] Though some disagreement arose within the Foreign Office about whether the level of reported State Department displeasure was a fabrication of journalists, there was consensus that officials at Washington were distressed about British dilatoriness in the matter.[59] Whilst the State Department's supposed irritation with the Baldwin government was being publicised, the American Department was waiting for a Washington Embassy report on aspects of Kellogg's 'model' treaty that had been advanced in December 1927.[60] The Washington Embassy had been told that since the renunciatory pact was 'out of the way', the Foreign Office would be able to concentrate on arbitration. But before the Foreign Office received the Embassy's report, the Cabinet decided that the question of arbitration was too important to be left to the consideration of a single department of state. The troubled atmosphere of Anglo-American relations, which had appeared to worsen after the formal American rejection of the compromise, caused the Cabinet to examine the matter of a new arbitration treaty. Since there was no contemplation about reserving those matters relating to 'vital interests', the Cabinet recognised that acceptance of Kellogg's 'model' treaty might effectively prohibit the application of British belligerent rights against the United States. Consequently, the Cabinet decided to have the renewal of the Anglo-American arbitration treaty examined by Salisbury's belligerent rights sub-committee.[61]

Since August 1927 both Baldwin and the King had been receiving letters from Lord Willingdon, the governor-general of Canada, suggesting that the United States was moving to detach Canada from the British Empire.[62] These worried reports began soon after William Phillips, the American ambassador at Brussels and a former assistant-secretary in the State Department, was appointed as the first American minister at Ottawa. Phillips, who in accepting the transfer to Ottawa took a demotion in rank, went to cement closer Canadian–American ties.[63] Willingdon's reports stressed that the Americans had no intention of physically conquering Canada and absorbing it into the United States; such a move would have dire political repercussions both in the United States and internationally. Willingdon observed, however, that the Americans were conducting an unprecedented economic penetration of Canada, a method of expansion that was far more effective and more profitable than outright annexation. As Willingdon told Baldwin:

I am quite clear that the great purpose of American policy is to do everything in their power to make Canadians feel that they, the Americans, who are their nearest neighbours and best customers, are really much better and more helpful friends to Canada than the people of the old motherland.

The Foreign Office was not ignorant of the growing Canadian dependence on American economic and financial resources,[64] nor were Foreign Office officials unaware that the Americans were only too willing to use their economic clout for political advantage.[65]

In response to this perceived American challenge to Imperial unity, the Baldwin government decided that its representation at Ottawa had to be improved. Since 1867 the sole British representative in Canada was the governor-general, the monarch's personal deputy. Traditionally, the governors-general of all dominions reported to the monarch and the prime minister and, if particular matters required specialist attention, individual departments of state were asked for comment. In 1925 the complexity of intra-Imperial relations forced Baldwin's government to create a new ministry, the Dominions Office, to deal with British–Dominions affairs.[66] A year later, at the Imperial Conference, the Baldwin government recognised the growing independence of the Dominions by conceding that they were 'autonomous communities within the British Empire, equal in status, in no way subordinate to one another in any aspect of their domestic or external affairs'.[67] The upshot was that the Canadian government immediately established a permanent diplomatic mission at Washington under Vincent Massey, a former Canadian cabinet minister – it had actually been in the planning stages before the Imperial Conference – and the Americans responded by sending Phillips to Ottawa.[68] Canadian–American relations warmed after this[69] and, except for Willingdon's reports and a few observations from Howard and his staff, London seemed to know less and less about what was happening on the other side of the Atlantic.

The problem came to a head in February 1928. On 2 February Howard wired that Kellogg was to make an official visit to Ottawa in a few days time but, as his itinerary was being handled by Massey and Phillips, Howard was unable to speculate about why the American secretary of state was going to Canada.[70] The Foreign Office was distressed at this development, concluding that the lack of information about the purpose of Kellogg's trip suggested 'the need of having someone in Ottawa to whom we can go direct for information'.[71] Though it developed that Kellogg went to Canada on a goodwill mission,[72] the problem of inadequate British representation at Ottawa remained. Supported by Chamberlain, Amery convinced the

Cabinet to establish a separate British political mission at Ottawa, to be independent of the governor-general.[73] By the summer of 1928 William Clark, the comptroller-general of the Department of Overseas Trade, a Foreign Office adjunct, was selected as the first British high commissioner to Canada; he was to begin his duties in December.

It followed from this that when the crisis in Anglo-American relations developed in the aftermath of the Anglo-French disarmament compromise, the question of Canadian–American relations became an important consideration for the Baldwin government. But a snag materialised, and this was the problem of which department of state, the Foreign Office or the Dominions Office, was responsible for monitoring Canadian–American relations. When Clark was selected as high commissioner, it was decided that he would report to the Dominions Office rather than the Foreign Office. This was to keep British relations with Canada on a special footing, since the Foreign Office handled Britain's relations with foreign states and not with members of the Empire. But the Foreign Office was responsible for monitoring Anglo-American relations. When those relations worsened in the autumn of 1928, it was decided that the Foreign Office and Dominions Office should both keep an eye on Canadian–American relations. This served to undermine further the role of the Foreign Office in determining British American policy. Moreover, Baldwin became convinced that the state of Anglo-American relations had a general impact on the unity of the Empire. He accordingly restructured the belligerent rights sub-committee by making Amery a full member.[74] Though Amery's selection was made purely on the basis of his ministerial responsibility for both the colonies and dominions, his imperialist sentiments put him in the camp of Bridgeman, Hankey, and the other hardliners. The position of the Foreign Office in creating British American policy was weakened by the decisions to expand the purpose and membership of the belligerent rights sub-committee.

Coolidge's call for American naval superiority

The lowest point to which Anglo-American relations fell during the period of Baldwin's second government occurred after 11 November 1928. On 5 November the Republican Party, with Hoover as its presidential hopeful, retained the White House and its majority in both houses of Congress.[75] Although Hoover's inauguration would not occur until March 1929, Coolidge was freed somewhat from the constraints of office. With the end of his presidency in sight, he was upset with the failure of his Administration to bring about some sort of international arms limitation agreement. In his Armistice Day speech, which achieved wide distribution in the United States because it was broadcast on radio, the president made an untypical foray into the realm of foreign policy by castigating the European Powers for their reliance on armaments.[76] They were to blame for the lack of progress in arms limitation. Coolidge singled out Britain for the policies it had followed respecting cruiser limitation from the Washington conference to the Anglo-French disarmament compromise. In a dramatic statement, the more so considering his parsimonious nature, the president put his authority behind a bill then before Congress that authorised the construction of fifteen new cruisers:

When we turn to the sea the situation is different. We have not only a long coast line, distant outlying possessions, a foreign commerce unsurpassed in importance, and foreign investments unsurpassed in amount, the number of our people and value of our treasure to be protected, but we are also bound by international treaty to defend the Panama Canal. Having few fuelling stations, we require ships of large tonnage, and, having scarcely any merchant vessels capable of mounting five- or six-inch guns, it is obvious that, based on positions, we are entitled to a larger number of warships than a nation having these advantages.

Coolidge was seeming to call for American naval superiority over Britain.

8 . THE AMERICAN QUESTION RESOLVED, NOVEMBER 1928 JUNE 1929

In a struggle between the United States and ourselves, it would not be the possession of a few 8″ gun ships more or less, but the relative economic strength of the two sides which would decide the day.

Wellesley, March 1929

The Foreign Office response to its critics

The unfavourable American reaction to the disarmament compromise provided the domestic critics of the Baldwin government's foreign policy with the opportunity to profit out of the souring of Anglo-American relations. They latched onto Coolidge's Armistice Day speech as proof that the American question had been mishandled. In late August Cecil had been sanguine about the direction of British foreign policy, chiefly because of the success of the renunciatory pact diplomacy.[1] Although puzzled about how the announcement of the compromise had been made, he thought the government would be able to wriggle out of any difficulty. A month later his opinion had changed. He considered using the League of Nations Union to take Baldwin's government to task over the agreement with the French,[2] but the timing was wrong. Baldwin had agreed to give the key-note address at the tenth anniversary celebrations of the Union. Despite the Union's leaders' antipathy toward the Conservative Party, a speech by the prime minister would add to the prestige of the League movement in Britain.[3] Realising that an attack on the government from a Union platform would be ill-advised, Cecil dissociated his criticism of Conservative foreign policy from the views of the Union. As soon as Parliament reconvened in November he spoke harshly about the government's disarmament record, basing his critique on the government's disregard for American sensitivity over naval issues.[4]

Cecil's barrage came just before the president's Armistice Day speech; it set the stage for attacks by Lloyd George and MacDonald in a Commons' debate on disarmament scheduled coincidentally two days after Coolidge's sabre-rattling. For Lloyd George, this debate fitted in well with his preparation for the anticipated general election. In August he and Philip Kerr, an adviser with decided pro-American tendencies, had drafted the Liberal Party manifesto that had a strong foreign policy plank declaring a commitment to a 'drastic all round cut in Armaments' and giving the poor state of Anglo-American relations prominence.[5] Before his Commons' speech Lloyd George had privately christened the Anglo-French compromise 'this sinister Pact'[6] and, in his Commons' denunciation of the Baldwin government's disarmament record, he deftly used the favourable domestic and international reaction to it as a symbol of all that was wrong with Conservative foreign policy.[7] Even an impartial observer like Tom Jones thought this indictment of the lack of progress towards international arms limitation was a success.[8] The Liberal leader, 'with something of his old eloquence and power', had raised the temperature of the debate.

MacDonald had also been readying his party in the summer and autumn of 1928 for the anticipated general election. The first chance to focus Labour disdain on the compromise and, thus, on Conservative foreign policy came in early October at the annual party conference.[9] In the first week of November, Philip Noel-Baker, a confidant of Cecil and an advocate of complete and universal disarmament, was priming MacDonald for the Commons' debate.[10] He felt that MacDonald's speech should lay the ground for the disarmament policy of the eventual Labour government, the basis of which would be 'whether the peace forces of Europe would rally to British leadership or not'. Noel-Baker also believed that Japan, Soviet Russia, and the United States would support 'any serious and radical proposals' which prime minister MacDonald would make – why these Powers which were at odds with one another in the Preparatory Commission would magically endorse such proposals was not explained. MacDonald was also asked to emphasise a point made by Cecil in the Lords: that the compromise was retrogressive as it pursued arms limitation and not disarmament. In the Commons MacDonald did attack the arrangement with the French as a symptom of Conservative preoccupation with security rather than disarmament.[11] But instead of concentrating on the poor state of Anglo-American relations,[12] he offered the argument that the unfavourable reaction to the compromise would not have happened had the Baldwin government been aware of the sensitivities of those countries affected by it.

Because Chamberlain was away, Baldwin felt he had to defend his ministry's disarmament record, a task requiring someone with authority both in the Cabinet and the Conservative Party.[13] Coolidge's Armistice Day speech, which 'intensely annoyed' Baldwin,[14] meant that his remarks would have to take into account both domestic critics and the Americans and, in speaking after Lloyd George who opened the debate, he dealt singly with each issue in the history of disarmament to 1928.[15] According to Jones, the speech amounted to 'a series of separate points, each made effectively but badly joined, and . . . lacking cumulative effect'.[16] Jones concluded, nevertheless, that the manner of Baldwin's delivery had so dampened the passions raised by Lloyd George that 'by the time the P.M. sat down one did not feel the House was dealing with an affair of really first-class importance'. It also blunted any impact MacDonald could hope to make for, unluckily, he spoke after Lloyd George and Baldwin. This debate represents the peak of domestic concern about the compromise, as Baldwin's performance stymied criticism by his Commons' opponents until at least the 1929 election campaign. More important, as far as Anglo-American relations were concerned, Coolidge never repeated his Armistice Day bluster, something Howard attributed to the president being disturbed by the 'reasoned' British response to his 11 November speech.[17]

Such calm did not ensue within the British government as the Foreign Office moved to recapture its primacy in the formal process that made British American policy. This began when Cushendun circulated a memorandum to the Cabinet on 14 November.[18] In a brilliant exposition of the crisis in Anglo-American relations, Craigie submitted that there were several indissoluble impediments in the way of good relations, 'which can at best only be slightly mitigated by tactful handling'. These included '[m]utual jealousy', 'the clash of differing national characteristics', 'intense trade rivalry', 'a determined competition between the two merchant marines', and 'the uneasy relationship between debtor and creditor'. Craigie reckoned that Anglo-American differences in late 1928 resulted from those permanent difficulties being exacerbated by a series of problems capable of solution – naval limitation, the arbitration treaty, the British Monroe doctrine, and belligerent rights. Though mentioning the reparations question which had reemerged with a German diplomatic campaign to get an early end to the Rhineland occupation, he felt this matter was not purely of Anglo-American concern.

Craigie judged that the resolvable issues were inter-connected, so that 'a failure to solve one of them may result in a state of suspended animation'. The Foreign Office believed it best to approach them collectively, thus, one over-all policy had to be devised to tackle each separate issue. More to the point, it would be essential to allow 'political considerations' taken within the context of the over-all policy to have equal weight with 'technical' ones – an obvious reproach of the hyper-critical attitude of the British navalists which had suffused official British discussion of the American question since the Coolidge conference. The essential point, however, remained: was it in Britain's interest to seek an accommodation with the United States?

The Foreign Office believed it was:

Great Britain is faced in the United States of America with a phenomenon for which there is no parallel in our modern history – a State twenty-five times as large, five times as wealthy, three times as populous, twice as ambitious, almost invulnerable, and at least our equal in prosperity, vital energy, technical equipment and industrial science. This State has risen to its present state of development at a time when Great Britain is still staggering from the effects of the superhuman effort made during the war, is loaded with a great burden of debt and is crippled by the evil of unemployment.

Craigie argued that if the resolvable problems continued unsettled, a number of uncomfortable situations might arise to the detriment of British power. Foremost would be the strain on intra-Imperial relations accentuated by developments like the growing warmth between Canada and the United States. The danger also existed that British diplomacy, generally, could suffer by domestic critics within Britain using the issue of poor Anglo-American relations to pillory the government. If those relations remained in their unordered condition or worsened, and Franco- and German-American relations improved, British influence in Europe might be diminished. Finally, since the Great War, Britain had been able to establish much-needed good financial and trading ties with the United States – the United States was Britain's best customer; continued strain in political relations could endanger important economic links. Craigie asserted that the United States felt the need to maintain good relations with Britain, but the Cabinet should not be blind to the fact the United States needed Britain less than Britain the United States.

If an accommodation with the United States was thought impractical, the Cabinet had two alternatives: 'the withdrawal from active co-operation with other nations in the solution of such questions as security, disarmament and reparations', or 'the continuation of the existing policy of co-operation with other Powers to the gradual exclusion of the United States'. Craigie dismissed both of these options. The first would mean rejecting all that British diplomacy had achieved since 1918 – the League Covenant, the Washington treaties, and, most important, Locarno. The certain result of this policy, Craigie surmised, would be a victory for the American 'Big Navy party', which could call for more naval construction because disarmament discussions had ended. The second alternative presupposed that a minimum of five Powers – Britain, France, Germany, Italy, and Japan – would join to exclude the United States from their deliberations. Craigie showed this to be barren. Germany was the key. He referred to the powerful voice of German-Americans, who would not support the estrangement of their country and Germany, and to American capital invested in Germany, a fact that spoke for itself. Moreover, recent moderation of Soviet Russia's foreign policy suggested that the Germans might find an ally in the east to balance what they perceived to be an increasing British commitment to France, indicated by the disarmament compromise.

Craigie proposed an early approach to the Americans on the naval question as this remained the main block in the way of good relations. If it could be removed, the task of eliminating the others would be that much easier. As the Foreign Office saw Coolidge to be less intractable in this matter than Hoover,[19] Craigie suggested that an approach be made before Coolidge left office in March 1929. Although Craigie recognised this might prove fruitless, the crisis in Anglo-American relations had to be resolved as quickly as possible.

Coming just three days after the Armistice Day speech and a day after the Commons' disarmament debate, this memorandum created a split in the Cabinet. On 19 November Churchill circulated a paper deploring the 'panic mood' of the Foreign Office about the American question.[20] He repeated the standard hard-liner argument that Britain had been giving into the United States for years, over Ireland, the war debt, and the Anglo-Japanese alliance, all to no avail. He saw the naval question as one best resolved by a formula of delay. Since Anglo-American relations were at their worst, by simply doing nothing, they were bound to improve. He particularly deprecated an early approach to Coolidge, a man he saw as merely 'a New England backwoodsman'. But all this was secondary in his submission. His primary purpose was to discredit Craigie and, hence, the Foreign Office. The first sentence of Churchill's paper was a blatant attempt at character assassination: 'If the essay by Mr Craigie on Anglo-American relations ... has no object than to inculcate meekness and caution, it need not be dealt with in detail.' But acknowledging that this might not be Craigie's aim, a disclaimer that damned with faint praise, the only lesson he felt he drew was that the Foreign Office was ready to set the stage for a capitulation on naval limitation and belligerent rights.

This deliberate misrepresentation of Craigie's case was not lost on Cushendun; he immediately took Churchill to task.[21] The Foreign Office was willing to consider the desirability of not approaching the Americans whilst Coolidge was president; this was not a *sine qua non*. However, Cushendun admonished the Cabinet 'not to be led away by the attractive vigour of Mr Churchill's literary style into supposing that he has demolished or indeed weakened in any degree, the significance of the picture presented by Mr Craigie'. There were dangers if Britain pursued policies without reference to the United States. For instance, Britain was committed to attend the next Preparatory Commission meeting when Cushendun was supposed to discuss with other delegates, including Gibson, formulae for naval limitation acceptable to the eventual Disarmament Conference. Clearly, Churchill's idea that the Baldwin government could continue 'jogging quietly on our path' was detached from reality. The effect of this Cabinet split, and of Coolidge's Armistice Day speech and the Commons' debate, convinced Baldwin that further discussion of the American question should await Chamberlain's return.[22] The Foreign Office had recaptured its primacy in the formal process that made British American policy.

The triumph of Austen Chamberlain's American policy

Chamberlain returned to work in late November. Cushendun and Salisbury sent him letters outlining the situation in Anglo-American relations that would greet him.[23] Cushendun ranged over the problems that the Foreign Office dealt with during his absence but, as he plainly told Chamberlain: 'By far the most important matter you will have to deal with on your return is that of Anglo-American relations in the most comprehensive meaning of the term.' He appended the White Paper on the compromise, the draft reply to the American rejection, and Craigie's memorandum. Chamberlain was told that the Foreign Office opposed despatching a strongly-worded note to the Americans, though Cushendun acknowledged that the Cabinet hard-liners were probably supported by a large section of British public opinion. About this, he acidly commented that 'that, of course, is very far from saying that they also have wisdom'. He recognised that 'the American attitude is arrogant and rude' but, as ably shown by Craigie, the Anglo-American crisis would only be exacerbated to the detriment of British interests if views like Churchill's were allowed to dominate. Cushendun's letter was a plea to Chamberlain to use his influence to bring the diverse elements of the debate on Anglo-American relations together. The belligerent rights sub-committee and the Cabinet committee on disarmament were 'still pottering along' without attempting to bring 'these various problems together to a focus where they can be examined as parts of a whole'.

Salisbury was preoccupied with the new arbitration treaty. The problem was to safeguard the application of belligerent rights, and there was just two ways to do this: by limiting the treaty to those matters covered by recognised international law – there were no codified rules governing maritime blockade – or by inserting a clause in the treaty that would put Parliament 'on the same footing' as the American Senate in accepting an arbitral award. He favoured the latter course but, claiming diffidence, he offered to discuss this and other aspects of Anglo-American relations with Chamberlain.

When Chamberlain returned to his desk, he received briefings on all aspects of Foreign Office work that had gone on whilst he was away. True to Cushendun's report, those relating to the American question were most important. One of the first papers he saw was a minute by Craigie taking issue with every point raised in Churchill's misrepresentation of the major Foreign Office memorandum.[24] Besides emphasising that he had advocated neither abandoning belligerent rights nor reducing the size of the Royal Navy, he reaffirmed that a policy of 'wise and deliberate inactivity' would fail to resolve the major political problems that separated Britain from the United States.

Chamberlain was also acquainted with his advisers' assessment of the Armistice Day speech. Although Coolidge seemed taken aback with the 'reasoned' British response, notably Baldwin's effort in the Commons,[25] Howard was reporting that American newspapers had given Coolidge's remarks 'wide-spread' approval.[26] The American Department contended that the president had adopted a truculent tone by believing that the failure of the naval conference in 1927 and the conclusion of the disarmament compromise had shown the Europeans cared little for disarmament; this belief was fostered by the 'Big Navy party'.[27] But by the time Howard received an advance copy of Coolidge's last message to Congress, which was to be delivered in early December, the president was assuming a more moderate stance,[28] the result of growing unfavourable reaction to the bombast of 11 November in the United States and abroad.[29] Despite this change in Coolidge's attitude and the reason for it, significant sections of American opinion still supported the sentiment of the Armistice Day speech. It was imperative that Britain avoid taking a line that would serve only to worsen relations. To underscore the need to patch up Anglo-Ameircan differences was a report by Walford Selby, Chamberlain's private secretary, which showed that poor Anglo-American relations were damaging the British position in Europe,[30] an eventuality predicted by Craigie.

Two minor crises arose at this time which, though coming to nothing in the end, reinforced the need to settle British difficulties with the United States. The first occurred when the chairman of the House of Representatives Committee on Naval Affairs, Fred Britten, proposed an Anglo-American inter-parliamentary conference on naval equality.[31] Britten became chairman of the House committee in June 1928, an event which prompted a warning from the Washington Embassy;[32] here was a man in a central position in American naval affairs who was a prominent member of the 'Big Navy party' and an anglophobe. In making his proposal, Britten telegraphed directly to Baldwin.[33] When asked about Britten's move, Kellogg thought that it was a tactic to secure appropriations for twenty-five, rather than fifteen new cruisers.[34] Although Kellogg refused to state publicly his opposition to Britten's scheme,[35] Baldwin and Chamberlain succeeded in checking the congressman with a conciliatory telegram explaining that, whilst Baldwin appreciated Britten's 'friendly sentiments', the matter could only be dealt with between executive branches of government.[36] To ensure that this position was not misrepresented by Britten's 'Big Navy' associates, or by domestic critics of Conservative disarmament policy, Baldwin repeated this line in the Commons.[37] Britten withdrew his proposal, but the lesson drawn from it was not lost. The continuing inability to effect further naval limitation had the potential of raising public hopes on both sides of the Atlantic about the chances of naval agreement, when the bases for such agreement did not yet exist. An excitement of public opinion could only worsen Anglo-American relations when an eventual agreement did not meet public expectations.

The second minor crisis centred on Borah's intention to introduce a resolution calling on Coolidge to convene a multilateral conference to codify international law. Far more than Britten, Borah worried the British. Howard reported Borah's intention on 15 November, and Cushendun was advised to order the ambassador not to approach Borah in the hope of dissuading him from introducing his resolution.[38] Cushendun did so, with Lindsay minuting that 'Senator Borah and his resolution are one of the elements which I fear make it impossible for us to pursue the policy of "jogging quietly along".'[39] But Howard decided that Borah had to be headed off. He took the initiative of seeing his close friend, James Garfield, the prominent Republican who was a friend of Hoover, and persuaded him that when he next saw the president-elect he should impress on him the dangers of a premature conference on international law.[40] Howard did not err in doing this; he had attended a belligerent rights sub-committee meeting in July when it was decided that, if Borah tried to get a conference on maritime law, a private approach would have to be made to the American government.[41] The Foreign Office supported Howard, though warning him to exercise careful diplomacy.[42] In early December, however, Borah changed his tactics by announcing that he would append his resolution to the fifteen cruiser bill then before Congress.[43] Though the chance of the resolution's adoption was enhanced,[44] the issue's immediacy receded. Garfield was to see Hoover, and the fifteen cruiser bill would not be voted on until early 1929.

The advent of the Borah resolution led Chamberlain and his advisers to draw a conclusion about the state of Anglo-American relations that dominated their thinking for the remainder of the second Baldwin government: the only way of resolving the resolvable problems with the United States was to settle the question of belligerent versus neutral rights.[45] Borah had brought to the surface, once again, the basic difficulty in Anglo-American relations that had been superseded temporarily by the renunciatory pact diplomacy and the aggravation kindled by the disarmament compromise. The Foreign Office remained convinced that by removing 'the blockade difficulty', tensions raised by the cruiser question would be reduced and the naval deadlock more easily broken.[46] A separate belligerent rights agreement would also mean that the question of whether the new arbitration treaty failed to reserve 'vital interests' could be ignored. But it was essential that a belligerent rights policy be decided and the Salisbury sub-committee, now also responsible for policy concerning the new arbitration treaty, should be the focus of the government's attention on the American question.

After assessing the state of Anglo-American relations that greeted him on his return, and being confronted immediately with the Britten and Borah proposals, Chamberlain took Cushendun's advice by bringing matters to a head. He began with a private conversation with Baldwin during the first week of December, a move which brought the prime minister fully over to the Foreign Office view. The proof of Baldwin's conversion lies in two conversations, a month apart, he had with Jones. On 1 November Baldwin felt that the disarmament problem was, perhaps, Britain's most critical problem. He remarked that: 'If I come back next year I will take up myself this question of disarmament.'[47] But after seeing Chamberlain, he had changed his mind completely:

I had an hour and a quarter with Austen this week, and we talked America. My own mind is shaping up this way: We must have no conference of experts, no conference on naval armaments. We shall not get any agreement until we face up to the freedom of the seas. Therefore we must face up and get the best maritime law we can. I think we had better have some preparatory preliminary conversations of a private kind to discover what it is the Americans want. Then we must have the conference . . . We must agree.[48]

This conversion was a signal victory for the foreign secretary.

Chamberlain did not stop there. At a Cabinet meeting the next day he suddenly and unexpectedly asked his colleagues for any observations on belligerent rights.[49] This was most unusual for a man who revelled in parliamentary and ministerial traditions, and who did his utmost to defend them – the subject was not on the Cabinet agenda, nor did Chamberlain clear his action beforehand with either Baldwin or Salisbury. A major discussion of belligerent rights ensued, nonetheless, though no decision was reached. A decision was not Chamberlain's purpose in any case; he simply wanted the Cabinet to recognise that the various aspects of the American question were inter-related.

His unorthodox action brought an immediate howl of protest from Hankey, who realised the hard-liners had been out-manoeuvred. He wrote to Salisbury charging that Chamberlain was seeking to circumvent the belligerent rights sub-committee, and that the Cabinet was being asked to make a hurried decision about a basic tenet of Imperial defence.[50] Hankey's rage was uncontrolled in private.[51] He claimed inaccurately that Chamberlain again favoured the freedom of the seas, and that the Foreign Office and diplomatic service, led by the 'traitorous' Tyrrell, were busy behind the scenes pressing the point. After consulting Baldwin, Salisbury responded to say that it would be impossible to circulate Hankey's critique of the foreign secretary.[52] Salisbury agreed that the work of the specialist advisory committees should not be short-circuited. In an apparent concession to Hankey, Salisbury suggested that the unscheduled discussion be considered as 'no more than a general ventilating of American policy taken as a whole'. But the substance of this letter amounted to another victory for Chamberlain, when Salisbury, in alluding to the 'general ventilating of American policy', pointed out:

Looked at from this point of view there may be a certain advantage in getting Ministers to see that each subdivision of American policy – Reply to their despatch; Disarmament; Arbitration; Belligerent Rights – must be regarded as a part of the whole, to which each Department must conform.

Although Salisbury indicated that he would willingly make a statement at the next Cabinet about the need for ministers to keep open minds – which he did[53] – it remains that both Baldwin and Salisbury now shared the Foreign Office view about a network of Anglo-American problems having to be approached collectively.

The belligerent rights sub-committee next met on 20 December.[54] Chamberlain began with a short statement explaining the approach to Hoover and emphasising that Howard had been instructed to make certain that Garfield's mission did not go beyond the new occupant of the White House. Chamberlain affirmed to his colleagues his conviction that belligerent rights remained the major Anglo-American problem. Discussion then considered the idea that the resolvable Anglo-American differences were connected. To facilitate debate, Salisbury and the Admiralty had prepared memoranda.[55] Salisbury tried to put the sub-committee's eleven months of sporadic study into perspective. He pointed out that almost the first decision made had been to keep belligerent rights as high as possible. Although no vote had yet been taken, he felt there was a consensus that some sort of agreement on those rights would have to follow. Also noting that belligerent rights should not be diminished, the Admiralty argued that there should be no discussions with the Americans unless the British were forced into them. Any agreement would fetter Britain unnecessarily.

Debate began with Salisbury stating the view elucidated in Craigie's major memorandum: 'there was a vicious circle consisting of Disarmament, Arbitration Treaties and Belligerent Rights. Each appeared to depend on the other.' Chamberlain added that 'in every other segment of the circle there was the sinister influence of Belligerent Rights'. He believed this lay at the bottom of the naval deadlock, and that this alone was why the arbitration treaty negotiations had stalled. All that the foreign secretary wanted was a decision about when it would be opportune to enquire into the official American attitude regarding belligerent rights. The Foreign Office could make no recommendations on this critical subject – Borah's resolution would certainly pass, thus, necessitating such recommendations – unless some idea of important American opinion was known. This could not be discovered unless Howard could begin talks with the State Department.

Bridgeman and Madden disagreed that belligerent rights were responsible for the naval deadlock. Bridgeman claimed that the loss of the right to blockade would mean that an even larger navy would have to be built. The political members of the sub-committee were not opposed to making any overtures to the Americans, but they deprecated doing so until after the 1929 general election. Even if a conference on maritime law was called, as might happen if Borah's resolution passed, it could not convene until the latter half of 1929. Salisbury and Chamberlain agreed, but were able to get consent that if a conference on maritime law was certain to be called – the Cabinet would have the final decision about the degree of certainty – 'private conversations' would be attempted with the American government.

The rest of this meeting concerned the effect that the renunciatory pact might have on the application of belligerent rights. The idea was that blockade and all it entailed would not always be anathema to the Americans. If, for instance, a state violated the renunciatory pact, the United States could not protest belligerent rights enforced against a pact-breaker. On this assumption, the sub-committee then discussed a notion that had been gaining currency in official circles in Britain during the autumn and winter of 1928: that there were really two types of wars, 'private' and 'public'. Salisbury, Chamberlain, Lindsay, Hurst, and Hankey had variously discussed this.[56] A 'public' war would be one involving a great many Powers united against a transgressor of peace, as might occur under the operation of the renunciatory pact or the League Covenant. A 'private' war, on the other hand, would be one between individual Powers for reasons of pure self-interest. Broad agreement existed within the sub-committee that if Britain was forced to enter into belligerent rights talks with the United States, either bilaterally or under the auspices of a multilateral conference, it would be advantageous 'to start from the basis of the [renunciatory] Pact'. It was assumed this would permit subsequent Anglo-American conversations to revolve around 'public' versus 'private' wars. Britain could then press for the highest possible rights in the case of 'public' war whilst, for 'private' war, concessions might have to be granted. The sub-committee's intention in this regard was explained by Hankey to the infirm Balfour:

Once we have a code drawn up for public wars we shall always be able to apply it *mutatis mutandis* to private wars, which, by the way, we should always try and induce the world to believe were public wars or else wars like the American operations in Nicaragua, which Phillip [sic] Kerr politely designates as police measures.[57]

It was decided that a special group composed of Hurst, Craigie, Gwyer, and Flint would examine which belligerent rights could be safely abandoned in an accommodation with the United States, whilst Hankey should analyse the feasibility of raising 'public' versus 'private' wars in any future negotiation with the United States.

Chamberlain's success at this meeting can be gauged by Bridgeman's anger at what had transpired. He complained bitterly to Baldwin, suggesting that Foreign Office fear of the United States was groundless.[58] The Admiralty was willing to let the Americans build as large a fleet as they wished; the essential point was to avoid formalising anything that amounted to an Anglo-American naval agreement. It was preferable if the United States increased its naval strength to something near Britain's, rather than have Britain reduce its to come into line with the United States. Only if the Americans decided to increase substantially their navy, should Britain abandon the one-power standard. For Bridgeman, this was the problem in relations with the United States. Hence, he could see no advantage to

British interests in sacrificing belligerent rights to assauge American opinion; significantly, he did not bother to mention any of the political considerations that had been discussed in Craigie's major memorandum. In a flight of fancy, Bridgeman even compared the Foreign Office to the League of Nations Union in its 'panic' about the poor state of Anglo-American relations.

His criticism was not restricted to the Foreign Office; Chamberlain, Cushendun, and even Salisbury were attacked as almost traitorous. Chamberlain was dismissed as 'far from well', a charge lacking truth. Cushendun, he believed, was not only unconcerned with Imperial unity, at the base of which stood the Royal Navy, but was infected with 'the Geneva microbe which gives all English people who get it the idea that they are always in the wrong and must give up something'. Salisbury was too preoccupied with the 'awful consequences' for Britain that would arise if the Americans remained unpacified. Like Churchill a month earlier, Bridgeman recommended that the wisest course was one of prudential calm.

The belligerent rights sub-committee did not meet again until 21 January. There was no use conferring until the reports from Hankey and the special group were in. Hankey busied himself over the Christmas holidays with his analysis, and he concluded that there was little to gain by trying to distinguish between 'public' and 'private' wars.[59] The difficulty derived from the uncertainty with which the United States would see a League war as 'public'. If an Anglo-American belligerent rights agreement was concluded, one precluding the enforcement of those rights in a 'private' war, there was no guarantee that a future American government would see the implementation of a British blockade, sanctioned under the Covenant as a legitimate aspect of a 'public' war. Contrary to what he had told Balfour, Hankey now doubted trying to convince international public opinion that private British wars were really public to justify enforcing blockade.

The special group, called the technical sub-committee, based its enquiry on the differences between the British and American approaches to the application of belligerent rights.[60] It compared British action in the Great War, in terms of the orders-in-council that gave a legal basis to the blockade and prize courts, with American rules for belligerent rights contained in the *United States Naval Instructions* which, though issued in 1917, were still in effect. Hurst and his colleagues concluded that there was just one major point of variance between established British practices and extant American rules. Thus, they surmised that the chance of getting an agreement with the Americans in which little would be given away was quite good.

Two events of political consequence also took place before the 21 January meeting of the sub-committee which made its work all the more important. First, the decision was made not to reply to the American note rejecting the compromise. As Chamberlain told Briand at the December League Council, Baldwin's government did this because of 'the very delicate discussions which were pending in the American Senate'.[61] Since no new proposals for naval limitation existed, a reply could only express disappointment that the compromise had not met with American approval. Nothing would be accomplished. The Baldwin government had decided that its efforts would be best channelled in the direction of the Preparatory Commission. This decision not to break the naval deadlock outside of the Commission, a ploy designed to permit the naval limitation issue to slide in order to cool the passions raised by the disarmament compromise, made the questions of arbitration and belligerent rights more pressing; neither of these issues could slide.

The second event occurred on 15 January when the Senate Foreign Relations Committee, with just a single dissenting vote, recommended ratification of the renunciatory pact. This overwhelming majority resulted from Borah, who had the committee's report make clear that the pact would not restrict American rights of self-defence – the Monroe doctrine was mentioned – and that American military or naval forces would not be used against pact-breakers.[62] Although Kellogg regretted reference to the Monroe doctrine,[63] it was an integral part of American policies of self-defence. By the same token, the 'British Monroe doctrine' was equally integral to British policies of Imperial defence. However, the differences between the two governments about their respective doctrines had not been resolved. It was certain that this tangled subject would be raised in the negotiation of the new arbitration treaty, since the Kellogg formula did not reserve matters of 'vital interest'. Protecting the 'British Monroe doctrine' against inroads by the Americans had fallen to the sub-committee.

In this way the debate on British American policy, at least that concerning the two most pressing problems, came to centre in the belligerent rights sub-committee by mid-January 1929. In one calendar year it had held only seven meetings. This desultory approach changed abruptly by the time of the eighth meeting, a situation attributable to the seriousness with which Chamberlain and others viewed the Anglo-American crisis. In a little over two months, the sub-committees would hold nine more meetings and conclude its business.

The importance of the eighth meeting, held on 21 January, comes from the reports by Hankey and the technical sub-committee.[64] Hankey's arguments against differentiating between 'public' and 'private' wars were persuasive. The sub-committee recognised the danger if any British government had to restrict belligerent rights because of an American judgement about whether a war involving Britain was 'public' or 'private'. Preserving belligerent rights in this way was rejected. If these rights were to be protected, another approach, one providing balance between Britain and the United States or, perhaps, giving Britain an advantage, would have to be found. The technical sub-committee's findings supplied the material for this alternative, and they served as the main group's basis of deliberation for the remainder of its existence.

Although Flint had a place on the technical sub-committee, the Admiralty could not accept that the British and American positions respecting the enforcement of belligerent rights were almost equal. This precipitated a heated exchange between the hard-liners, led at this stage by Madden, and the others, led by Chamberlain. The intriguing thing is that Hurst now sided with his political master in confronting the hard-liners; a year earlier Chamberlain had secured Tyrrell's place on the sub-committee as a means of countering Hurst's apparent intransigence over belligerent rights. Whilst still not wishing to surrender any British prerogatives, the technical sub-committee's enquiry had convinced Hurst that a belligerent rights agreement would not lead to an abandoning of fundamental aspects of Imperial defence. The exchanges between Madden and what was now a united Foreign Office concerned four specific points that the Admiralty contended, contrary to the technical sub-committee's conclusions, were not at all similar in the British and American views of belligerent rights. The detailed discussion of these four points – the right of diversion and detention, the right to visit and search a vessel under convoy, the right to arm merchant-men defensively, and the principle that a flag flown gave conclusive evidence of a neutral character – is not germane to this analysis.

What is notable is that the division in the main sub-committee became even more pronounced, and that the hard-liners now formed a minority.

Amery had immediately adhered to the hard-line after he attended his first meeting in November 1928.[65] His intransigence to an Anglo-American agreement was never hidden. As he told a subsequent meeting:

. . . even should low belligerent rights be accepted in peace, they were certain to go by the board in war. The whole idea was so absurd that no belligerent could be expected to stick by it; meanwhile, we might lose victory as a result of our relying on the false promise regarding the adherence of belligerents to a low standard of belligerent rights.[66]

The dominions secretary became one of the most obstructionist hard-liners. This was not surprising. It was unexpected that Salisbury, already amenable to the Foreign Office view of the Anglo-American crisis and how to resolve it, began to side openly with those who felt an accommodation of some sort was necessary. Although he continued to fulfil impartially his role as chairman, he tended, when he gave a personal opinion or commented on a particular point, to endorse Chamberlain's view that a belligerent rights agreement was in Britain's best interests. He emphasised this on 21 January by remarking that 'it seemed clear that we should have to consider the situation in which we had allies, as well as that in which we had no allies; in the latter case it was obvious that we could in no way imitate our actions of the late war, whereas with allies, we might well act in a similar manner'.[67] Britain would find it extremely difficult in the future, Salisbury reasoned, to enforce a maritime blockade without political or naval allies. Since the United States represented the greatest potential threat to a successful, unilateral imposition of belligerent rights, it was necessary before the situation arose to conclude some arrangement with the Americans. Although never guaranteeing that difficulties with other Powers could be eliminated, such an arrangement would remove the main impediment in the way of a future British blockade.

At the ninth meeting, held on 25 January, Salisbury circulated a draft report on arbitration which, he believed, possessed 'the mind of the sub-committee when they last discussed the question'.[68] Prior to any discussion, Chamberlain read aloud two news reports from *The Times* of that morning. The first related that Kellogg had publicly remonstrated against the British delay in continuing the new arbitration treaty correspondence. The second reported that Borah had finally introduced his resolution for a conference to codify maritime law – as an amendment to the fifteen cruiser bill – with a proviso that this conference should occur before that scheduled for naval disarmament in 1931. As Chamberlain pointed out yet again, arbitration, belligerent rights, and the naval deadlock were inter-twined.[69] The net effect of Salisbury's paper and the reports from the United States saw the sub-committee concentrate on arbitration during its ninth, tenth, and eleventh meetings.

At the ninth meeting, discussion ranged over three proposed amendments to the draft American treaty that Salisbury's report thought practicable. Two of them accentuated the division within the sub-committee. The first dealt with 'specific exception', that is, what Britain could reserve specifically from arbitration. Chamberlain took the view that protecting the 'British Monroe doctrine' was most important. The British, he pointed out, would only be able to reserve one 'vital interest' from the operation of the proposed treaty; this, because the Americans were only reserving one, their Monroe doctrine. Moreover, since the Americans had already concluded a number of Kellogg formula treaties with other Powers during 1928, notably with France, the British would *ipso facto* have to recognise the special status of the American Monroe doctrine. The Foreign Office felt that the vagueness of the 'British Monroe doctrine' which had been a hallmark of the note of 19 May 1928 could not be repeated. It must now be specific: 'There was no parallel between the reservation of the American Monroe doctrine and that which we wished to adopt regarding the Persian Gulf and Afghanistan.' The British would have to list the areas where their doctrine applied, namely Egypt and the Suez Canal. Bridgeman countered that a blanket reservation exempting all self-defence might suffice. As the Foreign Office and Admiralty views could not be reconciled, no decision about 'specific exemption' was reached at the ninth meeting.

Salisbury's second amendment proposed 'the limitation of subjects that could be arbitrated upon to those which were justicable under a recognised rule of law'. This would protect belligerent rights since there was no body of international law on the subject; assuming Borah's conference on maritime law or one like it never amounted to anything, belligerent rights would be exempt from arbitration. Finding nothing wrong with this, Chamberlain wanted assurances that British prize courts would be unaffected in the event some 'recognised rule of law' later emerged. His fears were eased by Hailsham who pointed out that the prize courts were national bodies and not susceptible to challenge by foreign governments. There seemed a consensus to protect belligerent rights by this means.

The tenth meeting of the sub-committee occurred on Friday, 1 February.[70] Salisbury observed that as there seemed to be a near consensus about the proposed amendments to the American draft that he had raised in his report, only a decision had to be made between Chamberlain's specific reference to Egypt and Suez and the broader mention of self-defence suggested by Bridgeman. The Admiralty had already circulated a paper which outlined Bridgeman's proposal in greater detail.[71] The key phrase was that Britain should not agree to arbitrate any matter:

[which] Affects or involves the maintenance of the integrity and security of all or parts of the British Empire, or involves the relations between the parts of the British Empire (or the special British interest or obligations in Egypt and the Sudan).

This amounted to a position that there was no British 'vital interest' to exempt from arbitration, except anything touching its right to defend the Empire. Chamberlain, Salisbury, and Hailsham immediately recognised that this would not meet with American approval. As Salisbury caustically remarked: 'if the Admiralty proposal were accepted it would be asked why we had given up "vital interests" and then proceeded to cover them with other words.' The hard-liners were intent on playing havoc with the Kellogg formula concerning vital interests. When Chamberlain and his supporters would not budge, Amery conceded that a Foreign Office suggestion in Salisbury's report, which came from Hurst, might work. This declared that no matter could be arbitrated which:

Depends upon or involves the maintenance of the policy proclaimed in the past by either High Contracting Parties in relation to particular areas wherein each party possesses special interests which it is bound to uphold . . .

Though avoiding mention of specific areas, the reference to proclaimed policy meant that only extant proclamations, the two Monroe doctrines, would be exempt from arbitration. With Amery's concession, the hard-liners caved in and the Foreign Office amendment was endorsed.

The matter of limiting arbitrable subjects to only those covered by recognised international law still worried Chamberlain and the

Foreign Office. The idea had originated with Hailsham, who thought it 'the least blatant method' of excepting belligerent rights from arbitration. Chamberlain agreed that it would work, but only until some conference, like that proposed by Borah, got busy and codified rules respecting maritime law. The foreign secretary argued that 'a definite attempt to exclude belligerent rights would merely hasten the day when a conference would be called to state and codify them'. Chamberlain cautioned that as far as belligerent rights were concerned, there was no unity of American opinion. The Administration seemed to have a policy, the Navy Department had its *Naval Instructions*, and 'the mass of uneducated public opinion . . . talked nothing but the "Freedom of the Seas" '. In gauging the uncertainty of American opinion, he suggested that it would be less than responsible to suggest that there was 'no accepted rule of law with regard to belligerent rights'. Such irresponsibility would be compounded if Britain maintained this position and refused subsequently to attend a conference to codify maritime law.

Discussion of Hailsham's amendment and the points raised by Chamberlain followed. The penalty for including a provision that would draw attention to belligerent rights was seen to be too great. Hailsham changed his opinion as the rest of the sub-committee seemed to appreciate Chamberlain's admonition. When it appeared that Hailsham's amendment was not about to be endorsed, the more so since its author had abandoned it, Bridgeman and Madden registered only mild protests; Salisbury indicated that in drafting his final report, he would not mention belligerent rights. Thus, the consensus that derived from the tenth meeting, the so-called 'Friday' policy, entailed a belief that in the new arbitration treaty there had to be relatively specific mention of the 'British Monroe doctrine' and no reference to belligerent rights.

Within a few hours of the tenth meeting, the hard-liners came to believe that the 'Friday' policy concerning belligerent rights had gone too far. This group included Amery, Bridgeman, Peel, Hankey, and Madden. In a crucial decision Cunliffe-Lister decided that the 'Friday' policy would safeguard belligerent rights, and the group of hard-liners was reduced by one more. To bolster their faltering position, Amery sent a Dominions Office official, Harry Batterbee, to see Balfour. Balfour had attended just one sub-committee meeting, though he had been kept informed of its deliberations by Hankey.[72] Batterbee elicited from Balfour a statement about the desirability of keeping belligerent rights amongst matters not to be the subject of arbitration. These views were put before the sub-committee members in the next couple of days in a campaign that seems to have been carefully orchestrated by Hankey.[73] At the next sub-committee meeting held on Monday, 4 February, the hard-liners, still without Cunliffe-Lister, united in their disapproval of not mentioning belligerent rights in the new arbitration treaty. Known as the 'Monday' policy, its advocates got Salisbury's agreement to include their dissenting view in his final report to the Cabinet.[74]

The final form of this first report was hammered out at the next two sessions of the sub-committee and circulated to the Cabinet on 13 February.[75] Although the Cabinet would yet have to decide whether to adopt the majority view, the 'Friday' policy, or the minority view, the 'Monday' policy, the sub-committee had endorsed strongly the Foreign Office case about not adding to the Anglo-American crisis by adopting a hard-line over arbitration. Salisbury, Hailsham, Cushendun, and Cunliffe-Lister all sided with Chamberlain against the intransigence of Bridgeman, Amery, and Peel. In another blow to the hard-liners, Balfour's continued support of the 'Monday' policy was not forthcoming; he decided that his absence from most of the sub-committee meetings mitigated against him signing anything. As a consequence, the Foreign Office had determined the course of this important aspect of British American policy, and it could look for powerful support within the Cabinet – Chamberlain and Salisbury – in the ensuing debate.

The second part of the sub-committee's mandate, the enquiry into belligerent rights, had only been eclipsed temporarily by the pressing nature of the arbitration treaty. The sub-committee had actually begun to deal with this in some detail whilst the final touches were being put on Salisbury's first report[76] and, considering the milieu in which discussion occurred – the simultaneous debate on arbitration, Borah's resolve to have an international conference on maritime law, the passage of the fifteen cruiser bill, and the after-shock of the Anglo-French disarmament compromise – it is surprising that this debate did not prove to be as emotive as that over arbitration.[77] Chamberlain and his supporters argued that some accommodation with the Americans on future blockade policy had to be arranged before differences in corollary areas like naval limitation could be resolved in Britain's favour. Expressed by Bridgeman, Madden, and Hankey, the Admiralty view was that there had to be a solution to naval limitation before there could be any attempt to resolve political differences. Despite this apparent schism, the Cabinet received a nearly unanimous second report – only Cushendun dissented.[78] The Cabinet was told that, except for Cushendun, it was agreed that belligerent rights should be kept as high as possible; the difficulty was that 'the undoubted trend of American opinion' seemed to endorse the concept of low rights. It was imperative, therefore, to avoid a conference whose purpose would be to codify maritime law. It was assumed that at such a conference, Britain would have trouble not only with the United States but also a number of European Powers. If a multilateral conference appeared inevitable, there was agreement that Hoover would have to be approached directly about the dangers from any attempt to codify maritime law.

The 'Friday' and 'Monday' policies were then proffered. This happened because a Foreign Office proposal was incorporated into the conclusions suggesting that the only way of avoiding a conference on maritime law would be to make sure that, upon concluding the 'Friday' policy arbitration treaty, a separate Anglo-American belligerent rights agreement be negotiated. The 'Monday' policy was included as an Admiralty warning about the dangers that might arise in concluding an arbitration treaty that did not reserve belligerent rights specifically. To avoid a conference on maritime law, the sub-committee also recommended arranging an Anglo-American belligerent rights agreement based on the *United States Naval Instructions* of 1917. This came from the technical sub-committee. Salisbury and his colleagues did feel, however, that if an international conference was unavoidable, one of the five principal naval Powers would be preferable to one attended by a number of countries. But regardless of the type of conference, preliminary talks would have to be held with the Americans 'in the hope of harmonising beforehand, as far as possible the views of the two Governments'.

Foreign Office dominance in this second report is clear. Although the *caveat* about the 'Friday' policy was included, it is the only point of note made by the hard-liners. The Foreign Office view about the need to confront Hoover if a maritime law conference seemed imminent became an essential feature of the sub-committee's recommendations. The level of anticipated Anglo-American conversations in the event that such a conference would be called indicates the power of the Foreign Office argument that Britain could not continue 'jogging quietly along'; it would be necessary to seek out the United States as an ally to protect British belligerent rights. By mid-March 1929 the Baldwin government had a blue-print to resolve Britain's differences with the United States, essentially a Foreign Office-inspired blue-print, and it merely had to be followed.

Baldwin used his influence to postpone Cabinet discussion of the two Salisbury sub-committee reports. Ostensibly this was because of the absence of key ministers[79] but, more probably, he wanted to keep Cabinet attention on more pressing domestic issues that were certain to be raised in the impending election campaign. Polling day was 30 May. There is no indication of Baldwin delaying discussion of Anglo-American relations out of fear of splitting the Cabinet. Most of the in-fighting and posturing that would probably occur had happened in the belligerent rights sub-committee. Besides, any approach to the Americans would have to come after the new government was formed.

Adding to the desirability of waiting to implement the sub-committee recommendations was the change in American government. In almost his last public words whilst president, Coolidge recanted the anglophobic and anti-European charges he had made on Armistice Day.[80] Though this derived from the unfavourable domestic and international reaction to these menacing words, the Foreign Office welcomed it as an indication that official American opinion was softening.[81] The rise of Hoover to the White House, though first greeted in London with trepidation,[82] was seen as a new departure in Republican foreign policy. The new president was going to take an active part in shaping his Administration's external policies. He admitted this to Howard two weeks after his inauguration, and in the same conversation he impressed on the ambassador his intention to do something to take the chill out of Anglo-American relations.[83] Though the Foreign Office recognised that Hoover's actions would speak louder than his words, there was some relief that he might not be the anglophobe he had seemed earlier.[84]

Two early actions suggested that he might meet the British half way in ameliorating Anglo-American differences. The first was selecting General Charles Dawes, who had been Coolidge's vice-president, as Houghton's replacement. Though forthright in public – his favourite curse earned him the nickname 'Hell and Maria' Dawes – he was an anglophile; the Foreign Office saw his appointment as 'proof of the importance attached by the new Administration to the maintenance of satisfactory Anglo-American relations'.[85] The second action came at the Preparatory Commission meeting held in April 1929. Craigie, who accompanied Cushendun, was permitted to seek out Gibson and, on a purely personal level, see what could be done to facilitate some agreement on naval limitation.[86] In these conversations Craigie was told that 'Mr Hoover was strongly of the opinion that at any meeting about the "naval" problem the "experts" should be kept in a separate room and only summoned when their advice was desired on some technical point.' More important, Gibson indicated that the new Administration was prepared to negotiate on the basis of a 'naval yardstick', a system that would consider the armament, tonnages and ages of vessels in calculating naval strength. Gibson could not provide the specific details of the 'yardstick' as they had not been finally determined. Though caution in dealing with the Americans was still important, the indication was that the chance of settling Anglo-American problems was more favourable.

This was not lost on Chamberlain. In February 1929 he had written a minute responding to a suggestion that Baldwin travel to the United States after the general election to settle Anglo-American differences.[87] Chamberlain felt that all the prime minister would, or should, be able to do would be to 'renew his personal relations' with Hoover. Since the Foreign Office conducted foreign policy, Chamberlain believed it would be preferable for him, as foreign secretary, to lead a negotiation team to Washington. But he would only do this if Britain could get 'an agreed basis for negotiation through the diplomatic channel' – a reflexion of his desire to avoid the ill-preparation that had preceded the Coolidge conference. By late April, with Hoover's apparent desire for Anglo-American accord, such a basis seemed possible; all that remained was for the Conservative government to consider the recommendations of the belligerent rights sub-committee. But the Conservatives lost the general election and the second Baldwin government gave up its seals of office on 4 June. It fell to others to settle Anglo-American differences. Needless to say, the groundwork for a *rapprochement* had been completed by the first week of March 1929 which reflected the Foreign Office perception of how to improve Anglo-American relations. Following the course charted by Salisbury's sub-committee, others would get the credit for settling Anglo-American differences that should have gone to Chamberlain, his Foreign Office, and Baldwin's second government.

Anglo-American relations, 1929–1930

MacDonald succeeded Baldwin as prime minister on 5 June 1929 and two days later, though in a minority in the House of Commons, the second Labour government took office.[88] Because MacDonald suppressed moves in his party to replace a number of the principal foreign and defence policy advisers that had achieved prominence under the Conservatives,[89] the basic structure of the foreign-policy-making élite that dealt with the American question remained unaltered. Lindsay and Wellesley stood as the government's senior diplomatic advisers, whilst Craigie and Thompson continued as the principal American specialists. Howard and the Embassy at Washington, coupled with BLINY, remained the primary link in the process that explained American developments to the diplomatists at London. The civil service advisers in other areas, from Willert to Hankey and Vansittart, went on as before which, for the American question, added continuity to policy.

Changes, of course, occurred at the top of the élite but, in terms of creating British American policy, the group of politicians involved was even smaller than that which emerged under Baldwin. As the reward for his anti-Baldwin, anti-Chamberlain activities after mid-1927, Cecil was given a room at the Foreign Office and ostensible control over British League policy; he also attempted to influence arms limitation policy when the occasion arose. Bridgeman's successor, Albert Alexander, was brought perforce into the debate on policy toward the United States when talk of naval arms limitation arose; but he does not seem to have had the same weight that Bridgeman was able to arrogate for himself. The real difference occurred at the highest political level. Arthur Henderson, a man with important Labour Party connexions – he was the party secretary from 1912 to 1935 – became foreign secretary. He wanted to be the principal architect of Labour foreign policy, a wish that resulted in a bitter dispute during the formation of the government over who would take the Foreign Office.[90] But unlike other areas of his jurisdiction, Henderson could not control British American policy. MacDonald's interest in Anglo-American relations, along with his prominence in the arms limitation debate after mid-1927, led him to keep the American question to himself. The improvement in the diplomatic atmosphere following Coolidge's recanting of his Armistice Day anglophobia, Dawes' posting to London, and Hoover's avowed desire to achieve naval arms limitation, suggested to MacDonald that he might benefit politically as the perceived healer of Anglo-American wounds.

On 10 June MacDonald received three memoranda from Craigie which discussed Anglo-American differences over belligerent rights, arbitration, and arms limitation.[91] He was told of the conclusions of the belligerent rights sub-committee about keeping those rights as high as possible and about the merit of the 'Friday' policy in pursuing a new arbitration treaty. Craigie emphasised the Foreign Office view that a belligerent rights agreement would be as beneficial to the Americans as the British, thus, the need to secure prior Anglo-American accord if an international conference to codify maritime law appeared imminent. MacDonald was also told that the Preparatory Commission was continuing its slow process of producing a single draft disarmament convention and the French, still Britain's principal European ally, would oppose any naval arms agreement that was not linked to the continuing talks at Geneva.

Like Chamberlain, MacDonald recognised that face-to-face talks with Hoover were essential to resolving Anglo-American differences and, taking Craigie's memoranda to heart, he acknowledged that the diplomatic ground would have to be secured before he could travel to the United States. He therefore held talks with Dawes and Gibson at London over the next four months to this end. To take the urgency out of belligerent rights at the outset of these talks, he was able to get Dawes to concur that any belligerent rights discussion would be inopportune whilst naval limitation was being examined.[92] After intense discussions that lasted into early October, a tentative basis for Anglo-American agreement on naval limitation emerged when MacDonald suggested that his government was willing to consider the possibility of the Americans arming enough of their 10,000-ton cruisers with six-inch guns to arrive at Anglo-American parity in vessels with eight-inch weapons. This had the merit of allowing the Americans to have eight-inch gun ships comprise the bulk of their cruiser fleet and the British possession of a large number of smaller vessels.[93] MacDonald and Dawes also agreed that a five Power naval conference should be convened once again and, as Washington and Geneva had already been the venues of conferences in 1921 and 1927, and as there was no desire to have one at Tokyo, that it should be held at London. To avoid the appearance of an Anglo-American *fait accompli* on naval limitation, invitations to the French, Italians, and

Japanese were sent just as MacDonald began his American tour in early October.[94]

The American tour was crucial as no Admiralty officials or men considered to be hard-liners accompanied the prime minister. Vansittart and Craigie were his advisers, indicating a desire to have discussions with political rather than technical experts; this approach corresponded with the Foreign Office perception of how to handle the American question that had emerged under Chamberlain's *régime*.[95] The talks with Hoover saw the limitation proposals that had been made during the MacDonald–Dawes conversations elaborated and refined – the Americans would build eighteen heavy cruisers and the British fifteen; this would hold the Japanese to only twelve under the 5:5:3 ratio. To compensate for American superiority in 10,000 tonners, the British would make up the difference with light cruisers. This was essentially what was agreed at the London naval conference six months later.[96] But more important than this there emerged a tacit understanding on belligerent rights that originated with Hoover. He suggested quite unexpectedly that food ships be excluded from detention and seizure during wartime. Whilst acknowledging that this had merit, MacDonald, Vansittart, and Craigie did not commit Britain one way or the other – though Hankey typically over-reacted when he read the report of this meeting and tried to prevent any formal agreement,[97] which, of course, the MacDonald mission had no intention of concluding. But as American worries about maritime blockade now seemed to be allayed, the issue of belligerent rights was buried and the basis of Anglo-American agreement on cruiser limitation had been achieved in discussions dominated by diplomats rather than sailors. The naval deadlock had been broken and the London naval conference which met from January to April 1930 succeeded because the world's two principal maritime Powers were now in agreement.

The arbitration treaty was resolved differently. Because he felt his government should decide between the merits of the 'Friday' and 'Monday' policies, MacDonald established an *ad hoc* Cabinet committee in July 1929 to formulate arbitration policy.[98] Both Henderson and Alexander sat on this committee but Henderson, marshalling the standard Foreign Office arguments about the dangers of specifically reserving belligerent rights, persuaded his colleagues that the 'Monday' policy was fraught with danger. To the chagrin of the Foreign Office, however, and the delight of Cecil,

Henderson also convinced the committee that exempting the 'British Monroe doctrine' might create problems.[99] He was able to get Cabinet agreement that it would be best to rely on the League of Nations in matters of arbitration; this seems to have devolved from Cecil.[100] In 1920 an amendment had been introduced to the Protocol of the International Court of Justice, a League appendage, to aid in arbitration and conciliation procedures.[101] It was not compulsory, hence, it was called the 'Optional Clause', but once states adhered to it they were bound to accept the jurisdiction of the Court without reservation in disputes involving the interpretation of treaties, all questions on international law, any 'breach of international obligation', and the level of award in the event such breach occurred. Baldwin's government had opposed this measure for a number of reasons,[102] but MacDonald's government decided that the 'Optional Clause' would serve as the sole arbitration agreement to which the British government would become a party. On 19 September, before MacDonald embarked on his American tour, Henderson signed the 'Clause' at Geneva. This ended any chance for bilateral arbitration treaties with other Powers. To obviate criticism from opponents in Britain about protecting belligerent rights, the Foreign Office issued a White Paper on the 'Optional Clause' which devoted one-third of its contents to why maritime blockade would not be affected by the arbitral procedures of the International Court.[103]

Nearly one year after Chamberlain left the Foreign Office, his Labour successors had completed a drive to resolve the outstanding problems in Anglo-American relations: in arbitration, naval arms limitation, and belligerent rights. As the Foreign Office had been preaching since late 1927, those problems had been inter-twined, with the solution or non-solution of each affecting that of the others. Chamberlain agreed, supporting as well the diplomatic impracticability of 'jogging quietly along'. This led to the influential role he took for himself in the final phase of Salisbury's belligerent rights sub-committee, a role which proved to be decisive in fixing the blue-print to resolve the American question that reached Baldwin's Cabinet in March 1929. Independently of the sub-committee, Chamberlain came to believe that he would probably have to visit the United States for face-to-face meetings with American leaders to effect an Anglo-American *rapprochement*. The fall of the Conservatives did not alter the basic Chamberlain strategy. Once MacDonald saw that the problems with the Americans were 'all hanging on one another', and an independent foreign policy would not solve them, he prepared the way for a journey to the United States. A naval compromise developed that eventually formed the basis of the London Naval Treaty; the Salisbury sub-committee requirement to keep belligerent rights as high as possible was fulfilled, followed by a firm stand on a new arbitration arrangement which saw this contentious issue slide into oblivion. Though the form of the final settlement of the American question was not exactly as Chamberlain thought it should be, it corresponded to his perception of how it had to be resolved.

NOTES

1 The second Baldwin government and the United States

1 This study limits those who make and implement British foreign policy to the narrow definition of the élite suggested in D. C. Watt, 'The Nature of the Foreign-Policy-Making Élite in Britain', in D. C. Watt, *Personalities and Policies. Studies in the formulation of British foreign policy in the twentieth century* (London, 1965), 1–15. This concept has been used in a few studies; for example, M. G. Fry, *Illusions and Security. North Atlantic Diplomacy 1918–22* (Toronto, 1972). On the nature of the élite, see J. Alt, 'Continuity, Turnover and Experience in the British Cabinet 1868–1970', in J. Alt and V. Herman (eds.), *Cabinet Studies* (London, 1974); P. W. Buck, *Amateurs and Professionals in British Politics 1918–59* (Chicago, 1963); W. L. Guttsman, 'Aristocracy and the Middle Class in the British Political Elite, 1886–1916', *BJS*, 5(1964), 12–32; B. J. C. McKercher, 'The British foreign-policy-making élite and its attitudes towards the United States, November 1924–June 1929' [unpublished Ph.D. dissertation] (London, 1979), Appendix I; Z. S. Steiner and M. L. Dockrill, 'The Foreign Office Reforms', *HJ*, 17(1974), 131–56, particularly Appendices I and II; and R. Wilkinson, 'Political Leadership and the Late Victorian Public School', *BJS*, 13(1962), 320–30.

2 Admittedly, this is a point of contention. C. M. Mason, 'Anglo-American Relations: Mediation and Permanent Peace', in F. H. Hinsley (ed.), *British Foreign Policy Under Sir Edward Grey* (Cambridge, 1977), 466–87; and D. C. Watt, 'America and the British Foreign-Policy-Making Élite, from Joseph Chamberlain to Anthony Eden, 1895–1956', in Watt, *Personalities and Policies*, 30–6 argue that the low point came between 1915–16.

3 On Anglo-American economic relations during the Great War, see K. M. Burk, 'The Diplomacy of Finance: British Financial Missions to the United States, 1914–1918', *HJ*, 22(1979), 351–72. For one example of Britain funding an ally's war effort, see Keith Neilson, *Strategy and Supply: the Anglo-Russian Alliance, 1914–1917* (forthcoming, Allen and Unwin).

4 See K. Middlemas and J. Barnes, *Baldwin. A Biography* (London, 1969), 128–36.

5 J. Carroll, 'America Reacts to the Balfour Plan: the debate over war debt cancellation', *Research Studies*, 41(1973), 107–17. Cf. S. Marks, 'The Myths of Reparations', *Central European History*, 11(1978), 231–55.

6 See Cmd. 1912; W. N. Medlicott, *Contemporary England 1914–1964* (London, 1976), 177–9; Middlemas and Barnes, *Baldwin*, 136–48. President Coolidge was impressed with the way Britain settled its war debt: see telegram – 7 Nov 1925, Howard [British ambassador, Washington] to Chamberlain [foreign secretary]: *DBFP 1A*, 871–3.

7 For the patterns of cooperation and compromise, see M. J. Hogan, *Informal Entente: the private structure of cooperation in Anglo-American economic diplomacy 1918–1928* (Columbia, Missouri, 1977). Cf. F. C. Costigliola, 'Anglo-American Financial Rivalry in the 1920s', *JEH*, 37 (1977), 911–34; M. P. Leffler, 'Political Isolationism, Economic Expansion, or Diplomatic Realism: American Policy Toward Western Europe, 1921–1933', *Perspectives in American History*, 8(1974), 413–61; C. P. Parrini, *Heir to Empire: United States economic diplomacy, 1916–1923* (Pittsburgh, 1969); and J. H. Wilson, *American Business and Foreign Policy, 1920–1933* (Lexington, Ky., 1971). On the British side, see letter – 3 Apr 1929, D'Abernon [former British ambassador, Berlin] to his wife: BM Add MSS 48936; and Viscount D'Abernon, 'The Economic Mission to South America', *JRIIA*, 9(1930), 568–82. Also see diary entries – 23, 24 & 27 Jul 1927, Evelyn Wrench [a founder of the English Speaking Union and an exponent of close Anglo-American ties]: BM Add MSS 59575.

8 M. L. Dockrill and J. D. Goold, *Peace Without Promise. Britain and the Peace Conferences 1919–23* (London, 1981), 37–8, 85.

9 An indication can be seen in A. Orde, *Great Britain and International Security 1920–1926* (London, 1978), 30–2.

10 Cf. Foreign Office, *Peace Conference Handbooks*, No. 47a: *Freedom of the Seas* (London, 1919); A. J. Marder, *From Dreadnought to Scapa Flow*, vol. V: *Victory and Aftermath, January 1918–June 1919* (London, 1970), 238–42; and S. W. Roskill, *Naval Policy Between the Wars*, vol. I: *The Period of Anglo-American Antagonism 1919–1929* (London, 1968), 80–3, 90–1, 100.

11 For example, despatch – 30 Oct 1924, Howard to MacDonald [prime minister]: FO 371/9618/6340/218.

12 K. Bourne, *The Foreign Policy of Victorian England 1830–1902* (Oxford, 1970); C. J. Lowe, *The Reluctant Imperialists*, 2 vols. (London, 1967); C. J. Lowe and M. L. Dockrill, *The Mirage of Power*, vol. I (London, 1972); and C. R. Middleton, *The Administration of British Foreign Policy, 1782–1846* (Durham, N.C., 1977).

13 See A. J. Sharp, 'The Foreign Office in Eclipse 1919–22', *History*, 61(1976), 198–218; and R. M. Warman, 'The Erosion of Foreign Office Influence in the Making of Foreign Policy, 1916–1918', *HJ*, 15(1972), 133–59. This prime ministerial group was the so-called 'Garden Suburb'. See P. Rowland, *Lloyd George* (London, 1975), 381; A. J. P. Taylor, *English History 1914–1945* (Harmondsworth, 1970), 112, 178, and 178n. The best study is J. Turner, *Lloyd George's Secretariat* (Cambridge, 1980).

14 For Baldwin's antipathy towards Lloyd George and its effect on Baldwin's style of leadership, see J. Campbell, 'Stanley Baldwin', in J. P. Mackintosh (ed.), *British Prime Ministers in the Twentieth Century*, vol. I:

Balfour to Chamberlain (London, 1977), 190–3. For Baldwin's disinterest in foreign affairs, see Lord Vansittart, *The Mist Procession* (London, 1958), 347. For Baldwin giving Chamberlain independence in foreign policy, see Middlemas and Barnes, *Baldwin*, 342–6.

15 Cf. *Ibid.*, 96–124; C. Petrie, *The Life and Letters of the Rt. Hon. Sir Austen Chamberlain*, vol. II (London, 1940), 186–206.

16 In the Spring of 1924, Chamberlain had been made chairman of the Conservative Party's 'Overseas Policy Committee', the mandate of which included foreign policy. See enclosure in letter – 8 Apr 1924, Salisbury [Conservative peer] to Cecil [Conservative peer]: BM Add MSS 51085.

17 Cf. the otherwise excellent J. Jacobson, *Locarno Diplomacy. Germany and the West, 1925–1929* (Princeton, 1972), 74–5; D. Johnson, 'Austen Chamberlain and the Locarno Agreements', *University of Birmingham Historical Journal*, 8(1961), 62–81; 'The Locarno Treaties', in N. Waites (ed.), *Troubled Neighbours. Franco-British Relations in the Twentieth Century* (London, 1971), 100–24.

18 D. Carlton, 'Great Britain and the Coolidge Naval Conference of 1927', *PSQ*, 83(1968), 573–98; 'Great Britain and the League Council Crisis of 1926', *HJ*, 11(1968), 354–64; 'The Anglo-French Compromise on Arms Limitation, 1928', *JBS*, 8(1969), 141–62.

19 Letter – 3 Nov 1924, Chamberlain to Ida, his sister: AC 5/1/339. C. Petrie, *A Historian Looks at His World* (London, 1972), 86–9 suggests Chamberlain's self-assessment is too harsh. Chamberlain could be charming, an indication of which can be seen in 'Draft Interview' – Apr 1928, Mackenzie [Associated Press, London]: FO 395/431/593/514.

20 A. Chamberlain, *Politics From the Inside: An Epistolary Chronicle, 1906–1914* (London, 1936).

21 For instance, A. G. Gardiner, 'Sir Austen Chamberlain': in A. G. Gardiner, *Portraits and Portents* (London, 1926), 106–13; and R. Rhodes James, *The British Revolution. British Politics 1880–1939* (London, 1978), 411.

22 D. H. Elletson, *The Chamberlains* (London, 1966), 172–3 *et passim*; P. Fraser, *Joseph Chamberlain, Radicalism and Empire, 1868–1914* (London, 1966), 226–51; and C. Petrie, *The Chamberlain Tradition* (London, 1938).

23 See Petrie, *Life and Letters*, vol. II, 132–4, 201–3, 213; and R. Rhodes James, *Memoirs of a Conservative. J. C. C. Davidson's Memoirs and Papers, 1910–37* (London, 1969), 28. Cf. Lord Beaverbrook, *Men and Power, 1917–1918* (London, 1956), xiii; *The Decline and Fall of Lloyd George* (London, 1963), 21–4, 222–3.

24 A. J. P. Taylor is the most prominent. See his *English History*, 103n, 406; *The Origins of the Second World War* (Harmondsworth, 1963), 81; *Beaverbrook. A Biography* (New York, 1972), 218.

25 A. Briggs, *Victorian People. A Reassessment of Persons and Themes 1851–67* (Harmondsworth, 1955), 9–22.

26 G. Kitson Clark, *An Expanding Society. Britain 1830–1900* (Melbourne, 1967), 44–6 discusses Joseph Chamberlain's use of the Education League to spread his views nationally.

27 Jacobson, *Locarno Diplomacy*, 75; and Johnson, 'Chamberlain', 67.
28 See E. Percy, 'Austen Chamberlain', *Pub. Admin.*, 15(1937), 125–7.
29 J. Connell, *The 'Office': A Study of British Foreign Policy and Its Makers, 1919–1951* (London, 1958), 70–1.
30 The best study is Jacobson, *Locarno Diplomacy*, 3–67. Also see S. E. Crowe, 'Sir Eyre Crowe and the Locarno Pact', *EHR*, 87(1972), 49–74; G. A. Grün, 'Locarno: Idea and Reality', *IA*, 31(1955), 477–85; F. S. Northedge, *The Troubled Giant. Britain Among the Great Powers, 1916–1939* (London, 1966), 248–72; and F. G. Stambrook, '"Das Kind" – Lord D'Abernon and the Origins of the Locarno Pact', *Central European History*, 1(1968), 233–63.
31 A. Chamberlain, 'Great Britain as a European Power', *JRIIA*, 9(1930), 180–8; letter – 10 Mar 1925, Selby [Chamberlain's private secretary] to Phipps [British *chargé d'affaires*, Paris]: FO 800/257; letter – 3 Feb 1926, Chamberlain to his wife: AC 6/1/636.
32 For example, Cabinet Conclusion 45(25)1: CAB 23/50.
33 Because Locarno was a mile-stone, the biographer of Churchill, the chancellor of the exchequer, claims his subject played a decisive part in Cabinet discussion of the treaty; see M. Gilbert, *Winston S. Churchill*, vol. V: *1922–1939* (London, 1976), 124–5. For the same reason, Lord Swinton, then P. Cunliffe-Lister, the president of the Board of Trade, says his role was crucial; see Viscount Swinton, *I Remember* (London, 1948), 162–3.
34 The literature on this subject is legion; for an overview see B. W. E. Alford, *Depression and Recovery?* (London, 1972); R. P. Arnot, *The Miners: Years of Struggle* (London, 1953); Gilbert, *Churchill*, vol. V, 65–329; Labour Research Department, *The Coal Shortage: why the miners will win* (London, 1926); Medlicott, *Contemporary England*, 223–41; Middlemas and Barnes, *Baldwin*, 278–341, 378–529; D. E. Moggridge, *The Return to Gold, 1925* (Cambridge, 1969); and G. A. Phillips, *The General Strike. The Politics of Industrial Conflict* (London, 1976).
35 Memorandum – 28 Mar 1925, Lampson; minute – 28 Mar 1925, Crowe [permanent under-secretary, Foreign Office]; minute – 28 Mar 1925, Chamberlain: all FO 371/10633/1747/6.
36 Letters – 8 & 21 Mar 1929, Hankey [Cabinet secretary] to Balfour [the lord president]: both BM Add MSS 49705.
37 French commentators were aware of Baldwin's tendency to support Chamberlain in times of crisis; see minute – 14 Jul 1927, Kenney [FO News Department]: FO 395/416/719/1.
38 Letter – 1 Dec 1924, Churchill to Chamberlain: FO 800/256.
39 This was an attempt to reduce naval expenditures, since the precluding of an Anglo-Japanese conflict meant fewer Royal Navy warships in the Pacific; see letter – 15 Dec 1924, Churchill to Chamberlain: *Ibid.*; CID Meeting 193: CAB 2/4; and Gilbert, *Churchill*, vol. V, 75–9.
40 The Foreign Office and the British Embassy at Washington aided the Treasury in spreading propaganda in the United States about the promptness with which the British war debt was paid; see letter – 8 Dec 1927, Leith Ross [Treasury] to Under-Secretary, FO: FO 371/12025/

7104/25; telegram (519) – 14 Dec 1927, FO to Howard: FO 371/12025/7155/25.

41 For example, letter – 17 Jun 1927, Pound to Keyes [commander-in-chief, Mediterranean Fleet]: KEYES 15/20.

42 Letter – 9 Jul 1927, Bridgeman to Baldwin: Bal MSS vol. 130.

43 For example, minute – 1 Feb 1927, Chamberlain; note – 1 Feb 1927, Bridgeman to Chamberlain: both FO 371/12035/771/93.

44 Amery's papers are closed to research, but there is his memoirs; see L. S. Amery, *My Political Life*, vols. I & II (London, 1953).

45 For example, letter – 9 Aug 1927, Willingdon [governor-general of Canada] to Baldwin: PREM 1/65.

46 For Baldwin's recognition of the power of the Cecil name, see Middlemas and Barnes, *Baldwin*, 243, 547–8, 704, 709.

47 See Cmd. 2029. Roskill, *Naval Policy*, vol. I, 372–3, 377–8 discusses the dispute and the work of Salisbury's committee.

48 For sympathetic appraisals of Cecil's character and actions in the 1920s, see D. Carlton, 'Disarmament with Guarantees: Lord Cecil 1922–1927', *Disarmament and Arms Control*, vol. 3, No. 2 (1965); H. Cecil, 'Lord Robert Cecil: A Nineteenth Century Upbringing', *History Today*, 25(1975).

49 Letter – 6 Nov 1924, Salisbury to Cecil: BM Add MSS 51085; 'Memorandum of conversation with the Prime Minister' – 11 Nov 1924, Cecil: BM Add MSS 51080; letter – 25 Jan 1925, Chamberlain to Salisbury: FO 800/257. Also see Johnson, 'Chamberlain', 67–8.

50 Cf. letter – 7 Jun 1927, Cecil to Irwin [viceroy of India]: BM Add MSS 51084; Cecil of Chelwood, *All the Way* (London, 1949), 185–7. See Carlton, 'League Council Crisis'; 'Coolidge Conference'; 'Anglo-French Compromise'; and G. A. Craig, 'The British Foreign Office from Grey to Austen Chamberlain': in G. A. Craig and F. Gilbert (eds.), *The Diplomats 1919–1939*, vol. I: *The Twenties* (New York, 1963), 42–7.

51 Letter – 4 Nov 1927, Cushendun to Chamberlain: FO 800/261. Cf. Lord Cushendun, 'Disarmament', *FA*, 7(1928), 77–93.

52 See P. Fraser, 'Arthur James Balfour': in Mackintosh, *Prime Ministers*, vol. I, 23–42.

53 For instance, see Earl of Balfour, 'On Anglo-American Friendship': in Balfour, *Opinions and Argument* (London, 1928), 241–7.

54 B. E. C. Dugdale, *Arthur James Balfour*, vol. II: *1906–1930* (London, 1936), 193–212; and K. M. Burk, 'British War Missions to the United States' [unpublished D.Phil. dissertation] (Oxford, 1976), 105–62.

55 There is a great deal of material on the Washington Conference; for an over-view, see J. B. Brebner, 'Canada, the Anglo-Japanese Alliance and the Washington Conference', *PSQ*, 50(1935), 45–57; Fry, *Illusions*, 154–86; Lowe and Dockrill, *Mirage of Power*, vol. II, 298–303; Roskill, *Naval Policy*, vol. I, 300–30; J. C. Vinson, *The Parchment Peace: the United States and the Washington Conference 1921–1922* (Athens, Ga., 1955). American historians, even those trained at British universities, persist in perpetuating the myth that Britain conceded complete naval parity to the United States at Washington; the most recent example is S. Marks, *The Illusion of Peace* (London, 1976), 41.

56 Percy of Newcastle, *Some Memories* (London, 1958), 9.
57 Memorandum – 16 Jan 1929, Percy: CP 10(29): CAB 24/201. Interestingly, Percy devoted fully one-third of his reflexions on Baldwin's second government to Anglo-American relations; Percy, *Memories*, 124–45.
58 S. W. Roskill, *Hankey Man of Secrets*, vol. II: *1919–1931* (London, 1972), 387. Also see Middlemas and Barnes, *Baldwin*, 317–18.
59 Roskill, *Hankey*, vol. II, 413–14; letter – 18 Aug 1925, Hankey to Cecil: BM Add MSS 51088.
60 Letter – 22 May 1924, Hankey to Smuts [South African statesman]: HNKY 4/16.
61 For Hankey's initial opposition to Locarno and its obligations, see diary entry – 22 Mar 1925: HNKY 1/17.
62 For example, letter – 17 Dec 1927, Hankey to Esher [Conservative peer]: HNKY 4/19.
63 Cf. the lists of Cabinet ministers from Baldwin's first and second governmentts in D. Butler and A. Sloman, *British Political Facts 1900–1975*, 4th ed. (London, 1975), 14–15, 17–18. For Baldwin's reduction of the landed interests element, see Campbell, 'Baldwin', 197–8, 202.
64 This did not mean that other aspects of foreign policy were equally ignored. William Joynson-Hicks, the home secretary, was violently anti-communist; see H. Florry, 'The Arcos Raid and the Rupture of Anglo-Soviet Relations, 1927', *JCH*, 12(1977), 707–23.
65 See A. Toynbee *et al.*, *Survey . . . 1924* (London, 1926), 1–80, 266–403; *1925*, vol. I (London, 1927), 189–269; *1925*, vol. II (London, 1928), 1–78, 310–95; *1926* (London, 1928), 1–80, 247–380; *1927*, 1–43, 83–114.
66 Letter – 10 Oct 1924, Chamberlain to his wife: quoted in Johnson, 'Chamberlain', 63.
67 Chamberlain turned down invitations to several functions at this time, always claiming the pressing demands of his new office; see letter 14 Nov 1924, Chamberlain to Laming [president of the Persia Society]; letter – 29 Nov 1924, Chamberlain to de Rothschild [of the bondholders of the Egyptian loan]: both FO 800/256.
68 Letter – 29 Apr 1925, Beaverbrook to Borden [former Canadian prime minister]: BBK MSS C/51. Johnson, 'Chamberlain' puts the foreign secretary's francophilia in its proper perspective. Chamberlain believed that when he spoke French his natural coldness disappeared; see letter – 2 Sep 1927, Chamberlain to Mary Carnegie [his step-mother]: AC 4/1/1282.
69 Letter – 22 Nov 1925, Lampson to D'Abernon: BM Add MSS 48929.
70 Letter – 21 Dec 1928, Lindsay to Chamberlain: AC 38/3/55.
71 Carlton, 'Anglo-French Compromise'; Cecil, *Great Experiment*, 185–8, 194–5; Craig, 'British Foreign Office', 46–7; and Middlemas and Barnes, *Baldwin*, 374–6.
72 A good survey of Tyrrell's character and early career is in Z. S. Steiner, *The Foreign Office and Foreign Policy, 1898–1914* (Cambridge, 1969), 118–19.

73 Middlemas and Barnes, *Baldwin*, 344.

74 Quoted in letter – 6 Jul 1928, Chamberlain to his wife: AC 6/1/717.

75 There is no historical treatment of Lindsay's career other than occasional mention in monographs that touch incidentally on his work; see Jacobson, *Locarno Diplomacy*, 126 *et passim*. An indication of how Lindsay approached his Berlin duties can be seen in letter – 17 Aug 1926, Lindsay to Howard: How MSS DHW 4/Personal/17.

76 For Wellesley's contribution to British East Asian policy, see W. R. Louis, *British Strategy in the Far East, 1919–39* (Oxford, 1971), 4–18 *et passim*. Wellesley was one of those rare élite members who felt that foreign and economic policies were kindred subjects; see V. A. H. Wellesley, *Diplomacy in Fetters* (London, 1945).

77 Vansittart, *Mist Procession*, 317–18.

78 See Chapter 2, below. Vansittart's most recent biographer is off the mark completely with the comment that Vansittart's time at the American Department was 'an uneventful period'; moreover, he sees fit to cover these four years in a single paragraph; see N. Rose, *Vansittart. A Study of a Diplomat* (London, 1978), 63.

79 On Vansittart's career before he went to the American Department, see *Ibid.*, 1–62. For Vansittart's critique of Chamberlain's francophilia, see Vansittart, *Mist Procession*, 317–18.

80 *Ibid.*, 347; Middlemas and Barnes, *Baldwin*, 345.

81 See Chapter 2, below.

82 The mission of Sir Horace Rumbold, the British minister at Berne for most of the Great War, is discussed fully in M. Gilbert, *Sir Horace Rumbold. Portrait of a Diplomat 1869–1941* (London, 1973), 137–81.

83 G. H. Thompson, *Front-Line Diplomat* (London, 1959), 65.

84 See D. H. Miller, *The Drafting of the Covenant*, vol. I (New York, 1928), *passim*.

85 See E. D. Canham, *Commitment to Freedom. The Story of 'The Christian Science Monitor'* (Cambridge, Mass., 1958), 195–254; J. E. Pollard, *The Presidents and the Press* (New York, 1947), 713–36; M. K. Singleton, *H. L. Mencken and the 'American Mercury' Adventure* (Durham, N.C., 1962); J. K. Winkler, *William Randolph Hearst. A New Appraisal* (New York, 1955). Cf. D. Perkins, 'The State Department and American Public Opinion': in Craig and Gilbert, *The Diplomats*, vol. I, 282–308. An example of an American journalist both influential and with decided ideas on foreign policy was Walter Lippmann, the editor of the *NY World*; see R. L. Zuercher, 'Walter Lippmann and His Views on American Foreign Policy' [unpublished Ph.D. dissertation] (Michigan State University, 1974).

86 On the News Department, see P. M. Taylor, *The Projection of Britain. British Overseas Publicity and Propaganda 1919–1939* (Cambridge, 1981), 11–14, 56–7; and memorandum – 17 Sep 1927, Yencken [News Department]: FO 395/423/993/993.

87 Such feelings did not diminish after Willert left the United States but, rather, they intensified; see A. Willert, *The Road to Safety. A Study in Anglo-American Relations* (London, 1952). For Willert's reminiscences of

this period in his career, see A. Willert, *Washington and Other Memories* (Boston, 1971), 147–52, 162–71.

88 Letter – 31 Aug 1927, M. MacDonald to his father: PRO 30/69/3/35. Willert's lectures were published as A. Willert, *Aspects of British Foreign Policy* (New Haven, Conn., 1928).

89 On Willert's selection to go to Williamstown, see memorandum [prepared for Tyrrell] – 17 Jan 1927, Yencken: FO 395/420/63/63; and letter – 4 Jul 1927, Willert to Howard: How MSS DHW 5/9. For Chamberlain's favourable assessment of Willert, see letter – 2 Jul 1928, Chamberlain to Hilda, his sister: AC 5/1/458.

90 Thompson, *Front-Line Diplomat*, 58.

91 E. Howard, 'British Policy and the Balance of Power', *APSR*, 19(1925), 261–7. Americans had generally become disenchanted with Europe and its affairs in the post-war period, especially anything to do with the League of Nations. A principal reason for this was the supposed European rejection of Wilson's attempt to build a 'new diplomacy' on the Fourteen Points; see J. D. Hicks, *Republican Ascendancy 1921–1933* (New York, 1960), 23–49; A. J. Mayer, *Politics and Diplomacy. Containment and Counterrevolution at Versailles, 1918–1919* (New York, 1969), 359–61. The problem of German 'war guilt' also had a bearing; see S. Adler, 'The War Guilt Question and American Disillusionment 1918–1929', *JMH*, 28(1956), 1–28.

92 Howard's career in these twenty years included resignation from the diplomatic service to run for parliament, as well as army service during the Boer War; see Howard of Penrith, *Theatre of Life*, vol. I: *Life Seen From the Pit 1863–1905* (London, 1935), 103–331.

93 *Ibid.*, vol. II: *Life as Seen From the Stalls 1905–1936* (London, 1936), 115–17, 492–3.

94 See Chapter 8, below.

95 For example, telegram – 15 Feb 1915, Bryan [US secretary of state] to Page [US ambassador, London]: *FRUS 1915*, vol. II, 105–7; telegram – 30 Mar 1915, Bryan to Page: *Ibid.*, 152–6. Cf. Foreign Office, *Peace Conference Handbooks*, No. 166: *President Wilson's Policy* (London, 1919), 49–57.

96 Howard, *Theatre of Life*, vol. II, 256.

97 *Ibid.*, 225.

98 For example, see letter – 1 Nov 1924, Tyrrell to Howard: How MSS DHW 1/28; letter – 15 Dec 1926, Vansittart to Howard: *Ibid.*, DHW 5/33.

99 This happened to Sir Charles Eliot, the ambassador at Tokyo, who was dropped from the diplomatic service after just five years at this senior post. See minute – 9 Jan 1925, Selby: FO 800/257; letters – 12 Jan, 18 Feb, & 31 Mar 1925, Chamberlain to Eliot: *Ibid.*; letters – 15 & 30 Jan, 4 Apr, & 2 May 1925: Eliot to Chamberlain: *Ibid.*

100 There seems to have been much non-governmental talk about replacing Howard in late 1928; see diary entries – 5 & 7 Dec 1928, Jones: in K. Middlemas (ed.), *Thomas Jones: Whitehall Diary*, vol. II (London, 1969), 159–62.

101 On the Protocol, see D. Marquand, *Ramsay MacDonald* (London, 1977),

351–6. Also see Medlicott, *Contemporary England*, 200–1; Northedge, *Troubled Giant*, 239–47; Taylor, *English History*, 277–9.

102 CID Meeting 192: CAB 2/4; and letter – 22 Dec 1924, Chamberlain to Howard: FO 800/256.

103 Letter – 9 Jan 1925, Howard to Chamberlain: FO 800/257.

104 Letter – 15 Feb 1925, Howard to Chamberlain: *Ibid.* Cf. D. D. Burks, 'The United States and the Geneva Protocol of 1924: "A New Holy Alliance"?', *AHR*, 64(1959), 891–905.

105 Report (CID 559B) – 23 Jan 1925: CAB 4/12; and memorandum – 27 Jan 1925, Chamberlain: CP 48(25): CAB 24/171.

106 For example, letter – 10 Jan 1927, Chamberlain to Spender [of *The Christian Science Monitor*]: FO 800/260.

107 For instance, see Thompson, *Front-Line Diplomat*, 62.

108 Howard went on such a trip in mid-1927. See despatch – 3 Jun 1927, Howard to Chamberlain: FO 371/12052/3485/673; and Howard, *Theatre of Life*, vol. II, 547–58.

109 The work of the British consulates in the United States added almost nothing to the Washington Embassy's political work; see the memoirs of the consul-general at San Francisco for this period, G. Campbell, *Of True Experience* (New York, 1947). Cf. D. C. M. Platt, *The Cinderella Service. British Consuls Since 1815* (London, 1971), 68–124, 240–2.

110 On BLINY, see B. J. C. McKercher, 'The British diplomatic service in the United States and the Chamberlain Foreign Office's perceptions of domestic America, 1924–1927: images, reality, and diplomacy', in B. J. C. McKercher and D. J. Moss (eds.), *Shadow and Substance in British Foreign Policy, 1895–1939. Memorial Essays in Honour of the late Professor C. J. Lowe* (forthcoming, University of Alberta Press); and Taylor, *Projection*, 68–77.

2 Foreign Office perception of Republican foreign policy

1 Letter – 12 Mar 1925, Hurst to Chamberlain: FO 371/10646/1490/1490.

2 For Kellogg's career prior to his service as ambassador, see D. Bryn-Jones, *Frank B. Kellogg. A Biography* (New York, 1937), 28–127.

3 For Chamberlain's unfavourable impression of Kellogg, see letter – 4 Jan 1925, Chamberlain to Hilda, his sister: AC 5/1/344.

4 Letter – 28 Jan 1925, Chamberlain to Howard: FO 800/257. Also see minute – 11 Jan 1925, R. I. Campbell; minute – 12 Jan 1925, Vansittart; minute – 13 Jan 1925, Tyrrell: all FO 371/10639/171/171.

5 Letter – 13 Feb 1925, Howard to Chamberlain: FO 800/257.

6 Minute – 26 Mar 1925, Hurst: FO 371/10646/1490/1490.

7 The blockade claims question had been raised previously in the Foreign Office but there had never been any urgency about a presentation. See letter – 23 Feb 1923, A. Lasker [chairman, US Shipping Board] to the accountant-general, Board of Trade; minute – 23 Nov 1923, Sperling [head, FO American Department]: both FO 371/8509/6893/240; minute – 3 Mar 1924, Malkin [assistant legal adviser, FO]; minute – 7 Mar 1924, R. I. Campbell: both FO 371/9602/1377/84.

8 This was the 'Laws of War' sub-committee; see CAB 16/55.
9 Memorandum on 'Default of the Southern States of the American Union' – 22 Apr 1925, Orchard [FO Library]: FO 371/10642/2235/367. More important, see letter – 21 Jul 1925, Vansittart to Administrator of Enemy Property, Admiralty, Air Ministry, Board of Trade, Colonial Office, India Office, Treasury, War Office: FO 371/10646/3251/1490; and the replies, letter – Aug 1925, Air Ministry to FO: FO 371/10646/4115/1490; letters – 22 Sep & 2 Oct 1925, Admiralty to FO: both FO 371/10646/4781/1490; letter – 22 Sep 1925, Board of Trade to FO: FO 371/10646/4824/1490; letter – 6 Oct 1925, Treasury to FO: FO 371/10646/5000/1490.
10 Memorandum – 7 Aug 1925, Hurst: FO 371/10646/4006/1490. Olds was Kellogg's only major political appointment whilst secretary of state; see G. H. Stuart, *The Department of State. A History of Its Organization, Procedure, and Personnel* (New York, 1949), 280–1.
11 Telegram (282) – 26 Oct 1925, Howard to FO: *DBFP 1A*, II, 865. Cf. memorandum (extract) – 24 Nov 1925, Olds: *FRUS 1926*, II, 216–17.
12 See minute – 13 Oct 1925, Vansittart, enclosing 'Memorandum respecting possible presentation of United States blockade claims against His Majesty's Government' – 12 Oct 1925, Craigie: both FO 371/10646/5106/1490.
13 Cd. 4179; Cd. 7714.
14 For the Order in Council, see *British Foreign and State Papers*, vol. CIX, 217–41. For analysis of the belligerent rights question before 1914, the best study is M. R. Pitt, 'Great Britain and Belligerent Maritime Rights From the Declaration of Paris, 1856, to the Declaration of London, 1909' [unpublished Ph.D. dissertation] (University of London, 1964). Also instructive is W. N. Medlicott, *The Economic Blockade*, vol. I (London, 1952), 1–10. For the British blockade imposed during the Great War, see A. C. Bell, *A History of the Blockade of Germany* (London, 1937); G. Hardach, *The First World War 1914–1918* (London, 1977), 11–34; M. C. Siney, *The Allied Blockade of Germany* (Ann Arbor, 1957).
15 Minute – 28 Oct 1925, R. I. Campbell: FO 371/10646/5376/1490.
16 Minute – 28 Oct 1925, Hurst: *Ibid.*
17 Minute – 29 Oct 1925, Vansittart; minute – 30 Oct 1925, Wellesley: both *Ibid.*
18 Minute – 31 Oct 1925 (1:30 a.m.), Chamberlain: *Ibid.*
19 Telegrams (235 & 238) – 2 & 3 Nov 1925, FO to Howard: *Ibid.*
20 Letter – 31 Oct 1925, Chamberlain to Ida, his sister: AC 5/1/367.
21 Despatch – 3 Nov 1925, Chamberlain to Howard: *DBFP 1A*, II, 867–8. Curiously, in his report of this conversation, Houghton made no mention of his equating the blockade claims with war debts; see telegram – 3 Nov 1925, Houghton to Kellogg: *FRUS 1926*, II, 214–15.
22 Minute – 5 Nov 1925, Craigie: FO 371/10646/5488/1490.
23 Telegram (295) – 4 Nov 1925, Howard to FO: FO 371/10646/5507/1490. Cf. memorandum – 4 Nov 1925, Kellogg: *FRUS 1926*, II, 215–16. The Cabinet was told for the first time of the American intentions on 11 Nov 1925; see Cabinet Conclusion 52(25)4: CAB 23/51.
24 Telegram (243) – 5 Nov 1925, FO to Howard: FO 371/10646/5507/1490.

25 Telegram (302) – 7 Nov 1925, Howard to Chamberlain: *DBFP 1A*, II, 871–3.

26 Minute – 9 Nov 1925, R. I. Campbell; minute – 10 Nov 1925, Craigie; minute – 10 Nov 1925, Chamberlain; minute – 11 Nov 1925, Tyrrell: all FO 371/10646/5580/1490.

27 Letter – 13 Mar 1925, Kingsbury to Thompson; despatch – 20 Mar 1925, Howard to Chamberlain: both FO 371/10646/1697/1490. Letter – 5 May 1925, Hughes [Board of Trade] to FO: FO 371/10646/2286/1490.

28 Minute – 9 Apr 1925, R. I. Campbell; minute – 15 Apr 1925, Vansittart: both FO 371/10646/1697/1490; minute – 5 May 1925, Craigie: FO 371/10646/2286/1490.

29 Memorandum – 8 May 1925, Craigie: *Ibid.*

30 For example, letter – 25 Jun 1925, Waley [Treasury] to Vansittart: FO 371/10646/3251/1490.

31 Minute – 10 Nov 1925, Chamberlain: FO 371/10647/5580/1490.

32 Telegram (326) – 26 Nov 1925, Howard to FO: FO 371/10647/5916/1490; memorandum – 4 Feb 1926, Kellogg: *FRUS 1926*, III, 217–18; telegram (82) – 30 Mar 1926, Howard to FO: FO 371/11162/1788/6.

33 Minute – 27 Nov 1925, Craigie: FO 371/10647/5916/1490; telegram (12) – 19 Jan 1926, FO to Howard: FO 371/11161/135/6.

34 A good summary is in a memorandum on 'United States Blockade Claims: Present Position' – 27 May 1926, American Department: FO 371/11162/2742/6.

35 See n. 33 above; and memorandum – 29 Mar 1926, Phenix: *FRUS 1926*, II, 222–4. Cf. memorandum on 'United States Blockade Claims' – 1 Apr 1926, R. I. Campbell: FO 371/11161/1665/6.

36 See W. J. Dennis, *Tacna and Arica; an account of the Chile–Peru boundary dispute and of the arbitration of the United States* [originally published in 1931] (Hamden, Conn., 1967); and L. E. Ellis, *Frank B. Kellogg and American Foreign Relations, 1925–1929* (New Brunswick, N.J., 1961), 86–96.

37 See telegram (59) – 16 Mar 1926, Howard to FO: FO 371/11161/1476/6. Cf. 'US and "Rights of Neutrals". War Claims Against Allies' – 17 Mar 1926, *Times*; and 'Borah's Proposal Shocks England' – 17 Mar 1926, *NY Times*. For insight into Borah and foreign policy, see L. Ashby, *The Spearless Leader. Senator Borah and the Progressive Movement in the 1920s* (Urbana, Chicago, London, 1972), 95–116; W. Lippmann, Concerning Senator Borah', *FA*, 4(1926), 211–22; R. J. Maddox, *William E. Borah and American Foreign Policy* (Baton Rouge, 1969).

38 Telegram (68) – 22 Mar 1926, Howard to FO: FO 371/11161/1609/6; telegram (73) – 26 Mar 1926, Howard to FO: FO 371/11161/1663/6.

39 Telegram (81) – 29 Mar 1926, Howard to Chamberlain: *DBFP 1A*, II, 880; despatch – 1 Apr 1926, Howard to Chamberlain: FO 371/11162/1993/6.

40 Chamberlain was particularly worried, as he believed that State Department lawyers were laying a trap for the British government through an unsuspecting Kellogg; see telegram (70) – 10 Apr 1926, Chamberlain to Howard: FO 371/11161/1665/6.

41 See memorandum on 'United States Blockade Claims: Present Position' –

27 May 1926, American Department: FO 371/11162/2742/6; and telegram (174) – 7 Jun 1926, Howard to FO: *DBFP 1A*, II, 889–90.

42 Telegram (116) – 25 Apr 1926, Howard to FO: minute – 27 Apr 1926, R. I. Campbell; minute – 28 Apr 1926, Craigie: all FO 371/11162/2226/6.

43 Telegram – 14 May 1926, Kellogg to Houghton: *FRUS 1926*, II, 227–9; memorandum on 'United States Blockade Claims: Present Position' – 27 May 1926, American Department: FO 371/11162/2742/6.

44 Minute – 7 Jul 1926, Craigie; minute – 8 Jul 1926, Vansittart: both FO 371/11162/3558/6. One example of a powerful influence on British public opinion being concerned that Britain had been giving too much away since 1918 can be seen in letter – 16 Jul 1925, Beaverbrook to Borden [former Canadian prime minister]: BBK MSS C/51.

45 'Sees Extortion in Rubber Prices. Hoover says America is mulcted of $600,000,000 a year by British monopoly' – 15 Dec 1925, *NY Times*; also see despatch – 19 Dec 1925, BLINY to FO: FO 371/11167/10/10. For an indication of Hoover's dynamism whilst he was the secretary of commerce, see J. Brandes, *Herbert Hoover and Economic Diplomacy; Department of Commerce Policy, 1921–1928* (Pittsburgh, 1962); and E. W. Hawley, 'Herbert Hoover, the Commerce Secretariat, and the Vision of an "Associated State", 1921–1928', *JAH*, 61(1974–75), 116–40.

46 The rest of this paragraph is based on a memorandum on the 'Short History of the Rubber Restriction Scheme' – February 1928, Beckett [Colonial Office]: FO 371/12831/1967/507.

47 Firestone's activities were reported regularly to the Foreign Office. See telegram (205) – 30 Jul 1926, Howard to FO: FO 371/11168/4080/10; and despatch – 4 Sep 1926, BLINY to FO: FO 371/11168/4952/10.

48 Letter – 22 Jan 1926, Steel-Maitland to Tyrrell; minute – 27 Jan 1926, R. I. Campbell: both FO 371/11167/489/10.

49 For example, 'The U.S. Rubber Complaints. Mr. Hoover Rebuked' – 29 Dec 1925, *Daily Mail*; 'Rubber Outcry "Ungenerous and Unjustified"' – 3 Jan 1926, *Sunday Express*; 'People in Glass Houses' (editorial) – 28 Dec 1925, *Morning Post*. For examples of comprehensive analyses of American press opinion on rubber, see memorandum – 19 Feb 1926, BLINY: FO 371/11167/1181/10; memorandum – 22 May 1926, BLINY: FO 371/11169/2960/10.

50 Memorandum – 7 May 1926, Broderick: FO 371/11162/2660/6.

51 Minute – 25 Aug 1926, Vansittart: FO 371/11163/4579/6; minute – 10 Sep 1926, Vansittart: FO 371/11163/4692/6.

52 Though echoing Vansittart's opinion of Phenix, Howard thought that he was good at handling Kellogg: 'He was always useful in smoothing the ruffled feathers of his somewhat irascible chief.' See letter – 21 Aug 1926, Howard to Vansittart: *Ibid*.

53 At its second and final look at blockade claims, on 14 July 1926, the Cabinet decided that for economic, legal, and strategic reasons there could be no arbitration; see Cabinet Conclusion 46(26)7: CAB 23/53.

54 'Meritorious' claims were those which, though arising from the blockade, did not call into question its application. For example, three meritorious

claims concerned the accidental sinking of vessels after their interception and whilst under the command of British officers.

55 The approximate value of the British 'make-weights' was £507,500; see minute – 9 Sep 1926, Craigie: FO 371/11164/4814/6.

56 Actually, Howard had reported that Olds would be in London; he had suggested to Tyrrell that a meeting be arranged with the American under-secretary; see letter – 25 Aug 1926, Tyrrell to Howard: DHW4/Personal/13.

57 Letter – 10 Sep 1926, Lewis to Dawson: Lewis MSS.

58 Letter – 10 Oct 1926, Tyrrell to Howard: How MSS DHW 5/9; letter – 12 Oct 1926, Broderick to Howard: How MSS DHW 5/25; minute – 22 Oct 1926, Craigie: FO 371/11164/5592/6; memorandum – 22 Oct 1926, Broderick: FO 371/11164/5700/6; memorandum – 19 Nov 1926, Craigie: *DBFP 1A*, II, 903–5.

59 The appraisal of Phenix being 'on the make' proved to be correct; see letter – 12 Oct 1926, Tyrrell to Howard: How MSS DHW 5/9.

60 For example, see 'Record of an Interdepartmental Meeting' – 15 Nov 1926, Craigie: FO 371/11164/6103/6; 'Record of an Interdepartmental Meeting' – 24 Nov 1926, Craigie: FO 371/11165/6494/6; 'Record of an Interdepartmental Meeting' – 8 Dec 1926, FO: FO 371/11166/6825/6.

61 For instance Hankey, so close to the Cabinet and with his Admiralty connexions, had only the sketchiest idea of how the controversy had been resolved; see letter – 12 Jan 1928, Hankey to Balfour: BM Add MSS 49705.

62 See Cmd. 2877; and *Arrangement . . . between the United States and Great Britain for the disposal of certain pecuniary claims arising out of the recent war* (Washington, 1927).

63 Telegram (332) – 29 Dec 1926, Howard to FO: *DBFP 1A*, II, 917–18.

64 See telegram (23) – 10 Jan 1927, Howard to FO: FO 371/12022/213/24; telegram (100) – 10 Feb 1927, Howard to FO: FO 371/12022/1015/24; despatch – 1 Apr 1927, Howard to Chamberlain: FO 371/12022/2204/24. Also see Bryn-Jones, *Kellogg*, 171–202, 211–21; and Ellis, *Kellogg*, 23–85, 105–56.

65 Telegram (161) – 18 Mar 1927, Howard to FO: FO 371/12022/1693/24.

66 Letter – 25 Mar 1927, Leith Ross [Treasury] to under-secretary, FO: FO 371/12022/1806/24.

67 Minute – 18 Mar 1927, R. I. Campbell; minute – 18 Mar 1927, Vansittart: both FO 371/12022/1657/24.

68 'Anglo-American Shipping Accord Reached' – 19 May 1927, *Baltimore Sun*.

69 For example, telegram (81) – 29 Mar 1926, Howard to FO: minute – 30 Mar 1926, R. I. Campbell: both FO 371/11162/1757/6.

70 Coolidge subsequently made no mention of foreign affairs in his memoirs; see C. Coolidge, *The Autobiography of Calvin Coolidge* (London, 1929).

71 Letter – 28 Jan 1925, Chamberlain to Howard: FO 800/257.

72 Telegram (174) – 7 Jun 1926, Howard to Chamberlain: *DBFP 1A*, II, 889.

73 Quoted in Ashby, *Spearless Leader*, 16.

74 On Borah's appointment as chairman of the Senate Foreign Relations Committee, see despatch – 13 Nov 1924, Howard to Chamberlain; minute

– 26 Nov 1924, R. I. Campbell; minute – 27 Nov 1924, Tyrrell: all FO 371/9636/6553/6359. When Borah was near death in January 1940, it was noted that Vansittart 'was glad of it and hoped that he would die because he had done so much mischief to the right causes'; quoted in diary entry – 19 Jan 1940, Crozier [editor, *Manchester Guardian*]: A. J. P. Taylor (ed.), *W. P. Crozier. Off the Record* (London, 1973), 125.

75 For example, minute – 5 Feb 1926, Craigie: FO 371/11167/636/10; minute – 16 Mar 1926, Vansittart: FO 371/11167/1449/10.

76 For example, minute – 10 Sep 1926, Vansittart: FO 371/11168/4769/10; minute – nd [probably 21 or 22 Dec 1926], R. I. Campbell: FO 371/11190/6741/330; minute – 31 Jan 1927, Vansittart to Chamberlain: FO 371/10235/771/93.

77 Despatch – 3 Jun 1927, Howard to Chamberlain: FO 371/12023/3487/24.

78 *Ibid.*

3 The onset of naval deadlock

1 Department of State, *Conference on the Limitation of Armament. Washington. November 12, 1921–February 6, 1922* (Washington, 1922), 406–17, 418–849, 1575–604.

2 Hicks, *Republican Ascendancy*, 146–7; D. R. McCoy, *Calvin Coolidge. The Quiet President* (New York, London, 1967), 363. During the 1924 presidential campaign, Coolidge had indicated that he would call for an international arms limitation conference 'as soon as conditions in Europe justify such a move'; see Roskill, *Naval Policy*, vol. I, 431.

3 Despatch – 22 Dec 1924, Howard to Chamberlain: FO 371/10636/77/49. American–Japanese problems derived from immigration restriction laws that had been enacted by some states, notably California, and which discriminated against East Asians; see despatch – 8 Dec 1924, Howard to Chamberlain: FO 371/9587/7005/2; and Hicks, *Republican Ascendancy*, 131–4.

4 Debates – 19 Dec 1924, House of Representatives: *Congressional Record*, vol. 66, Pt. 1, 854–7. See despatch – 31 Dec 1925, Tottenham to Howard, enclosed in despatch – 2 Jan 1925, Howard to Chamberlain: FO 371/10633/191/6.

5 Minute – 14 Jan 1925, R. I. Campbell; minute – 14 Jan 1925, Vansittart: both *Ibid.*

6 See minute – 15 Jan 1925, Tyrrell: *Ibid.*; minute – 4 Feb 1925, R. I. Campbell; minute – 4 Feb 1925, Vansittart: both FO 371/10636/588/49; minute – 5 Feb 1925, Vansittart: FO 371/10636/604/49.

7 Debates – 5 Feb 1925, House of Representatives: *Congressional Record*, vol. 66, Pt. 3, 2972–3; telegram (38) – 4 Feb 1925, Howard to FO: FO 371/10636/604/49.

8 Minute – 5 Feb 1925, R. I. Campbell; minute – 5 Feb 1925, Vansittart: both *Ibid.* This was also the Cabinet's opinion; see Cabinet Conclusion 24(25)5: CAB 23/50.

9 For example, 'Disarmament. Mr. Coolidge for meeting at Washington' – 9 Oct 1925, *Morning Post.*

10 Minute – 22 Oct 1925, Chamberlain: FO 371/10637/5122/49.
11 On the Preparatory Commission, see Cecil, *Great Experiment*, 171; Walters, *League of Nations*, 363–76; Wheeler-Bennett, *Disarmament*, 43–102.
12 From an extract of draft CID minutes in *DBFP 1A*, I, n.4, 189–90.
13 Telegram (256) – 5 Dec 1925, Chamberlain to Cecil: *Ibid.*, 217.
14 Telegram (402) – 9 Dec 1925, London [British Legation, Geneva] to Tyrrell: *Ibid.*, 231. For the invitation to the United States, see letter – 12 Dec 1925, Scialoja [League Council] to Kellogg: *FRUS 1926*, I, 40–2.
15 Telegram (348) – 17 Dec 1925, Howard to FO: *DBFP 1A*, I, 259–60.
16 Message to Congress – 4 Jan 1926, Coolidge: *FRUS 1926*, I, 42–4. Also see Ellis, *Kellogg*, 160.
17 For analyses of the 1926 election, see Hicks, *Republican Ascendancy*, 127–9; McCoy, *Coolidge*, 311–13. For an example of a contemporary attack on Coolidge and the Republican Party, see W. Lippmann, 'Calvin Coolidge: Puritanism De Luxe' [originally published in May 1926]: in W. Lippmann, *Men of Destiny* (New York, 1927), 10–17.
18 As, for instance, the question of United States relations with Nicaragua; see Ellis, *Kellogg*, 59–71.
19 *FRUS 1926*, I, vii–xxx.
20 Minute – 22 Dec 1926, Craigie: FO 371/11190/6741/330.
21 Minute – nd [probably 21 or 22 Dec 1926], R. I. Campbell: *Ibid.*; minute – 7 Jan 1927, R. I. Campbell: FO 371/12034/93/93.
22 'Says We Need a New Navy' – 27 Dec 1926, *NY Times*; minute – 13 Jan 1927, Vansittart: FO 371/12034/166/93; despatch – 7 Jan 1927, Howard to Chamberlain: FO 371/12035/342/93.
23 Despatch – 28 Jan 1927, BLINY to FO: FO 371/12036/877/128.
24 The invitations were despatched to the embassies in the respective capitals a week earlier; see telegram – 3 February 1927, Kellogg to Herrick [US ambassador at Paris] (*mutatis mutandis* to London, Rome, and Tokyo): *FRUS 1927*, I, 1–5.
25 Memorandum – 12 Feb 1927, R. H. Campbell: *DBFP 1A*, III, 568–71.
26 Cf. C. J. Lowe and F. Marzari, *Italian Foreign Policy 1870–1940* (London, 1975), 211–22; J. Néré, *The Foreign Policy of France from 1914 to 1945* (London, 1975), 132–3.
27 Telegram (85) – 13 Feb 1927, Tilley to Chamberlain: *DBFP 1A*, III, 572.
28 Memorandum – 19 Feb 1927, Japanese Embassy, Washington: *FRUS 1927*, I, 13–14.
29 See Cabinet Conclusion 10(27)1, and Appendix: CAB 23/54.
30 For the report of this conversation and a copy of the formal British reply, see despatch – 25 Feb 1927, R. H. Campbell to Howard: *DBFP 1A*, III, 576–8. Cf. telegram – 25 Feb 1927, Houghton to Kellogg: *FRUS 1927*, I, 22–3.
31 Memorandum – 5 Mar 1927, Grew: *Ibid.*, 23–4; telegram (139) – 5 Mar 1927, Howard to Chamberlain: *DBFP 1A*, III, 580. Also see J. C. Grew, *Turbulent Era. A Diplomatic Record of Forty Years, 1904–1945* (Boston, 1952), 696–7.
32 Telegram (117) – 8 Mar 1927, Tyrrell to Howard: *DBFP 1A*, III, 581.

33 Note – 11 Mar 1927, Grew to Matsudaira [*mutatis mutandis* to Howard]: *FRUS 1927*, I, 28. Memoranda were also sent to the French and Italian governments informing them of the conference and asking them to participate. These two governments eventually sent observers to Geneva.

34 For example, Carlton, 'Coolidge Naval Conference', 575; Cecil, *Great Experiment*, 185.

35 A good indication of American prescience here can be seen in Roskill, *Naval Policy*, vol. I, 500–1.

36 See Cmd. 2888; Toynbee *et al.*, *Survey of International Affairs 1927*, vol. I, 1–21 *passim*.

37 About Singapore, see Roskill, *Naval Policy*, vol. I, 339, 347–9, 400, 459–66. For Japanese concern about Singapore as late as two days before the conference began, see telegram (262) – 18 Jun 1927, Tilley to Chamberlain: *DBFP 1A*, III, 605. An excellent overview of Anglo-Japanese relations at this time is I. H. Nish, 'Anglo-Japanese Relations in the Shadow of the Washington Conference, 1922–29' (paper for the 1974 Mt. Kisco Conference) [unpublished]. I am indebted to Dr Nish for showing me this paper.

38 D. Borg, *American Policy and the Chinese Revolution, 1925–1928* (New York, 1947); T. Buckley, 'John Van Antwerp MacMurray. The Diplomacy of an American Mandarin': in D. R. Burns and E. M. Bennett (eds.), *Diplomats in Crisis. United States–Chinese–Japanese Relations, 1919–1941* (Santa Barbara, Oxford, 1974), 27–48.

39 For example, Lord Chatfield, *It Might Happen Again*, vol. I: *The Navy and Defence* (London, Toronto, 1947), 43; Chatfield was then the third sea lord. M. D. Kennedy, *The Estrangement of Great Britain and Japan 1917–35* (Manchester, 1969), 93; Kennedy was Reuters' man at Tokyo.

40 J. Daniels, *The Wilson Era*, vol. II: *Years of War and After, 1917–1923* (Chapel Hill, 1944), 367–88; G. T. Davis, *A Navy Second to None* (New York, 1940); Fry, *Illusions*, 40; H. and M. Sprout, *Toward a New Order of Sea Power* (Princeton, 1946), 64–5.

41 Lowe and Dockrill, *Mirage of Power*, vol. I, 96–8; Marder, *Dreadnought to Scapa Flow*, vol. I: *The Road to War* (London, 1961), 124–5; S. F. Wells, Jr, 'British Strategic Withdrawal from the Western Hemisphere 1904–6', *CHR*, 49(1968), 335–56.

42 Letter – 27 May 1927, Kellogg to Coolidge: *FRUS 1927*, I, 40–1.

43 Telegram – 5 Apr 1927, Chamberlain to Howard: *DBFP 1A*, III, 588–9.

44 Letter – 1 Apr 1927, Chamberlain to Cecil: BM Add MSS 51079.

45 Letter – 27 May 1927, Kellogg to Coolidge: *FRUS 1927*, I, 40–1.

46 At Washington, Hughes had ignored the US Navy Department's advice in his desire to get some sort of naval limitation; he actually excluded the American admirals from the drafting of the final American plan; see Roskill, *Naval Policy*, vol. I, 501. Cf. Ellis, *Kellogg*, 166.

47 'Verbatim Report of the First Plenary Session' – 20 Jun 1927: FO 371/12668/5772/61.

48 'Executive Committee Minutes' – 21 Jun 1927: FO 371/12669/5875/61.

49 See letter – 25 Feb 1927, Chamberlain to Bridgeman: FO 800/260; Roskill, *Naval Policy*, vol. I, 503.

50 There is no doubt that Britain had an overwhelming superiority in almost all classes of vessel; see Cmd. 2349; Cmd. 2590; Cmd. 2809; US Navy Department, *Annual Report of the Secretary of the Navy* [1923–26] (Washington, 1924–27); Anonymous, 'Comparative Tables of Armaments', *FA*, 4(1925), 158–9; 'Comparative Naval Strengths', *FA*, 5(1927), 425–6.

51 Roskill, *Naval Policy*, vol. I, 499–500.

52 'Verbatim Report of the First Plenary Session' – 20 Jun 1927: FO 371/12668/5772/61.

53 *Ibid.* Also see Cmd. 2964.

54 See *DBFP 1A*, III, 606–739; *FRUS 1927*, I, 46–159; M. J. Brode, 'Anglo-American Relations and the Geneva Naval Disarmament Conference of 1927' [unpublished Ph.D. dissertation] (University of Alberta, 1972); Carlton, 'Coolidge Naval Conference'; Ellis, *Kellogg*, 164–84; Roskill, *Naval Policy*, vol. I, 498–516; Toynbee *et al.*, *International Affairs 1927*, 43–82; Wheeler-Bennett, *Disarmament*, 103–27; B. H. Williams, *The United States and Disarmament* [originally published in 1931] (Port Washington, New York, London, 1973), 161–78.

55 Gilbert, *Churchill*, vol. V, 82–9, 101–5, 128–30; Middlemas and Barnes, *Baldwin*, 326–40; Roskill, *Naval Policy*, vol. I, 445–64. Also see the Naval Programme Committee Meetings (25)1 – (25)6: CAB 27/273.

56 The following is based on R. Humble, *Before the Dreadnought. The Royal Navy from Nelson to Fisher* (London, 1976), 114–15, 164–5, 195–6; Marder, *Dreadnought to Scapa Flow*, vol. I, 44–5; Roskill, *Naval Policy*, vol. I, 212–13, 324–6, 412–48 *passim*.

57 Telegram – 23 Jun 1927, Gibson to Kellogg: *FRUS 1927*, I, 52–3.

58 The Admiralty had argued originally that Britain required 79 cruisers: 25 for fleet work and, based on a formula combining the length of sea routes to be defended and the density of traffic, 54 for trade protection. The Admiralty had also contended that the United States would need just 50: 25 for fleet work and 25 for trade protection. See memorandum – 17 Mar 1927, Egerton [director of plans, Admiralty]: ADM 116/3371/02807.

59 Telegram (153) – 5 Jul 1927, Bridgeman to Baldwin: FO 371/12670/6269/61.

60 For the American concern about British merchantmen, see Ellis, *Kellogg*, 170. Bridgeman deprecated the idea of arming merchantmen; see telegram – 24 Jun 1927, Bridgeman to Howard: *DBFP 1A*, III, 616–17. Also see minute – 29 Jul 1927, Binney [Admiralty]: ADM 116/3371/02896.

61 'Verbatim Report of the First Plenary Session' – 20 Jun 1927: FO 371/12668/5772/61.

62 'Gibson . . . explained that American proposed maximum of 400,000 tons had not been fixed with the idea of suggesting to other countries limit to which they must descend but was simply largest figure to which American delegation expected to be able to obtain consent of Senate.': in telegram (168) – 10 Jul 1927, British delegation to FO: *DBFP 1A*, III, 662–3.

63 Memorandum – 6 Jul 1927, Japanese delegation: *FRUS 1927*, I, 76.

64 Telegram (26) – 25 Jun 1927, Bird [BLINY] to Willert: FO 395/421/615/

256; letter – 30 Jun 1927, Bird to Fletcher; minute – 18 Jul 1927, Fletcher; minute – 19 Jul 1927, Villiers [FO Western Department]; minute – 21 Jul 1927, Thompson; minute – 21 Jul 1927, Craigie: all FO 395/421/720/256; minute – 12 Jul 1927, Yencken [News Department]: FO 395/421/699/256; letter – 7 Jul 1927, Steward to Yencken: FO 395/422/728/256.

65 'Verbatim Report of the Second Plenary Session' – 14 Jul 1927: FO 371/12672/6773/61. Also see Cmd. 2964.

66 Telegram (190) – 14 Jul 1927, Bridgeman to Baldwin and the Cabinet: *DBFP 1A*, III, 681.

67 Telegram (194) – 17 Jul 1927, Bridgeman to Baldwin: *Ibid.*, 690–1.

68 A good condensation of Gibson's criticism can be found in Toynbee *et al., International Affairs 1927*, 62–3.

69 Telegram (194) – 17 Jul 1927, Baldwin to Bridgeman: *DBFP 1A*, III, 698. Also see Cabinet Conclusion 40(27)4c, and Appendix; Cabinet Conclusion 41(27)1: both CAB 23/55. Also important is memorandum – 21 Jul 1927, Hankey: CP 211(27): CAB 24/188.

70 Middlemas and Barnes, *Baldwin*, 370.

71 Churchill had been lobbying against formal British agreement to Anglo-American naval parity since late June 1927; see memorandum – 29 Jun 1927, Churchill: CP 189(27): CAB 24/187. Also see Cabinet Conclusion 43(27)1, and Appendices: CAB 23/55.

72 For instance, memorandum – 21 Jul 1927, Birkenhead: CP 210(27): CAB 24/188.

73 Memorandum – 26 Jul 1927, na: CP 212(27): *Ibid.*

74 Cabinet Conclusion 44(27), and Appendices: CAB 23/53. Also see speech – 27 Jul 1927, Chamberlain: *H of C Debs*, vol. 209, Cols. 1246–9; speech – 27 Jul 1927, Salisbury: *H of L Debs,* vol. 68, Cols. 933–6.

75 Some historians have since argued that Shearer accomplished nothing at Geneva; see Brode, 'Anglo-American Relations', Appendix I. This was not the view of the Foreign Office News Department; see memorandum – 15 Aug 1927, Steward: FO 395/422/862/256. In 1929 Shearer brought a law-suit against the firms that hired him to disrupt the Coolidge conference. He did this to collect monies that these firms still supposedly owed him for his disruptive work; see Roskill, *Naval Policy*, vol. I, 506.

76 Cf. telegram (134) – 29 Jul 1927, Chamberlain to Bridgeman: *DBFP 1A*, III, 706–7; telegram – 30 Jul 1927, Kellogg to Gibson: *FRUS 1927*, I, 141.

77 See telegram – 28 Jul 1927, Gibson to Kellogg: *Ibid.*, 137–8. For Dulles' views about disarmament that were published in April 1927, see A. Dulles, 'Some Misconceptions About Disarmament', *FA*, 5(1927), 413–24.

78 Telegram (145) – 3 Aug 1927, Chamberlain to Bridgeman: *DBFP 1A*, III, 722–3.

79 'Verbatim Report of the Third Plenary Session' – 4 Aug 1927: FO 371/12674/7499/61.

80 Press reports indicated that official opinion seemed to regard the conference's failure as less than a disaster. For example, see 'Failure at Geneva. The conference "adjourned"'; 'Statement by Mr. Kellogg. Failure not final' – both 5 Aug 1927, *Times*; 'Naval Parley Ends in No

Agreement . . . Closing scenes amicable'; 'Kellogg Sees Basis for Naval Accord' – both 5 Aug 1927, *NY Times*. Editorial opinion, on the other hand, tended to apportion blame; see 'The Conference Adjourns' (editorial) – 5 Aug 1927, *Times*; 'Back to Direct Negotiations' (editorial) – 5 Aug 1927, *NY Times*. The Times had actually looked with disfavour on the Coolidge conference from the outset; see Anonymous, *History of The Times*, vol IV, Pt 2 (London, 1954), 806–7.

4 Belligerent versus neutral rights

1 This figure has been computed in Cecil, 'Nineteenth Century Upbringing'.

2 Dugdale, *Balfour*, vol. II, 187.

3 See letter – 19 Feb 1926, Chamberlain to D'Abernon: FO 800/259; letter – 5 Apr 1926, Chamberlain to Ida, his sister: AC 5/1/376; letters – 21 & 24 Mar 1926, Cecil to Baldwin: BM Add MSS 51080. Carlton, 'League Council Crisis' is notable only for accepting uncritically Cecil's anti-Chamberlain bias.

4 The rest of this paragraph is based on the following: letters – 27 Oct 1926, 4 Nov 1926, 2 Mar 1927, 7 Jun 1927, 29 Sep 1927, Cecil to Irwin [viceroy of India]: all BM Add MSS 51084; letter – 13 Mar 1927, Cecil to Chamberlain: *Ibid.*, 51079; letters – 8 Apr 1927, 31 Jul 1927, Cecil to Salisbury: *Ibid.*, 51086; letter – 6 Apr 1927, Cecil to Baldwin: Bal MSS vol. 130. Also see Cecil, *Great Experiment*, 187–90; *All the Way*, 191–2; Middlemas and Barnes, *Baldwin*, 371–2.

5 Letter – 10 Aug 1927, Cecil to Chamberlain: BM Add MSS 51079.

6 Letter – 29 Sep 1927, Cecil to Irwin: *Ibid.*, 51084.

7 Letter – 18 Jul 1927, Cecil to Salisbury: BM Add MSS 51086.

8 Telegram (213) – 29 Jul 1927, Bridgeman to the Cabinet: *DBFP 1A*, III, 704–5.

9 Letter – 31 Jul 1927, Cecil to Salisbury: BM Add MSS 51086.

10 The best summary of the resignation is found in memorandum – 30 Aug 1927, Hankey: CAB 21/297. Chamberlain's private correspondence with Cecil on the resignation question is retained in BM Add MSS 51079. Also see Cecil, *Great Experiment*, 187–90; Middlemas and Barnes, *Baldwin*, 371–2; Roskill, *Hankey*, vol. II, 441–4.

11 For example, see *The Times* of 30 Aug 1927.

12 Letter – 2 Sep 1927, Cecil to Salisbury: BM Add MSS 51086.

13 Memorandum – 11 Oct 1927, Craigie: *DBFP 1A*, IV, 382–4.

14 Some historians argue that Coolidge did not want another term as president; see J. L. Blair, 'I do not choose to run for President in Nineteen Twenty-Eight', *Vermont History*, 30(1962). Howard agreed with this view; despatch – 5 Aug 1927, Howard to Chamberlain: FO 371/12039/4793/128.

15 R. H. Ferrell, *The American Secretaries of State and Their Diplomacy*, vol. XI: *Frank B. Kellogg – Henry L. Stimson* (New York, 1963), 101–2.

16 Letter – 26 Jul 1927, Wilmot Lewis to Howard: How MSS DHW 5/9.

17 Letter – 16 Jun 1927, Chamberlain to Hilda, his sister: AC 5/1/420.

18 Letter – 3 Aug 1927, Howard to Baldwin: Bal MSS vol. 130.
19 Telegram (329) – 14 Jul 1927, Howard to Chamberlain: *DBFP 1A*, III, 680.
20 Letter – 1 Aug 1927, Chamberlain to Mary Carnegie: AC 4/1/1277.
21 See telegram (un) – 6 Jul 1927, Howard to Chamberlain: *DBFP 1A*, III, 641–2. Kellogg complained later of British duplicity over what had occurred at the Jones–Admiralty meeting; see letter – 23 Sep 1927, Lamont [prominent Republican and vice-president of J. P. Morgan] to Cecil: BM Add MSS 51144.
22 Despatch – 3 Aug 1927, Howard to Chamberlain: *DBFP 1A*, III, 723–5.
23 Letter – 7 Aug 1927, Chamberlain to Mary Carnegie: AC 4/1/1278.
24 Despatch – 12 Aug 1927, Howard to Chamberlain: FO 371/12040/4935/133.
25 Minute – 23 Aug 1927, Thompson; minute – 24 Aug 1927, Craigie: both *Ibid.*
26 Memorandum – 24 Aug 1927, Craigie: FO 371/12040/5042/133.
27 Minute – 25 Aug 1927, Wellesley; minute – 25 Aug 1927, Chamberlain: both FO 371/12040/4935/133.
28 Despatch – 5 Aug 1927, Howard to Chamberlain: FO 371/12039/4793/128.
29 Letter – 29 Jul 1927, Howard to Chamberlain: *DBFP 1A*, III, 708–9.
30 Letter – 10 Aug 1927, Chamberlain to Howard: *Ibid.*, 729–31.
31 See Cmd. 1987; Cmd. 1988; Cmd. 2301; Cmd. 2768; H. D. Hall, 'The Genesis of the Balfour Declaration of 1926', *JCPS*, 1(1963), 169–93; R. A. Preston, *Canada and Imperial Defence* (Durham, N.C., 1967); P. G. Wrigley, *Canada and the Transition to Commonwealth. British–Canadian Relations 1917–1926* (Cambridge, New York, London, Melbourne, 1977), especially 248–77.
32 Letter – 1 Sep 1927, Howard to Chamberlain: *DBFP 1A*, III, 736–9.
33 Letter – 23 Jun 1927, Howard to Chamberlain: FO 800/261. Chamberlain later repeated this argument; see letter – 7 Aug 1927, Chamberlain to Mary Carnegie: AC 4/1/1278.
34 Letter – 21 Jul 1927, Howard to Chamberlain: FO 800/261; also see telegram (343) – 21 Jul 1927, Howard to Chamberlain: *DBFP 1A*, III, 700–1. Howard's views were supported by Wilmot Lewis; see letter – 26 Jul 1927, Wilmot Lewis to Howard: How MSS DHW 5/9.
35 Despatch – 5 Aug 1927, Howard to Chamberlain: FO 371/12040/4794/133.
36 This would have been true had the Labour Party been in power; a good indication of Labour Party thinking on Imperial security can be found in 'Notes on Imperial Strategy' – Jun 1927, Bennett [for the Advisory Committee on Imperial Questions, International Department, Labour Party]: PRO 30/69/5/153.
37 Minute – 16 Aug 1927, Thompson; minute – 17 Aug 1927, Craigie; marginal comment [on Craigie's minute] – 17 Aug 1927, Wellesley; minute – 17 Aug 1927, Chamberlain; letter – 26 Aug 1927, Chamberlain to Howard: all FO 371/12040/4794/133.
38 For a report of Jones' interview with the press and an analysis of

American newspaper comment, see despatch – 18 Aug 1927, Howard to Chamberlain: FO 371/12035/5073/93.

39 See minute – 10 Sep 1927, Thompson: FO 371/12035/5309/93; telegram (422) – 26 Sep 1927, Howard to FO: FO 371/12035/5650/93; despatch – 23 Sep 1927, BLINY to FO: FO 371/12035/5846/93; despatch – 13 Oct 1927, Howard to Chamberlain: FO 371/12035/6205/93.

40 Telegram (472) – 5 Nov 1927, Howard to Chamberlain: FO 371/12035/6445/93.

41 Speech – 16 Nov 1927, Cecil: *H of L Debs*, vol. 69, Cols. 84–94; also see telegram (488) – 21 Nov 1927, Howard to FO: FO 371/12035/6776/93. Although the initial American reaction to Cecil's resignation had been bad, the issue had seemed to die from lack of interest; see memorandum – 11 Oct 1927, Craigie: *DBFP 1A*, IV, 382–4.

42 Speech – 23 Nov 1927, Bridgeman: *H of C Debs*, vol. 210, Cols. 2186–98; see also telegram (492) – 24 Nov 1927, Howard to FO: FO 371/12035/6842/93.

43 Articles on the freedom of the seas had begun to appear as well; see Anonymous, 'Is there any maritime law', *New Republic*, LIII(Dec 1927); J. T. Gerould, 'Great Britain's opposition to the freedom of the seas', *Current History*, No. 27 (Oct 1927), 112–15.

44 See speech – 6 Dec 1927, Coolidge: *FRUS 1927*, I, v–xxvi. Cf. minute – 8 Dec 1927, Craigie; initialled – 8 Dec 1927, Wellesley; minute – 9 Dec 1927, Tyrrell to Baldwin: all FO 371/12036/7090/93.

45 British newspapers also started using the term; see 'U.S. Congress and Cruisers. "Big Navy Group's" Demands' – 6 Nov 1927, *The Times*.

46 Letter – 18 Feb 1929, Casey [of the Australian High Commission, London] to Craigie: FO 371/13519/1281/30.

47 Letter – 6 Mar 1929, Craigie [drafted by Thompson] to Casey: *Ibid*.

48 For instance, see 'America's Naval Ambitions. "Disaster" at Geneva' – 4 Sep 1927, Simonds: *Sunday Times*.

49 For Beaverbrook on the United States and naval limitation, see letter – 14 Nov 1927, Beaverbrook to Bennett [leader of the Canadian Conservative Party]: BBK MSS A 65/50. At this time Vansittart recorded: 'The sub-editor of one of the cheaper papers told me the other day that he could at any moment double his circulation by open hostility to America': minute – 7 Nov 1927, Vansittart: FO 371/12041/6689/133.

50 For Baldwin, see speech at 'The International Peace Bridge' [between Ontario and New York] – 7 Aug 1927, Baldwin: in S. Baldwin, *Our Inheritance. Speeches and Addresses* (London, 1928), 153–4. For Balfour, see minute – 5 Aug 1927, Hankey, enclosed in letter – 5 Aug 1927, Hankey to Balfour: BM Add MSS 49704; and 'Lord Balfour and America. A Personal Statement' – 7 Aug 1927, *Observer*. For Bridgeman, see 'Disarmament and Security. Mr. Bridgeman and the Geneva Conference' [speech at the Junior Imperial League] – 25 Oct 1927, *The Times*; W. C. Bridgeman, 'Naval Disarmament', *JRIIA*, 6(1927), 335–49. For Churchill, see speech on the 'Failure of the Geneva Conference' [at Haslemere] – 6 Aug 1927, Churchill: in R. Rhodes James (ed.), *Winston*

S. Churchill. *His Complete Speeches, 1897–1963*, vol. IV: *1922–1928* (New York, London, 1974), 4323–5.

51 For instance, J. L. Garvin, the strongly atlanticist editor of *The Observer*, wrote that ton for ton Anglo-American cruiser parity meant naval inferiority for Britain; see 'The Upas Tree' [editorial] – 27 Nov 1927, *Observer*. For Garvin's support of Anglo-American harmony, 'the greatest of his causes', see K. Garvin, *J. L. Garvin. A Memoir* (London, Melbourne, Toronto, 1948), 192.

52 Cf. 'Great Britain and the United States' [editorial] – 5 Aug 1927, *Washington Post*; 'Navy Day' [editorial] – 27 Oct 1927, *Ibid.*

53 This became the preserve of the pacifist far-left; see P. J. Noel-Baker, *Disarmament and the Coolidge Conference* (London, 1927).

54 The rest of this paragraph is based on Marquand, *MacDonald*, 467–9; diary entry – 8 Sep 1927, Scott [editor, *Manchester Guardian*]: BM Add MSS 50907; letter – 15 Sep 1927, Scott to MacDonald; letter – 26 Sep 1927, MacDonald to Snowden [member, Labour shadow cabinet]: both PRO 30/69/5/38.

55 'Disarmament and Security. Mr Lloyd George on armaments' – 25 Oct 1927, *The Times*. Also see letter – 25 Oct 1927, Murray [of the League of Nations Union] to Lloyd George: LG MSS G 31/2/60. For general discussion of Lloyd George and the Liberals at this time, see K. O. Morgan, *The Age of Lloyd George. The Liberal Party and British Politics, 1890–1929* (London, New York, 1971), 96–110. Of interest is P. Raffo, 'The Founding of the League of Nations Union', *CJH*, 12(1977), 193–206; and H. R. Winkler, *The League of Nations Movement in Great Britain, 1914–1919* (New Brunswick, N.J., 1952).

56 For example, letters – 6 & 13 Jan 1928, Murray to Chamberlain; and letters – 11 & 28 Jan 1928, Chamberlain to Murray: all FO 800/262. For an objective criticism of the Chamberlain–Briand–Stresemann triangle, see J. Jacobson, 'The Conduct of Locarno Diplomacy', *RP*, 34(1972), 67–81.

57 See letters – 5 & 16 Nov 1926, 14 Aug 1927, Murray to Cecil: all BM Add MSS 51132.

58 For a particularly vicious attack, see 'Disarmament. Mr. Lloyd George on Locarno. Foreign secretary criticised' – 8 Nov 1927, *The Times*.

59 Letter – 10 Dec 1927, Borah to Lloyd George: LG MSS G 31/2/74.

60 Speech – 16 Nov 1927, Bridgeman: *H of C Debs*, vol. 210, Col. 1013. Also see Gilbert, *Churchill*, vol. V, 247–52. Influential naval officers were not happy with this reduction; see letter – 12 Dec 1927, Beatty to Keyes: KEYES 15/1.

61 This motion and the debate that it spawned can be found in *Ibid.*, Cols. 2089–198. MacDonald was warned by a member of his party with Admiralty connexions not to raise the question of the freedom of the seas, as it could hurt the Labour Party; see letter – 1 Nov 1927, Ammon to MacDonald: PRO 30/69/5/38.

62 See letters – 18 Nov 1927, 25 & 28 Mar 1928, Cecil to Bridgeman; letters – 21 Nov 1927, 26 & 30 Mar 1928, Bridgeman to Cecil: all BM Add MSS 51099.

63 Letter – 26 Nov 1927, Chamberlain to Ida, his sister: AC 5/1/428. Responsible quarters agreed with Chamberlain, suggesting that the MacDonald–Lloyd George attacks confused rather than clarified the issue; see 'Darkness and Light' [editorial] – 25 Nov 1927, *The Times*.

64 Chamberlain stated privately that he thought that this was one of the main reasons for the conference's failure; see letter – 7 Aug 1927, Chamberlain to Mary Carnegie: AC 4/1/1278.

65 Speech – 10 Nov 1927, Wemyss: *H of L Debs*, vol. 69, Cols. 19–20.

66 Letter – 11 Nov 1927, Hankey to Balfour: BM Add MSS 49704.

67 See 'Sir A. Geddes on the United States. Difficulties of mutual understanding' [speech to the English Speaking Union, Manchester] – 16 Nov 1927, *The Times*.

68 Hankey attended this meeting as well. This paragraph is based on letter – 14 Dec 1927, Hankey to Madden [first sea lord]: CAB 21/310; and diary entry – 13 Dec 1927, Hankey: HNKY 1/8.

69 Non-governmental discussion of Anglo-American relations on both sides of the Atlantic was also beginning to emerge in a few influential journals. For example, Anonymous [P. Kerr], 'The Naval Conference', *RT*, 68(Sep 1927), 659–83; 'J.M.G.', 'Naval Strategy', *NB*, 6(Nov 1927), No. 52; 'Cecil vs. the Admirals', *NB*, 7(Nov 1927), No. 3; L. Y. Spear, 'Battleships or Submarines', *FA*, 6(1927), 106–15.

70 See letters – 15 & 22 Sep 1927, Howard to Tyrrell: both *DBFP 1A*, IV, 360–2, 370–1.

71 Memorandum – 16 Oct 1927, Chamberlain to Tyrrell: *Ibid.*, 392–4.

72 Memorandum – 19 Oct 1927, Vansittart, enclosing memorandum – 17 Oct 1927, Craigie: *Ibid.*, 394–412. Craigie had actually begun this memorandum before Chamberlain's request.

73 Howard was ordered subsequently to 'avoid any conversation with anyone – officially or otherwise – which might engage us in discussions on these delicate matters until they have been considered here'; see letter – 28 Oct 1927, Tyrrell to Howard: *Ibid.*, 427–8.

74 Minute – 20 Oct 1927, Chamberlain: FO 371/12040/6073/133.

75 Minute – 25 Oct 1927, Craigie: *Ibid.*

76 See D. M. Smith, *The Great Departure. The United States and World War I, 1914–1920* (New York, London, 1965), 51–6.

77 Memorandum – 26 Oct 1927, Chamberlain: *DBFP 1A*, IV, 415–16.

78 Chamberlain never said that belligerent rights had to be reduced; he suggested that the possibility of reducing them be studied. His critics continue to maintain incorrectly that he was willing to compromise no matter what; for example, see Roskill, *Hankey*, vol. II, 451.

79 See memorandum – 16 Nov 1927, Vansittart, enclosing memorandum – 16 Nov 1927, Craigie: *DBFP 1A*, IV, 440–5; memorandum – 17 Nov 1927, Thompson: *Ibid.*, 445–7; memorandum – 21 Nov 1927, Locker Lampson [parliamentary under-secretary, FO]: *Ibid.*, 447–50.

80 Letter – 31 Oct 1927, Hankey to Chamberlain: FO 371/12041/6763/133. A memorandum – 31 Oct 1927, Hankey, enclosed with this letter, has been removed from the FO Archives; a copy can be found as CP 286(27),

Appendix I: CAB 24/189. Roskill, *Hankey*, vol. II, 451–3 overstates Hankey's role in this issue.

81 On the Declaration of London, see Pitt, 'Belligerent Maritime Rights', 370–436. Before Hankey raised the issue, Chamberlain had asked Craigie why he did not mention the Declaration in his major memorandum; Craigie replied that he felt the Declaration would be unimportant in an approach to the Americans. See minute – 20 Oct 1927, Chamberlain; minute – 25 Oct 1927, Craigie: both FO 371/12040/6073/133.

82 Memorandum – 10 Nov 1927, Hurst: *DBFP 1A*, IV, 433–9.

83 For discussion of League sanctions policy, see Walters, *League of Nations*, 41–3, 53.

84 Hurst did not discuss the possibililty of Britain being a covenant-breaker because in 'such a war Great Britain would never carry the Dominions with her, and it is an eventuality which need not be considered'.

85 Memorandum – 14 Nov 1927, Chamberlain: *DBFP 1A*, IV, 433.

86 Minute – 16 Nov 1927, Chamberlain: FO 371/12041/6811/133.

87 Letter – 10 Nov 1927, Chamberlain to Hankey; letter – 12 Nov 1927, Hankey to Chamberlain: both FO 800/261.

88 Cabinet Conclusion 57(27)7: CAB 23/55.

89 Memorandum – 5 Dec 1927, na: BR 1; memorandum – 19 Jan 1928, na: BR 1A: both CAB 16/79.

90 Baldwin's idea in having 'expert assessors' and the role he envisaged for them is explained in letter – 2 Dec 1927, Hankey to Bridgeman: CAB 21/307.

91 *Ibid.*

92 Letter – 6 Jan 1928, Chamberlain to Hankey: *Ibid.* Roskill, *Hankey*, vol. II, 453 claims that Hankey neutralised Tyrrell's effectiveness as a supporter of a possible agreement with the Americans before the first sub-committee meeting. There is no empirical basis for this assertion.

93 Letter – 16 Jan 1928, Hurst to Chamberlain; minute – 17 Jan 1928, Baldwin, on letter – 17 Jan 1928, Chamberlain to Baldwin: all CAB 21/307.

94 Memorandum – 26 Oct 1927, Chamberlain: *DBFP 1A*, IV, 415–16; memorandum – 14 Nov 1927, Chamberlain *Ibid.*, 433; memorandum – 16 Nov 1927, Craigie: *Ibid*, 440–5.

95 Letter – 19 Dec 1927, Pound to Keyes KEYES 15/20. Locker-Lampson was the Foreign Office parliamentary under-secretary, but rarely had he anything to do with the formulation and implementation of policy.

96 Pope-Hennessy had supplemented his first record of his talk with General Brown with another paper; see memorandum – 10 Oct 1927, Pope-Hennessy: *DBFP 1A*, IV, 388–91. See also minute – 25 Oct 1927, Craigie; minute – 26 Oct 1927, Wellesley; minute – 27 Oct 1927, Chamberlain: all FO 371/12040/6213/133.

97 Diary entries – 18 Oct & 15 Nov 1927, Domvile: DOM 43. Like Stopford, however, Domvile believed in the efficacy of an anti-American Anglo-Japanese alliance; he told this to Chilton, the counsellor at the British Embassy at Washington, who was in London on leave in January

1928: letter – 27 Jan 1928, Chilton to Howard: How MSS DHW 4/Official/23.
98 Letter – 12 Dec 1927, Beatty to Keyes: KEYES 15/1.
99 See letter – 11 Nov 1927, Hankey to Balfour: BM Add MSS 49704; and diary entries – 12, 13, 14, 16, & 18 Dec 1927, Hankey: HNKY 1/8.
100 Wickham Steed had said essentially the same thing in the United States in late October 1927; see despatch – 4 Nov 1927, Howard to Chamberlain: *DBFP 1A*, IV, 430–2.
101 See above, pp. 94–5.
102 Roskill, *Hankey*, vol. II, 453–4 makes this claim. An indication of the range of individuals Hankey told about the enquiry can be seen in letter – 5 Nov 1927, Hankey to Richmond [principal, Imperial Defence College]: CAB 21/307; letter – 17 Dec 1927, Hankey to Stamfordham [private secretary to the King]; letter – 21 Dec 1927, Hankey to Esher [Conservative peer]: both CAB 21/310.

5 The pact to renounce war

1 'Statement to the Associated Press' – 6 Apr 1927, Briand: *FRUS 1927*, II, 611–13.
2 Telegram – 22 Jun 1927, Whitehouse [US *chargé* at Paris] to Kellogg: *Ibid.*, 615–16.
3 Letter – 28 Dec 1927, Kellogg to Claudel: *Ibid.*, 626–7; letter – 28 Dec 1927, Kellogg to Claudel: *FRUS 1928*, II, 810–12. Also see Cmd. 3109; and Department of State, *Notes Exchanged between France and the United States . . . on the subject of a multilateral treaty for the renunciation of war* (Washington, 1928).
4 R. H. Ferrell, *Peace In Their Time. The Origins of the Kellogg–Briand Pact* (New Haven, 1952), 6, 134–5 compares the Root and Kellogg formulae.
5 The following paragraph is based on letter – 6 Jan 1928, Claudel to Kellogg, enclosing letter – 5 Jan 1928, Briand to Kellogg: *FRUS 1928*, I, 1–2; letter – 11 Jan 1928, Kellogg to Claudel: *Ibid.*, 3–5; letter – 21 Jan 1928, Claudel to Kellogg: *Ibid.*, 6–8.
6 Department of State, *Arbitration Treaty with France . . . signed [at] Washington, 6 February 1928* (Washington, 1928).
7 Letter – 27 Feb 1928, Kellogg to Claudel: *FRUS 1928*, I, 9–11.
8 F. B. Kellogg, 'The War Prevention Policy of the United States', *FA, Special Supplement*, 6(1928), i–xi.
9 See Walters, *League of Nations*, 258–9.
10 Letter – 26 Mar 1928, Claudel to Kellogg: *FRUS 1928*, I, 15–19.
11 For the British case, see letter – 13 Apr 1928, Houghton to Chamberlain: Cmd. 3109.
12 'French Draft Treaty' – nd [received 20 Apr 1928]: *FRUS 1928*, I, 32–4.
13 Kellogg had agreed already to this in a private conversation with Claudel; see memorandum – 27 Feb 1928, Phenix: *Ibid.*, 11–12.
14 For example, see minute – 6 Mar 1928, Craigie: FO 371/12789/1467/1.
15 Letter – 31 Oct 1927, Cecil to Murray: BM Add MSS 51132. This must be compared with Cecil's retrospective protests of innocence on this

issue: 'Only constant vigilance by the officers of the League of Nations Union prevented the Union from becoming an electoral ally of the Opposition': Cecil, *Great Experiment*, 192–3.

16 See above, pp. 88–9, especially n. 56 and n. 57.

17 See letter – 6 Mar 1928, Cecil to MacDonald, enclosing draft letter to Baldwin; letters – 8 & 12 Mar 1928, MacDonald to Cecil; letters – 9, 13, & 14 Mar 1928, Cecil to MacDonald: all PRO 30/69/5/39; letters – 8 & 14 Mar 1928, Murray to Lloyd George; letter – 13 Mar 1928, Lloyd George to Murray: all LG MSS G 4/1. Also see D. S. Birn, 'The League of Nations Union and Collective Security', *JCH*, vol. IX, No. 3(1974), 131–59.

18 For example, see Viscount Cecil, 'American Responsibilities for Peace', *FA*, 6(1928), 357–8; *International Arbitration: Being the Burge Memorial Lecture for 1928* (Oxford, 1928). For a Foreign Office appraisal of Cecil's efforts, specifically his *Foreign Affairs* article, see minute – nd [probably 18 Mar 1928], Thompson: FO 371/12790/1879/1.

19 Despatch – 17 Feb 1928, Howard to Chamberlain: FO 371/12790/1879/1.

20 For instance, see 'One Great Treaty to Outlaw all Wars' [W. E. Borah] – 5 Feb 1928, *NY Times*. Also see Ferrell, *Kellogg–Briand Pact*, 161–4.

21 Minute – 5 Mar 1928, Thompson: FO 371/12789/1467/1.

22 Minute – 2 Apr 1928, Craigie: FO 371/12790/2241/1.

23 Williams' subsequent editorial was marked with both caution and optimism; see 'Pacts and Armaments' – 4 Apr 1928, *The Times*.

24 Minute – 4 Apr 1928, Craigie: FO 371/12790/2241/1.

25 Telegram (538) – 30 Dec 1927, Howard to Chamberlain: *DBFP 1A*, IV, 480–1.

26 Diary entry – 6 Mar 1928, Castle [State Department]: quoted in Ferrell, *Kellogg–Briand Pact*, 165.

27 Letter – 13 Feb 1928, Chamberlain to Howard: *DBFP 1A*, IV, 551–4.

28 Despatch – 3 Apr 1928, Chamberlain to Dormer [British *chargé d'affaires*, Tokyo]: FO 371/12790/2479/1.

29 As late as 20 March, Chamberlain wrote that the French and Americans had to 'work out their ideas or at least finish their correspondence' before the Foreign Office should assess seriously the situation: see minute – 20 Mar 1928, Chamberlain: FO 371/12790/1815/1.

30 Minute – 20 Apr 1928, Hurst: *DBFP 1A*, V, 608–13.

31 Hurst based this analysis on the French conditions listed in Briand's 26 March letter to Kellogg; when Hurst began this paper, the French draft treaty had not been received by the Foreign Office.

32 The Declaration of February 1922, which gave Egypt independence, saw Britain reserve four matters to its 'absolute discretion': the security of the communications of the British Empire in Egypt, that is, the Suez Canal; the defence of Egypt against all foreign aggression and interference, direct or indirect; the protection of foreign interests and minorities; and matters relating to the Sudan. See Cmd. 1592; Cmd. 1617.

33 For a 'List of British Commitments in relative Order of Importance', see memorandum – 10 Apr 1926, Gregory [assistant under-secretary, FO]:

DBFP 1A, I, 880–1; and supplementary memorandum – 26 Apr 1927, na: *Ibid.*, III, 802.

34 On the Monroe doctrine, see T. A. Bailey, 'The Lodge Corollary to the Monroe Doctrine', *PSQ*, 48(1933), 220–39; A. Iriye, *From Nationalism to Internationalism. U.S. Foreign Policy to 1914* (London, Henley, Boston. 1977), 8–9, 104–9, 248–50; F. Merk, *The Monroe Doctrine and American Expansion* (New York, 1966); D. Perkins, *A History of the Monroe Doctrine*, rev. ed. (Boston, 1963).

35 Telegram (127) – 22 Apr 1928, Howard to Chamberlain: *DBFP 1A*, V, 614.

36 Minute – 24 Apr 1928, Hurst: *Ibid.*, 618–19.

37 Minute – 23 Apr 1928, Thompson: FO 371/12790/2750/1.

38 For instance, *Ibid.*; and minute – 24 Apr 1928, Oliphant [acting assistant under-secretary, FO]: FO 371/12790/2730/1.

39 For Kellogg's speech, see J. W. Wheeler-Bennett, *Information on the Renunciation of War, 1927–8* (London, 1928), 107–10. Analyses of this speech are in Ellis, *Kellogg*, 205–6; Ferrell, *Kellogg–Briand Pact*, 173–6.

40 See Ellis, *Kellogg*, 205, n. 26.

41 Notably in despatch – 20 Apr 1928, BLINY to FO: FO 371/12791/2903/1.

42 Memorandum – 3 May 1928, Chamberlain: CP 148(28): CAB 24/194.

43 For the German 'success', see Toynbee *et al.*, *Survey of International Affairs*, *1928*, 20. For insight into German reasons for embracing Kellogg's pact with a bear-hug, see Jacobson, *Locarno Diplomacy*, 192. Also see telegram (21) – 27 Apr 1928, Lindsay to FO; letter – 1 May 1928, Chancery, British Embassy, Berlin to FO Central Department: both FO 371/12791/2853/1.

44 The rest of this paragraph is based on minute – 7 May 1928, Hurst: FO 371/12791/3022/1.

45 For examples of concern by other departments of state about the proposed pact and British interests, see memorandum – 15 May 1928, Bridgeman: CP 159(28): CAB 24/195; letter – 14 May 1928, Monteath [India Office] to Selby: FO 371/12792/3336/1. For the Cabinet's deliberations, see Cabinet Conclusions 27(28)8 & Appendix, and 28(28)2 & Appendix: both CAB 23/57. For the British reply, see letter – 19 May 1928, Chamberlain to Houghton: Cmd. 3109. For Howard's instructions, see telegram (208) – 16 May 1928, Chamberlain to Howard: *DBFP 1A*, V, 658–9. Also of interest is letter – 20 May 1928, Howard to his wife: How MSS DHW3.

46 Memorandum – 21 May 1928, Hurst: FO 371/12792/3492/1. Kellogg was informed about the 'gratification' of the French public to the British note; see telegram – 21 May 1928, Herrick to Kellogg: *FRUS 1928*, I, 71.

47 See above, p. 110, n. 32.

48 See Cecil, *Great Experiment*, 194; and letter – 30 Jul 1928, Gilbert Murray to MacDonald: PRO 30/69/5/39.

49 The German government replied on 27 April; the Italian on 4 May; the British on 19 May; and the Japanese on 26 May. The French draft treaty of 20 April amounted to the official French reply.

50 *H of C Debs*, vol. 217, Cols. 433–78.

51 J. R. MacDonald, 'War and America', *The Nation* (2 May 1928).

52 Letter – 4 May 1928, Fletcher to Willert: FO 371/12792/3266/1.

53 *H of L Debs*, vol. 71, Cols. 4–30.

54 For example, 'Lords Acclaim Kellogg's Pact to Outlaw War. Prompt acceptance by Britain is urged' – 16 May 1928, *Philadelphia Public Ledger*. Also see minute – 17 May 1928, Thompson: FO 371/12792/3319/1.

55 Except for the French, who they kept fully informed, the British let their European associates know only the general lines of their thinking prior to 19 May. For the Belgian example, see memorandum – 17 May 1928, Selby: FO 371/12792/3440/1.

56 Cf. telegram – 21 May 1928, Kellogg to Houghton: *FRUS 1928*, I, 69–71; letter – 22 May 1928, Houghton to Chamberlain: FO 371/12792/3491/1.

57 For Chamberlain's report of this conversation, see letter – 25 May 1928, Chamberlain to Howard: *DBFP 1A*, V, 669–73. Cf. telegram – 25 May 1928, Houghton to Kellogg: *FRUS 1928*, I, 72–3.

58 Soon after his arrival in Britain, Houghton made it plain that he was a germanophile; see telegram (670) – 27 Apr 1925, Chamberlain to Howard: FO 371/10639/2199/171. Houghton made his pro-German feelings known to Lucy Baldwin, the prime minister's wife; see memorandum – 5 Jul 1925, Lucy Baldwin: Bal MSS vol. 108.

59 Chamberlain was stretching the truth a bit in his reconstruction of Locarno's origins; see Jacobson, *Locarno Diplomacy*, 12–26.

60 Telegram (106) – 23 May 1928, Dormer to FO; minute – 23 May 1928, Thompson; minute – 24 May 1928, Wellesley: all FO 371/12792/3516/1.

61 The Baldwin government was in the midst of breaking off diplomatic relations with the Soviet Union; see Florry, 'Arcos Raid'; Middlemas and Barnes, *Baldwin*, 457–8; Medlicott, *Contemporary England*, 209.

62 Chamberlain's willingness derived from an earlier misunderstanding about how the final form of the pact would be determined. Howard had initially reported that Kellogg preferred a meeting of foreign ministers to discuss the draft; this idea was opposed subsequently by Kellogg, who claimed that he had never made the suggestion and, moreover, that he actually favoured an exchange of interpretive notes. See telegram (120) – 13 Apr 1928, Howard to Chamberlain: *DBFP 1A*, IV, 645–6; and telegrams (141, 145) – 3 and 5 May 1928, Howard to Chamberlain: *Ibid.*, 646, 652. An interesting light was then shed on this issue: 'Mr. Castle admitted to Mr. Chilton yesterday that he had no doubt that Secretary of State had said he thought meeting of foreign ministers would be useful. Mr. Kellogg often got worked up and said things which he forgot afterwards': in telegram (un) – 5 May 1928, Howard to FO: FO 371/12791/3015/1.

63 Telegram (178) – 30 May 1928, Howard to Chamberlain: *DBFP 1A*, V, 674. The line that Howard was to take in this conversation with Kellogg, which was to be exactly the same as that Chamberlain was to take with Houghton, was sketched in letter – 15 May 1928, Chamberlain to Howard: FO 800/262.

64 Minute – 31 May 1928, Thompson: FO 371/12793/3697/1; minute – 31

May 1928, Craigie; minute – 31 May 1928, Wellesley; minute – 31 May 1928, Chamberlain: all FO 371/12793/3700/1.

65 Despatch – 18 May 1928, BLINY to FO: FO 371/12793/3672/1.

66 Minute – 30 May 1928, Thompson; minute – 1 Jun 1928, Craigie; minute – 1 Jun 1928, Wellesley: all *Ibid.*

67 Telegram (179) – 30 May 1928, Howard to FO: *DBFP 1A*, V, 674–5.

68 BLINY concluded that American press opinion had not much altered after the publication of the British note of 19 May; see despatch – 25 May 1928, BLINY to FO: FO 371/12793/3858/1.

69 Letter – 12 Jun 1928, Craigie to R. I. Campbell: FO 371/12792/3418/1.

70 See letter – 20 Jun 1928, Fletcher to Craigie: *Ibid.*

71 Memorandum – 7 Jun 1928, Craigie: FO 371/12793/3886/1.

72 See minute – 8 Jun 1928, Craigie: *Ibid.*; and telegram (un) – 8 Jun 1928, Tyrrell to Chilton: *DBFP 1A*, V, 684–5.

73 See telegrams (un) – 9, 11, & 12 Jun 1928, Chilton to Tyrrell: all *Ibid.*, 690–1, 696–7.

74 Minute – 15 Jun 1928, Craigie: FO 371/12793/4062/1. Also see minute – 11 Jun 1928, Craigie: FO 371/12793/3972/1; and minute – 12 Jun 1928, Craigie: FO 371/12793/4051/1.

75 Letter – 5 Jun 1928, Hurst to Malkin [assistant legal adviser]: FO 371/12793/3700/1.

76 Hurst showed this letter to both Craigie and Murray before he sent it to Malkin; he recorded their comments in post-script – nd, Hurst: *Ibid.*

77 Telegram (134) – 9 Jun 1928, Dormer to FO: FO 371/12793/3958/1.

78 Telegram (135) – 11 Jun 1928, Dormer to FO: FO 371/12793/4048/1. Also see I. H. Nish, *Japanese Foreign Policy, 1869–1942* (London, 1977), 293–4.

79 Minute – 14 Jun 1928, Craigie; minute – 14 Jun 1928, Hurst; minute – 14 Jun 1928; Wellesley; minute – 20 Jun 1928, Murray; minute – 21 Jun 1928, Monteagle: all FO 371/12793/4048/1; and, memorandum – 18 Jun 1928, Craigie; minute – 19 Jun 1928, Murray; minute – 19 Jun 1928, Monteagle; minute – 20 Jun 1928, Palairet [Northern Department]; minute – 20 Jun 1928, Mounsey [Far Eastern Department]; minute – 20 Jun 1928, Wellesley: all FO 371/12794/4462/1.

80 See letter – 23 Jun 1928, Atherton [US *chargé* at London] to Chamberlain: Cmd. 3153. The fourteen governments included the original five, plus Belgium, Czechoslovakia, Poland, the five Dominions, and India. For an analysis of the second Kellogg note, see Toynbee *et al.*, *Survey of International Affairs, 1928*, 23–4.

81 Minute – 25 Jun 1928, Craigie; minute – 25 Jun 1928, Malkin; minute – 25 Jun 1928, Wellesley: all FO 371/12794/4282/1.

82 Minute – 25 Jun 1928, Chamberlain: *Ibid.*

83 Telegram (46) – 26 Jun 1928, Malkin to Hurst: *DBFP 1A*, V, 718–19.

84 Telegram (372) – 27 Jun 1928, Hurst to Malkin: FO 371/12794/4442/1.

85 See telegram (75) – 30 Jun 1928, Hurst to Chamberlain: *DBFP 1A*, V, 748. For a record of the Hurst–Fromageot discussions, see despatch – 29 Jun 1928, Hurst to Chamberlain, enclosing memorandum – 29 Jun 1928, Hurst: *Ibid.*, 731–6.

86 Minute – 3 Jul 1928, Craigie; minute – 4 Jul 1928, Wellesley: both FO 371/12795/4529/1.

87 The FO News Department, for instance, outlined a procedure to be used if news of the Berlin talks leaked out; see minute – 6 Jul 1928, Willert to Wellesley; minute – 6 Jul 1928, Wellesley: both FO 371/12795/4818/1.

88 The rest of this paragraph is based on despatch – 9 Jul 1928, Hurst to Chamberlain: *DBFP 1A*, V, 764–7.

89 For an indication of British press opinion favour, see minute – 29 Jun 1928, Norton [FO News Department]: FO 371/12795/4521/1.

90 A copy of this note was appended to Hurst's report; see n. 88, above.

91 Minute – 3 Jul 1928, Chamberlain: FO 371/12794/4469/1; and telegrams (un) – 3 & 4 Jul 1928, Chamberlain to Chilton: *DBFP 1A*, V, 749–50, 752–3.

92 Cf. telegrams (un) – 3 & (2) 6 Jul 1928, Chilton to Chamberlain: *Ibid.*, 750, 756–9; and telegram – 6 Jul 1928, Kellogg to Herrick: *FRUS 1928*, I, 102–3.

93 Minute – 9 Jul 1928, Craigie, enclosing memorandum – 9 Jul 1928, Craigie; minute – 9 Jul 1928, Wellesley; minute – 9 Jul 1928; Hurst: all FO 371/12795/4612/1.

94 Memorandum – 29 Jun 1928, Foreign Office: CP 212(28): CAB 24/196. This paper was based on the minutes found in n. 79, p. 122, above.

95 See Cabinet Conclusions 35(28)1 & 36(28)1: both CAB 23/58.

96 Cabinet Conclusions 38(28)2 & 39(28)6: both *Ibid.* For the British note see letter – 18 Jul 1928, Chamberlain to Atherton: Cmd. 3153.

97 Memorandum – 11 Jul 1928, Balfour: CP 223(28): CAB 24/196.

98 Letter – 13 Jul 1928, Chamberlain to Balfour: FO 800/263; letter – 13 Jul 1928, Hankey to Balfour: BM Add MSS 49705.

99 Letter – 29 Jun 1928, Fletcher to Craigie, enclosing memorandum – 29 Jun 1928, BLINY; minute – 12 Jul 1928, Craigie: all FO 371/12795/4607/1.

100 See letter – 9 Jul 1928, Chamberlain to Ida, his sister: AC 5/1/459.

101 Despatch – 25 Jul 1928, Chilton to Chamberlain: *DBFP 1A*, V, 777–9.

102 See letter – 6 Jul 1928, Fletcher to Craigie: FO 371/12796/4867/1; letter – 11 Jul 1928, Fletcher to Willert: FO 371/12797/5109/1; despatch – 20 Jul 1928, BLINY to FO: FO 371/12797/5265/1.

6 Arbitration, belligerent rights and disarmament

1 The rest of this paragraph is based on telegrams (538 & 539) – 30 Dec 1927, Howard to Chamberlain: both *DBFP 1A*, IV, 480–1.

2 Minute – 2 Jan 1928, Vansittart: FO 371/12789/2/1.

3 Minute – 4 Jan 1928, Vansittart: FO 371/12789/68/1.

4 See above, p. 212, n. 53.

5 Minute – 4 Jan 1928, Wellesley; minute – 5 Jan 1928, Hurst; minute – 5 Jan 1928, Wellesley: all FO 371/12789/68/1.

6 Minute – 6 Jan 1928, Chamberlain: *Ibid.*

7 Letter – 6 Jan 1928, Chamberlain to Hankey: FO 800/262.

8 Letter – 8 Jan 1928, Hankey to Hermon-Hodge [secretary, Belligerent Rights Sub-Committee]: CAB 21/307.

9 See BR 1st Minutes: CAB 16/79.

10 Hankey afterward expressed surprise at this statement; see diary entry – 11 Jan 1928, Hankey: HNKY 1/8. If he had not misinterpreted the reason why the Foreign Office advocated an Anglo-American belligerent rights agreement, there would have been no surprise. Roskill, *Hankey*, vol. II, 454–5 reproduces Hankey's surprise without question.

11 Fletcher was reporting that for the first time since he had been in the United States, 'serious-minded people' were discussing the possibility of an Anglo-American war; see letter – 13 Dec 1927, Fletcher to Willert; minute – 3 Jan 1928, Vansittart: both FO 395/421/1317/154.

12 The Foreign Office was aware that *The Chicago Tribune*, in anti-British terms, was discussing possible American acquisition of the British West Indies; see despatch – 23 Sep 1927, BLINY to FO: FO 371/12035/5846/93; despatch – 30 Sep 1927, Howard to Chamberlain: FO 371/12035/5931/93; minute – 20 Dec 1927, Willert; minute – 21 Dec 1927, Willert; minute – 29 Dec 1927, Thompson; minute – 30 Dec 1927, Vansittart: all FO 395/420/1298/75.

13 Letter – 4 Nov 1927, McNeill to Chamberlain: FO 800/261.

14 Hankey and Cushendun had had a heated argument about belligerent rights just before the first sub-committee meeting; see diary entry – 11 Jan 1928, Hankey: HNKY 1/8.

15 Minute – 13 Jan 1928, Vansittart: FO 371/12789/150/1.

16 For example, see despatch – 6 Jan 1928, Graham [British ambassador, Rome] to Chamberlain; minute – 11 Jan 1928, Craigie; minute – [12?] Jan 1928, Vansittart: all FO 371/12789/177/1; and telegram (4) – 10 Jan 1928, Tilley to FO: FO 371/12789/224/1.

17 Department of State, *Arbitration Treaty with France*.

18 The Foreign Office followed this question with interest; see memorandum – 13 Jan 1928, Craigie: FO 371/12789/150/1; minute – 8 Feb 1928, Craigie: FO 371/12789/928/1.

19 Minute – 18 Jan 1928, Vansittart: FO 371/12789/318/1.

20 See Cabinet Conclusion 1(28)2: CAB 23/57; despatch – 30 Dec 1927, Howard to Chamberlain: *DBFP 1A*, IV, 482; memorandum – 24 Jan 1928, Chamberlain to the Cabinet: *Ibid.*, 510–26.

21 Letter – 1 Feb 1928, Phipps [counsellor, British Embassy, Paris] to Vansittart: FO 371/12789/875/1.

22 BR 2nd Minutes: CAB 16/79.

23 Fromageot's worth as an effective, informal link between the British and French Foreign Offices had been demonstrated often. For instance, he had confided in Hurst that one of the reasons Paris opposed a multilateral renunciatory pact was because of uncertainty of French relations with a few important Powers; Italy and Spain were mentioned specifically; see minute – [19?] Jan 1928, Hurst: FO 371/12789/592/1.

24 For Chamberlain's concern about the excitability of public opinion, see minute – 12 Sep 1927, Chamberlain to Tyrrell, on letter – 1 Sep 1927, Howard to Chamberlain: FO 800/261.

25 See above, p. 129–30.
26 The 1928 US Naval Bill was accompanied by the usual anglophobia; see telegram (1) – 1 Jan 1928, Howard to FO: FO 371/12802/3/3; despatch – 20 Jan 1928, Howard to Chamberlain: FO 371/12802/734/3; telegram (36) – 23 Jan 1928, Howard to FO: FO 371/12809/545/36; letter – 25 Jan 1928, Willert to Craigie: FO: 371/12809/725/36.
27 Hankey probably became acquainted with Craigie's view in a private conversation; there is no record. Craigie, who attended this meeting, did not record his opposition to what Hankey said.
28 Memorandum – 18 Jan 1928, Chamberlain, covering telegram – 29 Dec 1927, Howard to Tyrrell: BR 10: CAB 16/79.
29 Memorandum – 26 Jan 1928, Hankey: BR 15: *Ibid.* This must be compared with letter – 4 Jun 1928, Hankey to Howard: How MSS DHW 5/9.
30 Cabinet Conclusion 6(28)3: CAB 23/57.
31 See minute – 23 Feb 1928, Craigie; marginal comment and minute – both 23 Feb 1928, Wellesley; minute – 24 Feb 1928, Craigie: FO 371/12824/994/154; memorandum – 3 Mar 1928, Chamberlain: CP 76(28): CAB 24/193; circular despatch – 15 Mar 1928, Amery to the governments of Canada, Australia, New Zealand, the Union of South Africa, the Irish Free State, and Newfoundland: FO 371/12824/1859/154.
32 Telegram (114) – 13 Mar 1928, Chamberlain to Howard: *DBFP 1A*, IV, 601.
33 Despatch – 5 Jul 1927, Chamberlain to Howard: *Ibid.*, III, 636–7.
34 See Toynbee *et al.*, *Survey of International Affairs 1928*, 48–60; Walters, *League of Nations*, 363–72; Wheeler-Bennett, *Disarmament*, 58–67.
35 See Cmd. 2888.
36 The relevant portions of the two draft conventions are in Cmd. 3211.
37 Chamberlain reflected on this initiative three months later: 'I did not desire to intervene in discussion on disarmament but you and others strongly urged that no agreement would ever be reached if matter were left in hands of French Ministry of Marine and that the only chance of succeeding was that I should take it up with M. Briand. Accordingly, as you will remember, I spoke to him in March . . .': quoted in telegram (64) – 7 Jun 1928, Chamberlain to Cushendun and the Cabinet: *DBFP 1A*, V, 683–4.
38 This key meeting has been recorded in several places: for a truncated version, see Cmd. 3211; for fuller versions, see memorandum – 10 Mar 1928, British Delegation, Geneva: *DBFP 1A*, IV, 593–6; memorandum – 10 Mar 1928, Chamberlain: CP 81(28): CAB 24/193; and, PRA Meeting 27(6), Appendices I & II: CAB 27/361.
39 Carlton, 'Anglo-French Compromise', 146.
40 See PRA Meeting 27(6), Appendix I: CAB 27/361.
41 The British proposals were:
'Limitation to be effected by classes as follows:-
1. Capital Ships.
2. Aircraft carriers.
3. Cruisers between 10,000 and 7,000 tons.
4. Surface vessels under 7,000 tons.

5. Submarines.
6. Small vessels exempt from limitation.
States would be allowed to transfer tonnage from a higher to a lower category in all classes, excluding 1 and 2, subject to there being a limit to the proportion of total tonnage which might be utilised for submarines.
   States with a total tonnage, including class 6, not exceeding 80,000 tons to be subject to no classification.'
Quoted in Cmd. 3211.

42 Cecil, *Great Experiment*, 194; Marquand, *MacDonald*, 471.
43 Carlton, 'Anglo-French Compromise', 144, 161.
44 PRA Meeting (27)6, plus Appendices: CAB 27/361.
45 Cabinet Conclusion 50(27)9: CAB 23/55.
46 For a report of this meeting, see *DBFP 1A*, IV, 533, n. 3. Also of interest is H. Kelly, *Autobiography* [unpublished MSS], 37–49: KEL 6.
47 Telegram (33) – 14 Mar 1928, Kelly to deputy chief of the Naval Staff: *DBFP 1A*, IV, 603, plus n. 1 & n. 3.
48 See letter – 21 Mar 1928, Kelly to Cushendun: FO 800/228.
49 BR 3rd Minutes: CAB 16/79. Also see despatch – 5 Apr 1928, Chamberlain to Howard: *DBFP 1A*, IV, 641–4.
50 Through a private letter from Chilton, in London in January on leave, Howard knew of the work of the belligerent rights sub-committee; see letter – 27 Jan 1928, Chilton to Howard: How MSS DHW 4/Official/23.
51 See telegrams (121 & un) – 19 & 20 Apr 1928, Craigie to FO: *DBFP 1A*, V, 604–6; telegram (122) – 19 Apr 1928, Howard to Chamberlain: *Ibid.*, 603; memoranda – 1 & 8 Jun 1928, Craigie: BR 37 & BR 38: both CAB 16/79.
52 Minute – 23 Feb 1928, Thompson; minute – 24 Feb 1928, Craigie: both FO 371/12809/1208/36; despatch – 29 Feb 1928, Howard to Chamberlain: FO 371/12809/1776/36; letter – 9 Mar 1928, Howard to Chamberlain: FO 371/12810/1896/36.
53 There was also French worry about Germany's intention to secure an early end to the Rhineland occupation; this question is discussed in Jacobson, *Locarno Diplomacy*, 143–75.
54 Letter – 24 May 1928, Wigram [first secretary, British Embassy, Paris] to Cadogan: *DBFP 1A*, V, 667–8.
55 The course of these negotiations can be followed in Cmd. 3211; Carlton, 'Anglo-French Compromise', which must be read with an eye to its anti-Conservative, anti-Chamberlain bias; Kelly, *Autobiography*, 38–49; and Toynbee *et al.*, *Survey of International Affairs 1928*, 61–81.
56 Telegram (56) – 3 Jun 1928, Chamberlain to Tyrrell: *DBFP 1A*, V, 679–80; memorandum – 9 Jun 1928, Chamberlain: CP 184(28): CAB 24/195.
57 Telegram (40) – 5 Jun 1928, Cushendun to Chamberlain, enclosing minute – nd, Madden: *DBFP 1A*, V, 680.
58 Cabinet Conclusion 31(28)1, and Appendix: CAB 23/58.
59 Letter [extract] – 5 Jun 1928, Kelly to Admiralty: *DBFP 1A*, V, 681–2. Also see Kelly, *Autobiography*, 42–4.
60 Telegram (71) – 27 Jun 1928, Cushendun to Chamberlain: *DBFP 1A*, V, 725–6. This was repeated to FO three days later; see letter – 30 Jun 1928,

Henderson [British Embassy, Paris] to Villiers [FO Western Department]: *Ibid.*, 748–9.
61 Memorandum – 9 Jun 1928, Chamberlain: CP 183(28); memorandum – 16 Jun 1928, Cushendun: CP 189(28); memorandum – 18 Jun 1928, Salisbury: CP 193(28): all CAB 24/195.
62 Telegram (71) – 27 Jun 1928, Cushendun to Chamberlain: *DBFP 1A*, V, 725–6.
63 'Record . . . of a second conversation with the French Naval Representative' – 27 Jun 1928, Kelly; 'Record . . . of a conversation with the Italian Naval Representative' – 28 Jun 1928, Kelly; 'Record . . . of a conversation with Viscount Kato' – 28 Jun 1928, Kelly: all *Ibid.*, 726–9. Kelly was unable to talk to the American naval representative, Admiral Long, who was not at Geneva at this time; he lamented retrospectively about this inability to consult Long; see Kelly, *Autobiography*, 45.
64 Memorandum – 11 Jul 1928, Kelly: *DBFP 1A*, V, 769–70. Also see Kelly, *Autobiography*, 44.
65 Despatch – 23 Jul 1928, Henderson to Chamberlain, enclosing note – 20 Jul 1928, French FO to British Embassy, Paris: in both Cmd. 3211 and *DBFP 1A*, V, 775–7.
66 See PRA Meeting (27)10: CAB 27(361); and 'Committee on Policy. Third Report' – 24 Jul 1928, Salisbury: CP 253(28): CAB 24/197.
67 Cabinet Conclusion 41(28)7: CAB 23/58.
68 Despatch – 27 Jul 1928, Chamberlain to Henderson: *DBFP 1A*, V, 779–80.
69 Letter – 28 Jul 1928, Crewe to Briand: Cmd. 3211.
70 Telegram – 30 Jul 1928, Chamberlain to Chilton [Washington], Dormer [Tokyo], and Graham [Rome]: *Ibid.* and *DBFP 1A*, V, 781–2.

7 The crisis in Anglo-American relations

1 For indications of Chamberlain's poor physical condition, see letters – 29 Jun & 2 Jul 1928, Chamberlain to his wife: AC 6/1/708 & 713.
2 *H of C Debs*, vol. 220, Cols. 1837–8. An extract of this statement is in Cmd. 3211.
3 Petrie, *Chamberlain*, vol. II, 327 lists his complaints: dyspepsia, neuritis, pneumonia. Churchill's assertion that Chamberlain suffered a stroke is unsupported by any evidence; see Gilbert, *Churchill*, vol. V, 300.
4 See letter – 2 Aug 1928, Kellogg to Chilton; telegram – 2 Aug 1928, Kellogg to Atherton; telegram – 2 Aug 1928, Coolidge to Kellogg: all *FRUS 1928*, I, 266–7.
5 This conversation is recorded in telegram – 4 Aug 1928, Atherton to Kellogg: *Ibid.*, 272–3. Cf. telegram (54) – 5 Aug 1928, Chamberlain to Rumbold [British ambassador, Berlin]; telegram (271) – 7 Aug 1928, Chamberlain to Chilton: both *DBFP 1A*, V, 784–5.
6 See memorandum – 7 Aug 1928, Craigie: *Ibid.*, 785–6.
7 Cf. records in despatch – 10 Aug 1928, Cushendun to Chilton: *Ibid.*, 791–3; and telegram – 10 Aug 1928, Atherton to Kellogg: *FRUS 1928*, I, 273–5.

8 Telegram (un) – 10 Aug 1928, Cushendun to Chilton: *DBFP 1A*, V, 788–90.

9 Telegram (un) – 11 Aug 1928, Chilton to Cushendun: *Ibid.*, 794.

10 Telegram – 3 Aug 1928, Kellogg to Coolidge: *FRUS 1928*, I, 268–9.

11 Telegram (un) – 17 Aug 1928, Chilton to FO: FO 371/12798/5754/1.

12 Minutes – 20 & 24 Aug 1928, Thompson: *Ibid.*

13 For instance, see A. J. Ward, *Ireland and Anglo-American Relations, 1899–1921* (London, 1969).

14 See letter – 13 Sep 1928, Wilberforce to Willert: FO 371/12811/6705/39.

15 Telegram (384) – 27 Aug 1928, Hoare to FO: FO 371/12799/5984/1.

16 Minute – 27 Aug 1928, Thompson: *Ibid.*; minute – 29 Aug 1928, Thompson; minute – 29 Aug 1928, Murray; telegram (298) – 30 Aug 1928, FO to Hoare: all FO 371/12799/6026/1.

17 Despatch – 26 Jul 1928, Chilton to Chamberlain, enclosing despatch – 23 Jul 1928, Knothe [assistant British naval attaché] to Chilton; minute – 9 Aug 1928, Thompson: all FO 371/12810/5455/36.

18 For an indication of the problems caused by press speculation, see minute – 28 Aug 1928, Thompson: FO 395/424/1269/2.

19 Minute – 30 Aug 1928, Thompson: FO 371/12828/6293/406.

20 See 'United States and British Policy. Feeling of distrust' – 30 Aug 1928, *Daily Telegraph*. Also see minutes – 30 & 31 Aug 1928, Thompson; minute – 30 Aug 1928, Snow [FO American Department member who dealt with Latin American affairs]: all FO 371/12828/6293/406.

21 Minute – 31 Aug 1928, Willert; minute – 3 Sep 1928, Lindsay: both *Ibid.*

22 Record of a Conversation – 5 Sep 1928, Lindsay: *DBFP 1A*, V, 807–9.

23 Telegram (278) – 13 Sep 1928, Chilton to Birkenhead [acting foreign secretary whilst Cushendun was at Geneva]: *Ibid.*, 815.

24 Telegram (un) – 16 Sep 1928, Chilton to Birkenhead: *Ibid.*, 815–16. Also letter – 13 Sep 1928, Wilberforce to Willert: FO 371/12811/6705/39.

25 Despatch – 6 Sep 1928, Chilton to Cushendun: FO 371/12800/6563/1. Also see minute – 29 Aug 1928, Thompson: FO 371/12799/6263/1, which is a comment on 'Extension of Peace Pact. US invitation to all nations' – 29 Aug 1928, *The Times*. This article speculated on the possibility of the pact and the new naval construction bill going through Congress together.

26 A full report of this situation is in despatch – 13 Sep 1928, Chilton to Cushendun: FO 371/12800/6697/1.

27 Letter – 19 Sep 1928, Howard to Craigie: FO 371/12823/6652/133.

28 See Roskill, *Naval Policy*, vol. I, 547, especially n. 5.

29 'London and Paris in Naval Entente, Says Secret Note. Purported letter of Chamberlain to Briand reveals sea pact between Powers' – 25 Aug 1928, *NY World*. See letter – 31 Aug 1928, Lindsay to Cushendun: *DBFP 1A*, V, 805–6.

30 Telegram (un) – 4 Aug 1928, Rumbold to Chamberlain: *Ibid.*, and Cmd. 3211. Cf. Jacobson, *Locarno Diplomacy*, 190–2.

31 Telegrams – 14 & 22 Sep 1928, Kellogg to Fletcher [US ambassador at Rome]; telegram – 18 Sep 1928, Fletcher to Kellogg: all *FRUS 1928*, I, 280–2. Also see Toynbee *et al.*, *Survey of International Affairs 1928*, 72.

32 Telegram (4) – 9 Aug 1928, Dormer to Cushendun: *DBFP 1A*, V, 788;

letter – nd [telegraphed to London on 29 Sep 1928], Tanaka [Japanese prime minister] to Dormer: Cmd. 3211.

33 Letter – 28 Sep 1928, Houghton to Cushendun; and *Note Verbale* – 6 Oct 1928, Ministry of Foreign Affairs, Rome: both *Ibid.* For the US Navy Department's assessment of the compromise, see Roskill, *Naval Policy*, vol. I, 547–8.

34 See despatch – 14 Sep 1928, BLINY to FO: FO 371/12800/6708/1.

35 For arguments deprecating publication, see minutes 27 & 31 Aug 1928, R. H. Campbell; minute – 28 Aug 1928, Thompson; minute – 29 Aug 1928, Wellesley: all FO 395/424/1269/2. On the value of publication, see memorandum – 5 Oct 1928, Bridgeman: CP 291(28): CAB 24/197. Of interest are diary entries – 1 & 10 Oct 1928, Jones: *Whitehall Diary*, vol. II, 144, 147.

36 For instance, see minute – 4 Sep 1928, Selby to Cushendun, on letter – 31 Aug 1928, Lindsay to Cushendun; letter – 4 Sep 1928, Cushendun to Lindsay; letter – 8 Sep 1928, Lindsay to Cushendun: all FO 800/228.

37 The best analysis of the *New York American*'s revelation is in Toynbee *et al.*, *Survey of International Affairs 1928*, 75.

38 Telegram (286) – 23 Sep 1928, R. I. Campbell to Cushendun; telegram (320) – 26 Sep 1928, Cushendun to R. I. Campbell: both *DBFP 1A*, V, 825–7. Also see letter, with enclosures – 26 Sep 1928, Chilton to Kellogg: *FRUS 1928*, I, 286–90.

39 Cabinet Conclusion 44(28)4: CAB 23/58.

40 Telegram (173) – 29 Sep 1928, Tyrrell to Cushendun: *DBFP 1A*, V, 829–30; and letter – 8 Oct 1928, Tyrrell to Cushendun: FO 800/228.

41 Cf. letter – 20 Oct 1928, Tyrrell to MacDonald: PRO 30/69/5/39.

42 'Papers collected for the White Paper' – Oct 1928, na: CP 292(28): CAB 24/197. The eventual White Paper was Cmd. 3211.

43 See Cabinet Conclusions 46(28)2 & 47(28)1: both CAB 23/59. For the difficulties in coordinating simultaneous Anglo-French publication, see letter – 18 Oct 1928, Cushendun to Tyrrell: FO 800/228. Also see diary entry – 10 Oct 1928, Jones; and letter – 11 Oct 1928, Jones to Hankey: both *Whitehall Diary*, vol. II, 147, 149–50.

44 Letter – 9 Sep 1928, Bridgeman to Baldwin: Bal. MSS vol. 163.

45 Memorandum – 5 Oct 1928, Bridgeman: CP 291(28): CAB 24/197.

46 Letters – 2 & 11 Oct 1928, Hankey to Jones; and letter – 9 Oct 1928, Jones to Hankey: all *Whitehall Diary*, vol. II, 144–5, 146, 147–9.

47 The Germans had begun a diplomatic campaign to achieve an early end to the French occupation of the Rhineland; see Jacobson, *Locarno Diplomacy*, 187–207.

48 For example, letter – 25 Oct 1928, Hankey to Balfour: BM Add MSS 49705.

49 Memorandum – 12 Oct 1928, Percy: CP 301(28): CAB 24/198.

50 See Percy, *Memories*, 124–45 *passim* for indications of his pan-Anglo-Saxonism.

51 PRA Meeting (27)12: CAB 27/361.

52 PRA Meeting (27)13: *Ibid.*

53 Minute – 20 Apr 1928, Adam [FO Treaty Department]: FO 371/12825/

2673/154; minute – 2 May 1928, Thompson: FO 371/12825/2934/154; telegram (183) – 3 May 1928, Chamberlain to Howard: *DBFP 1A*, V, 645; telegram (151) – 9 May 1928, Howard to Chamberlain: *Ibid.*, 656; minute – 10 May 1928, Thompson; minute – 11 May 1928, Hurst: both FO 371/12825/31145/154; minute – 19 May 1928, Thompson to Hurst; minute – 21 May 1928, Hurst: both FO 371/12825/3764/154. Also see telegram – 22 May 1928, Kellogg to Houghton: *FRUS 1928*, I, 947.

54 Despatch – 23 Aug 1928, Chilton to Cushendun: FO 371/12825/6703/154.

55 Minute – 5 Sep 1928, Herbert [Egyptian Department]; minute – 11 Sep 1928, Thompson: both *Ibid.*

56 The State Department was in the midst of producing a major paper on the Monroe doctrine, examining its origins, original purpose and the like. It was an important reassessment of this key declaration. See State Department, *Memorandum on the Monroe Doctrine: prepared by J. Reuban Clark, Under-Secretary of State* (Washington, 1928).

57 See letter – 25 Oct 1928, Hankey to Balfour: BM Add MSS 49705.

58 For instance, 'New Friction Between Britain and USA' – 22 Oct 1928, *Daily Herald*; 'Arbitration with USA. Cause of British Delay. Unreserved Areas' – 23 Oct 1928, *The Times*.

59 See minute – 23 Oct 1928, Thompson; minute – 23 Oct 1928, Craigie both FO 371/12825/7429/154.

60 Letter – 11 Oct 1928, Thompson to R. I. Campbell: FO 371/12825/7095/1.

61 Cabinet Conclusion 47(28)5: CAB 23/59.

62 For instance, letter – 9 Aug 1927, Willingdon to Baldwin; letter – 13 Feb 1928, Willingdon to the King: both PREM 1/65; and letter – 6 Nov 1927, Willingdon to Baldwin: Bal MSS vol. 96.

63 See W. Phillips, *Ventures in Diplomacy* (London, 1955). The best over-view of official American perceptions of Canada at this time is in P. Kasurak, 'American foreign policy officials and Canada, 1927–1941: a look through bureaucratic glasses', *International Journal*, 32(1977), 544–58.

64 See despatch – 5 May 1926, Broderick to Chamberlain: FO 371/11192/2703/779; despatch – 13 Jun 1926, Pack [commercial secretary, British Embassy, Washington], to Chamberlain: FO 371/11192/3216/779; despatch – 28 Jul 1926, Pack to Chamberlain: FO 371/11192/4310/779; despatch – 27 Oct 1926, Chilton to Chamberlain: FO 371/11192/5922/779. Also of interest is J. W. Dafoe, 'Canada and the United States', *JRIIA*, 9(1930), 721–38.

65 For instance, memorandum – 29 Jan 1926, Department of Overseas Trade; minute – 8 Feb 1926, R. I. Campbell: both FO 371/11183/562/95.

66 J. A. Cross, 'Whitehall and the Commonwealth. The Development of British Departmental Organisation for Commonwealth Affairs', *JCPS*, 2(1964), 197–202.

67 See Hall, 'Balfour Declaration of 1926'; Wrigley, *British–Canadian Relations*, 248–77.

68 See telegram (223) – 30 Oct 1926, FO to Chilton: FO 371/11193/5756/977; letter – 17 Nov 1926, Moyer [private secretary to Mackenzie King] to Antrobus [Dominions Office]; minute – 18 Nov 1926, Craigie: both FO

371/11193/6096/977; letter – 24 Mar 1927, Massey to Tyrrell: FO 371/12020/2704/14.

69 There was one irritation in Canadian–American relations in 1927, during the Coolidge naval conference. First, the Americans insisted on counting the Canadian navy as part of the Royal Navy when calculating the tonnage ratios for cruisers, destroyers, and so on. Then the Americans excluded the Canadian delegates from their cherished role as middlemen between Britain and the United States – which had emerged at the Washington conference. See D. C. Watt, 'Imperial Defence and Imperial Foreign Policy, 1911–39: The Substance and the Shadow': in Watt, *Personalities and Policies*, 152.

70 Telegram (53) – 2 Feb 1928, Howard to FO: FO 371/12833/804/804.

71 Minute – 3 Feb 1928, Thompson; minute – 3 Feb 1928, Craigie; minute – nd [probably 3 Feb 1928], Wellesley; marginal comment – 3 Feb 1928, Chamberlain: all *Ibid.*

72 Letter – 23 Feb 1928, Batterbee [Dominions Office] to Craigie: FO 371/12833/1350/804.

73 See N. Hillmer, 'A British High Commissioner for Canada', *Journal of Imperial and Commonwealth History*, 1(1973–74).

74 Note – 19 Oct 1928, Secretary, Belligerent Rights Sub-Committee: BR 43: CAB 16/79.

75 Hicks, *Republican Ascendancy*, 201–14 discusses this election.

76 Office of the President, *Address of President Coolidge at the observance of the 10th anniversary of the armistice, under the auspices of the American Legion* (Washington, 1928).

8 The American question resolved

1 Letter – 30 Aug 1928, Cecil to Irwin: BM Add MSS 51084.

2 Letter – 8 Oct 1928, Cecil to Murray: BM Add MSS 51132.

3 The Conservative Central Office was not unaware of the power of the League issue in domestic British politics; see letter – 20 Dec 1927, Cecil to Davidson [Conservative Party chairman]: BM Add MSS 51080; letter – 18 Oct 1928, Pembroke Wicks [Conservative Central Office] to Vansittart: Bal. MSS vol. 132.

4 *H of L Debs*, vol. 72, Cols. 84–91.

5 See letter – 2 Aug 1928, Kerr to Lloyd George, enclosing 'Draft Manifesto' – Jul 1928, Kerr; letter – 11 Aug 1928, Lloyd George to Kerr, enclosing minute – nd, Lloyd George; letter – 28 Aug 1928, Kerr to Lloyd George, enclosing 'Draft Manifesto' – Aug 1928, Kerr: all LG MSS G 12/5.

6 Letter – 31 Oct 1928, Lloyd George to Garvin: LG MSS G 8/5.

7 *H of C Debs*, vol. 222, Cols. 721–38.

8 Diary entry – 13 Nov 1928, Jones: *Whitehall Diary*, vol. II, 157.

9 Marquand, *MacDonald*, 471.

10 Letter – 1 Nov 1928, Noel-Baker to MacDonald, enclosing memorandum [memorandum not in folio]; letter – 8 Nov 1928, Noel-Baker to MacDonald: both PRO 30/69/5/39.

11 *H of C Debs*, vol. 222, Cols. 755–64.
12 This he did outside of Parliament; see Marquand, *MacDonald*, 472–4.
13 Diary entry – 1 Nov 1928, Jones: *Whitehall Diary*, vol. II, 154.
14 Diary entry – 12 Nov 1928, Jones: *Ibid.*
15 *H of C Debs*, vol. 222, Cols. 738–55.
16 Diary entry – 13 Nov 1928, Jones: *Whitehall Diary*, vol. II, 157. Baldwin's stilted delivery probably resulted from the mass of information he received on disarmament. For just the Admiralty's submission, see diary entry – 12 Nov 1928, Domvile: DOM 44; letters – 12 & 13 Nov 1928, Domvile to Vansittart [latter enclosing note – Oct 1928, Domvile]: all Bal MSS vol. 131.
17 Telegram (359 & 360) – 28 Nov 1928, Howard to FO: FO 371/12813/8182/39.
18 Memorandum – 14 Nov 1928, Cushendun, enclosing memorandum – 12 Nov 1928, Craigie: *DBFP 1A*, V, 857–75.
19 For example: 'Mr. Hoover is nothing less than a cold, aggressive nationalist – an efficient calculating machine who will push commercial and maritime competition with this country to the utmost': in minute – 29 Oct 1928, Thompson: FO 371/12812/7450/39.
20 Memorandum – 19 Nov 1928, Churchill: *DBFP 1A*, V, 883–5. Also see Gilbert, *Churchill*, vol. V, 307–8.
21 Memorandum – 24 Nov 1928, Cushendun: *DBFP 1A*, 890–1.
22 Cabinet Conclusion 52(28)5: CAB 23/59.
23 Letter – 22 Nov 1928, Cushendun to Chamberlain; letter – 22 Nov 1928, Salisbury to Chamberlain: both FO 800/263.
24 Minute – 26 Nov 1928, Craigie; initialled – 26 Nov 1928, R. H. Campbell; initialled – 27 Nov 1928, Wellesley; initialled – 28 Nov 1928, Lindsay, Chamberlain: all FO 371/12812/8078/39.
25 Minute – 29 Nov 1928, Craigie; initialled – 30 Nov 1928, Lindsay, Chamberlain: all FO 371/12813/8182/39.
26 Despatch – 16 Nov 1928, Howard to Cushendun; minute – 28 Nov 1928, Thompson; minute – 30 Nov 1928, Craigie; minute – 1 Dec 1928, Wellesley; minute – 3 Dec 1928, Lindsay; minute – 3 Dec 1928, Chamberlain: all FO 371/12812/8128/39.
27 Memorandum on 'Mr. Coolidge's speech and the tactics of the Big Navy Party' – 19 Nov 1928, Craigie: FO 371/12812/7921/39.
28 Telegram (359 & 360) – 28 Nov 1928, Howard to FO: FO 371/12813/8182/39; and speech – 3 Dec 1928, Coolidge: *FRUS 1929*, I, v–xxx.
29 For the onset of unfavourable reaction in the United States, see n. 28, immediately above. For one example of unfavourable international reaction, see despatch – 23 Nov 1928, Dodds [first secretary, British Embassy, Stockholm] to Cushendun: FO 371/12812/8146/39.
30 Memorandum – 23 Nov 1928, Selby: *DBFP 1A*, V, 886–9. Also see the minutes on this memorandum: minute – 26 Nov 1928, Lindsay; minute – 2 Dec 1928, Chamberlain: both FO 800/263.
31 Telegram (355) – 28 Nov 1928, Howard to Chamberlain: *DBFP 1A*, V, 893.

32 Despatch – 8 Jun 1928, Chilton to Chamberlain: FO 371/12811/4146/39.

33 Telegram (un) – 26 Nov 1928, Britten to Baldwin: FO 371/12813/8224/39.

34 Telegram (359) – 28 Nov 1928, Howard to Chamberlain: *DBFP 1A*, V, 894. Also see telegram (61 & 62) – 28 Nov 1928, Armstrong [British consul-general, New York City] to FO: FO 371/12813/8183/39.

35 Telegram (364) – 1 Dec 1928, Howard to Chamberlain: *DBFP 1A*, V, 909.

36 See minutes (2) – 3 Dec 1928, Craigie; minute – 3 Dec 1928, Lindsay; minute – 3 Dec 1928, Chamberlain; telegram (un) – 3 Dec 1928, Baldwin to Britten: all FO 371/12813/8238/39. Also see telegrams (414 & 417) – 3 Dec 1928, Chamberlain to Howard: *DBFP 1A*, V, 910–11.

37 *H of C Debs*, vol. 223, Col. 829.

38 Minute – 16 Nov 1928, Craigie; minute – 17 Nov 1928, Wellesley: both FO 371/12823/7862/133. The possibility of Borah calling for such a conference had been raised in the summer of 1928, and a suggestion of Howard's to use Vincent Massey as a means of heading off the senator had been vetoed by the Foreign Office; see letter – 2 Aug 1928, Howard to Craigie; minute – 17 Aug 1928, Craigie; minute – 18 Aug 1928, Wellesley; minute – 1 Sep 1928, Lindsay: all FO 371/12823/5809/133; and letter – 2 Sep 1928, Craigie to Howard: How MSS DHW 5/9.

39 Minute – 27 Nov 1928, Lindsay: FO 371/12823/8079/133.

40 Letter – 30 Nov 1928, Howard to Chamberlain: *DBFP 1A*, V, 906–9.

41 See BR 4th Minutes: CAB 16/79.

42 Minute – 10 Dec 1928, Lindsay to Vansittart; minute – 11 Dec 1928, Chamberlain to Lindsay: both FO 371/12823/8765/133. Also see letter – 18 Dec 1928, Chamberlain to Howard: *DBFP 1A*, V, 926.

43 Telegram (366) – 1 Dec 1928, Howard to FO: FO 371/12823/8232/133.

44 Letter – 20 Dec 1928, Howard to Chamberlain: *DBFP 1A*, V, 927–8.

45 For the genesis of this, see minute – 26 Nov 1928, Thompson; minute – 26 Nov 1928, Craigie; minute – 27 Nov 1928, Wellesley: all FO 371/12823/8079/133.

46 For an exception, see memorandum – 25 Jan 1929, Malkin: *DBFP 1A*, VI, 626–8.

47 Diary entry – 1 Nov 1928, Jones: *Whitehall Diary*, vol. II, 155.

48 Diary entry – 6 Dec 1928, Jones: *Ibid.*, 161.

49 Cabinet Conclusion 55(28)1: CAB 23/59.

50 Letter – 10 Dec 1928, Hankey to Salisbury, enclosing memorandum – nd, Hankey: CAB 21/320; and diary entry – 8 Dec 1928, Hankey: HNKY 1/8.

51 Diary entries – 4 & 7 Dec 1928, Hankey: *Ibid.*

52 Letter – 11 Dec 1928, Salisbury to Hankey: CAB 21/320.

53 See Cabinet Conclusion 56(28)2: CAB 23/59.

54 BR 7th Minutes: CAB 16/79.

55 Memorandum – Aug 1928, Admiralty: BR 39; memorandum – 17 Dec 1928, Salisbury: BR 54: both *Ibid.*

56 See letter – 14 Dec 1928, Lindsay to Selby: *DBFP 1A*, V, 921–2; minute –

17 Dec 1928, Lindsay to Chamberlain: FO 371/12823/8682/133; diary entry – 17 Dec 1928, Hankey: HNKY 1/8.

57 Letter – 20 Dec 1928, Hankey to Balfour: CAB 21/320.

58 Letter – 23 Dec 1928, Bridgeman to Baldwin: Bal. MSS vol. 163.

59 Memorandum – 31 Dec 1928, Hankey: BR 57: CAB 16/79; and diary entry – 26 Jan 1929, Hankey: HNKY 1/8.

60 See BR(T) Meetings 1–8: CAB 16/80; and 'Report of the Technical Sub-Committee' – 17 Jan 1929: both in *Ibid.* and CAB 16/79.

61 Cabinet Conclusion 55(28)2: CAB 23/59; and memorandum – 13 Dec 1928, Chamberlain: *DBFP 1A*, V, 918–19.

62 Telegram (37) – 15 Jan 1929, Howard to FO: FO 371/13530/340/35.

63 Telegram (42) – 16 Jan 1929, Howard to FO: FO 371/13530/371/35.

64 BR 8th Minutes: CAB 16/79.

65 See his remarks in BR 5th Minutes: *Ibid.*

66 BR 12th Minutes: *Ibid.*

67 BR 8th Minutes: *Ibid.*

68 BR 9th Meeting; and 'Draft First Interim Report on the Renewal of the Arbitration Treaties' – 13 Jan 1929, Salisbury: BR 62: both *Ibid.* He was referring to the sixth meeting of the sub-committee.

69 For the Foreign Office view of these events, see telegram (64) – 25 Jan 1929, Howard to FO; minute – 28 Jan 1929, Thompson; minute – 28 Jan 1929, Craigie; minute – 28 Jan 1929, Wellesley; minute – 29 Jan 1929, Chamberlain: all FO 371/13518/617/30. Cf. diary entry – 26 Jan 1929, Hankey: HNKY 1/8. *The Times*' reports are produced verbatim in the records of the ninth meeting of the sub-committee.

70 BR 10th Meeting: CAB 16/79.

71 Memorandum – 31 Jan 1929, Bridgeman: *Ibid.*

72 See letters – 9 Nov & 20 Dec 1928, 7 Jan 1929, Hankey to Balfour: all CAB 21/320.

73 Memorandum – 4 Feb 1929, Batterbee: BR 72: CAB 16/79; letter – 4 Feb 1929, Hankey to Salisbury; letter – 6 Feb 1929, Batterbee to Hankey: both CAB 21/310.

74 BR 11th Meeting: CAB 16/79.

75 BR Meetings 12–13: both *Ibid.*; 'First Report of the Sub-Committee of the Committee of Imperial Defence on Belligerent Rights' – 13 Feb 1929: *DBFP 1A*, VI, 839–53.

76 See BR Meetings 12–13: CAB 16/79.

77 BR Meetings 12–16: *Ibid.*

78 'Second Report of the Sub-Committee of the Committee of Imperial Defence on Belligerent Rights' – 6 Mar 1929: *DBFP 1A*, VI, 854–80.

79 See letters – 8 & 21 Mar 1929, Hankey to Balfour: both BM Add MSS 49705.

80 Office of the President, *Address of President Coolidge . . . 22 February 1929* (Washington, 1929).

81 Minute – 25 Feb 1929, Thompson: FO 371/13510/1365/12; minute – 13 Mar 1929, Thompson; minute – 15 Mar 1929, Craigie: both FO 371/13510/1802/12. For why Coolidge's attitude changed, see letter – 21 Jan 1929, Mrs T. W. Lamont [wife of prominent Republican] to Cecil:

BM Add MSS 51144; despatch – 1 Mar 1929, Howard to Chamberlain: FO 371/13510/1802/12.

82 Minute – 9 Nov 1928, Wellesley: FO 371/12812/7952/39; minute – 28 Nov 1928, Thompson; minute – 29 Nov 1928, Craigie: both FO 371/12812/8126/39.

83 Telegram (143) – 17 Mar 1929, Howard to Chamberlain: FO 371/13541/1932/279.

84 Minute – 23 Apr 1929, Thompson; minute – 24 Apr 1929, Wellesley: both FO 371/13511/2799/12.

85 Telegram (140) – 13 Mar 1929, Howard to FO; minute – 14 Mar 1929, Thompson; minute – 19 Mar 1929, Craigie: all FO 371/13548/1864/1864; minute – 5 Apr 1929, Craigie: FO 371/13548/2429/1864.

86 The rest of this paragraph is based on letter – 20 Apr 1929, Cushendun to Chamberlain: FO 800/263.

87 Minute – 13 Feb 1929, Chamberlain: FO 371/13541/1040/279.

88 On the 1929 General Election, see E. A. Rowe, 'The British General Election of 1929' [unpublished B.Litt. dissertation] (Oxford, 1960).

89 For the case of Vansittart, see Rose, *Vansittart*, 66. Willert had been a target of the Labour Party's radicals since the fall of the first Labour government; they believed he had contributed to the Zinoviev crisis; see the private proposals contained in 'The Foreign Office and Labour Governments' – Feb 1925, Trades Union Congress and Labour Party, Joint International Department: PRO 30/69/5/132.

90 On Henderson's struggle to secure the Foreign Office, see D. Carlton, *MacDonald Versus Henderson. The Foreign Policy of the Second Labour Government* (New York, 1970), 15–16.

91 Memoranda on the 'Question of an Agreement with the United States in regard to Maritime Belligerent Rights', the 'Question of the conclusion of an Anglo-American Arbitration Treaty', and '... the Naval Disarmament Question' – all 10 Jun 1929, Craigie: all PRO 30/69/1/267.

92 This conversation was reported in despatch – 24 Jun 1929, Henderson to Howard: *DBFP II*, I, 8–10. Also see memorandum – 25 Jun 1929, MacDonald; and memorandum – 25 Jun 1929, Lindsay; both *Ibid.*, 10–13.

93 Letter – 9 Sep 1929, MacDonald to Dawes: *Ibid.*, 69–71.

94 See letter – 17 Sep 1929, MacDonald to Dawes; draft note of invitation to the Naval Conference – nd, Foreign Office; letters (2) enclosing memoranda – 18 & 19 Sep 1929, Dawes to MacDonald: all *Ibid.*, 83–6, 91–2. Also see memorandum – 25 Sep 1929, Lindsay: *Ibid.*, 97–8; and 'Note of Invitation to the Naval Conference' – 7 Oct 1929, British Government: *Ibid.*, 103–5.

95 Diary entry – 3 Oct 1929, Jones: *Whitehall Diary*, vol. II, 212–13.

96 Cf. memorandum – 4–10 Oct 1929, MacDonald: *DBFP II*, I, 106–16; H. C. Hoover, *Memoirs: The Cabinet and the Presidency, 1920–1933* (London, 1952), 345; and Cmd. 3547.

97 See Roskill, *Hankey*, vol. II, 491–2.

98 See CAB 27/392. Besides the foreign secretary and first lord, the lord

chancellor, the secretary for India, the lord president, and the secretary for both the colonies and dominions were members.

99 Carlton, *MacDonald Versus Henderson*, 76.
100 Cecil, *Great Experiment*, 201–5.
101 See Walters, *League of Nations*, 125–6, 274–5.
102 Chamberlain's antipathy toward it seems to have derived from it being integral to the Geneva Protocol, which the Baldwin government rejected in 1925 and on whose ruins Chamberlain built Locarno; see Jacobson, *Locarno Diplomacy*, 14–26.
103 Cmd. 3452.

BIBLIOGRAPHY

UNPUBLISHED SOURCES

Private Papers

Papers of Max Aitken, first Baron Beaverbrook
  House of Lords Record Office, London (BBK MSS)
Papers of Stanley Baldwin, first Earl Baldwin of Bewdley
  The University Library, Cambridge (Bal MSS)
Papers of Arthur Balfour, first Earl Balfour
  British Library, London (BM Add MSS 49683–49962)
Papers of Robert Cecil, Viscount Cecil of Chelwood
  British Library, London (BM Add MSS 51071–51157)
Papers of Austen Chamberlain
  Public Record Office, London (FO 800/256–263)
  The University of Birmingham, Birmingham (AC)
Papers of Edgar D'Abernon, first Viscount D'Abernon of Esher
  British Library, London (BM Add MSS 48928–48936)
Papers of Barry Domvile
  National Maritime Museum, Greenwich (DOM)
Papers of David Lloyd George, first Earl Lloyd-George of Dwyfor
  House of Lords Record Office, London (LG MSS)
Papers of Maurice Hankey, Baron Hankey
  Churchill College, Cambridge (HNKY)
Papers of Esme Howard, first Baron Howard of Penrith
  Cumbria County Record Office, Carlisle (How MSS)
Papers of Howard Kelly
  National Maritime Museum, Greenwich (KEL)
Papers of Roger Keyes, first Baron Keyes
  Churchill College, Cambridge (KEYES)
Papers of Wilmot Lewis
  The Times Archives, London (Lewis)
Papers of James Ramsay MacDonald
  Public Record Office, London (PRO 30/69)
Papers of Ronald McNeill, first Baron Cushendun
  Public Record Office, London (FO 800/228)
Papers of Charles Scott
  British Library, London (BM Add MSS 50907)

Papers of Evelyn Wrench
   British Library, London (BM Add MSS 59541–59575)

Government Archives

Admiralty
   ADM 116 Political Correspondence
        /3371 Limitation of Armaments (1927)
Cabinet
   CAB 2 Committee of Imperial Defence
         /4 Minutes
   CAB 4 Committee of Imperial Defence
        /12 Memoranda
   CAB 16 Committee of Imperial Defence. *Ad Hoc* Sub-committees
        /55 Laws of War Sub-committee
        /79 Belligerent Rights Sub-Committee
        /80 Technical Sub-committee on Belligerent Rights
   CAB 21 Registered Files
        /297 Resignation of Lord Cecil (1927)
        /307, 310, 320 Belligerent Rights – Freedom of the Seas (1928–1929)
   CAB 23 Cabinet
        /49–60 Minutes (November 1924–May 1929)
   CAB 24 Cabinet
        /164–207 Memoranda
   CAB 27 Committees. General Series
        /273 Naval Programme (1925)
        /355 Naval Programme (1927)
        /361 Meetings: Reduction and Limitation of Armaments Policy
        /392 Arbitration (1929)
 Foreign Office
   FO 371 General Correspondence. Political
      American Department (1924–1929)
      Western Department (1927–1928)
   FO 395 General Correspondence. News Department
      (1924–1929)
Prime Minister's Office
   PREM 1 Correspondence and Papers
           /65 Appointment of the first British High Commissioner to Canada

PUBLISHED SOURCES

Official Publications

Great Britain

Foreign Office. *British Foreign and State Papers*. vol. CXI
   Peace Conference Handbooks. No. 147a: *Freedom of the Seas* (London, 1919)

Peace Conference Handbooks. No. 166: *President Wilson's Policy* (London, 1919)
Documents on British Foreign Policy. Series 1A. 6 vols. (London, 1966–77)
Documents on British Foreign Policy. Series II. vol. I (London, 1946)
House of Commons Debates. 5th Series. vols. 188–234
House of Lords Debates. vols. 56–78
White Papers
Cmd. 1592: *Correspondence Respecting Affairs in Egypt*
Cmd. 1617: *Despatch to His Majesty's Representatives Abroad Respecting the status of Egypt*
Cmd. 1912: *Arrangements for the Funding of the British War Debt to the United States*
Cmd. 1938: *Recommendations of the National and Imperial Defence Committee*
Cmd. 1987: *Imperial Conference, 1923. Summary of Proceedings*
Cmd. 1988: *Imperial Conference, 1923. Appendices to the Summary of the Proceedings*
Cmd. 2029: *Report of the Sub-Committee of the Committee of Imperial Defence on National and Imperial Defence*
Cmd. 2301: *Correspondence with the Governments of the Self-Governing Dominions, relating to consultation on Matters of Foreign Policy and General Imperial Interest*
Cmd. 2349: *Fleets: (British and Foreign Countries). Return showing the Fleets of the British Empire, the United States of America, France, Japan, Italy, Russia, and Germany, on 1 February 1925*
Cmd. 2590: *Fleets: (British and Foreign Countries). Return showing the Fleets of the British Empire, the United States of America, France, Italy, Japan, Russia, and Germany, on 1 February 1926*
Cmd. 2681: *Report of the Council of the League of Nations on the First Session of the Preparatory Commission for the Disarmament Conference. Geneva, 26 May 1926*
Cmd. 2768: *Summary of the Proceedings of the Imperial Conference, 1926*
Cmd. 2769: *Appendices to the Summary of the Proceedings of the Imperial Conference, 1926*
Cmd. 2809: *Fleets: The British Empire and Foreign Countries. Particulars of the Fleets of the British Empire, the United States of America, Japan, France, Italy, Germany, and the Soviet Union on 1 February 1927*
Cmd. 2877: *Notes Exchanged between H.M. Government and the Government of the United States of America regarding the disposal of certain Pecuniary Claims arising out of the recent War. Washington, 19 May 1927*
Cmd. 2888: *Report of the British Representatives on the Preparatory Committee of the League of Nations for the Disarmament Conference. Third Session. Geneva, 21 March–26 April 1927*
Cmd. 2964: *Geneva Conference (Naval Armaments). Speeches at the Plenary Sessions by the Rt. Hon. W. C. Bridgeman, M.P., First Lord of the Admiralty. (June–August 1927)*
Cmd. 3109: *Correspondence with the United States Ambassador respecting the United States proposal for the renunciation of War*
Cmd. 3153: *Further correspondence with the Government of the United States of America respecting the United States proposal for the renunciation of War*
Cmd. 3211: *Papers Regarding the Limitation of Naval Armaments*

Cmd. 3452:   *Memorandum on the Signature by His Majesty's Government in the United Kingdom of the Optional Clause of the Statute of the Permanent Court of International Justice*

Cmd. 3547:   *Memorandum on the results of the London Naval Conference from January 21 to April 15 1930*

United States

Congressional Record. vols. 66–72

Department of the Navy. *Annual Report of the Secretary of the Navy* (Washington, 1924–1929)

Department of State. *Conference on the Limitation of Armament. Washington. November 12, 1921 – February 6, 1922* (Washington, 1922)

  Arrangement . . . between the United States and Great Britain for the disposal of certain pecuniary claims arising out of the recent war (Washington, 1927)

  Arbitration Treaty with France . . . signed [at] Washington, 6 February 1928 (Washington, 1928)

  Notes exchanged between France and the United States . . . on the subject of a multilateral treaty for the renunciation of war (Washington, 1928)

  Memorandum on the Monroe Doctrine: prepared by J. Reuban Clark, Under-secretary of State (Washington, 1928)

  Papers Relating to the Foreign Relations of the United States: 1925. 2 vols. (Washington, 1940); *1926.* 2 vols. (1941); *1927.* 3 vols. (1942); *1928.* 3 vols. (1942–1943); *1929.* 3 vols. (1943–1944)

Office of the President. *Address of President Coolidge at the observance of the 10th anniversary of the armistice, under the auspices of the American Legion* (Washington, 1928)

  Address of President Coolidge . . . 22 February 1929 (Washington, 1929)

Newspapers

Baltimore Sun	*Morning Post*	*Sunday Express*
Daily Herald	*New York Times*	*Sunday Times*
Daily Mail	*New York World*	*The Times*
Daily Telegraph	*The Observer*	*Washington Post*
Manchester Guardian	*Philadelphia Public Ledger*	

Biographies, Diaries, Memoirs, Speeches

Amery, L. S. *My Political Life.* vols. I & II (London, 1953)

Ashby, L. *The Spearless Leader. Senator Borah and the Progressive Movement in the 1920s* (Urbana, Chicago, London, 1972)

Baldwin, S. *Our Inheritance. Speeches and Addresses* (London, 1928)

Balfour, the Earl of. *Opinions and Argument* (London, 1928)

Beaverbrook, Lord. *Men and Power, 1917–1918* (London, 1956)

  The Decline and Fall of Lloyd George (London, 1963)

Bryn-Jones, D. *Frank B. Kellogg. A Biography* (New York, 1937)

Campbell, G. *Of True Experience* (New York, 1947)

Campbell, J. *Lloyd George: the Goat in the Wilderness, 1922–1931* (London, 1977)

Cecil of Chelwood, Viscount. *International Arbitration: Being the Burge Memorial Lecture for 1928* (Oxford, 1928)
A Great Experiment (London, 1941)
All the Way (London, 1949)

Chalmers, W. S. *The Life and Letters of David, Earl Beatty* (London, 1951)

Chamberlain, A. *Down the Years* (London, 1935)
Politics from the Inside: An Epistolary Chronicle, 1906–1914 (London, 1936)

Chatfield, Lord. *It Might Happen Again*. vol. I: *The Navy and Defence* (London, Toronto, 1947)

Coolidge, C. *The Autobiography of Calvin Coolidge* (London, 1929)

Craigie, R. L. *Behind the Japanese Mask* (London, 1945)

Daniels, J. *The Wilson Era*. vol. II: *Years of War and After, 1917–1923* (Chapel Hill, 1944)

Dugdale, B. E. C. *Arthur James Balfour*. vol. II: *1906–1930* (London, 1936)

Elletson, D. H. *The Chamberlains* (London, 1966)

Ellis, L. E. *Frank B. Kellogg and American Foreign Relations, 1925–1929* (New Brunswick, New Jersey, 1961)

Fraser, P. *Joseph Chamberlain, Radicalism and Empire, 1868–1914* (London, 1960)

Garvin, K. *J. L. Garvin. A Memoir* (London, Melbourne, Toronto, 1948)

Gilbert, M. *Sir Horace Rumbold. Portrait of a Diplomat 1869–1941* (London, 1973)
Winston S. Churchill. vol. V: *1922–1939* (London, 1976)

Grew, J. C. *Turbulent Era. A Diplomatic Record of Forty Years, 1904–1945* (Boston, 1952)

Grey of Fallodon, Viscount. *Twenty-Five Years 1892–1916*. 2 vols. (London, 1925)

Hoover, H. C. *Memoirs: The Cabinet and the Presidency, 1920–1933* (London, 1952)

Howard of Penrith, Lord. *Theatre of Life*. 2 vols. (London, 1935–1936)

James, R. Rhodes. *Memoirs of a Conservative. J. C. C. Davidson's Memoirs and Papers, 1910–1937* (London, 1969)
Churchill: A Study in Failure 1900–1939 (London, 1970)
ed. *Winston S. Churchill. His Complete Speeches, 1897–1963*. vol. IV: *1922–1928* (New York, London, 1974)

Johnson, E. ed. *The Collected Writing of John Maynard Keynes*. vol. XVI: *Activities 1914–1918. The Treasury and Versailles* (London, 1971)

Kellogg, F. B. 'The War Prevention Policy of the United States'. *FA. Special Supplement*. 6(1928), i–xi

Maddox, R. J. *William E. Borah and American Foreign Policy* (Baton Rouge, 1969)

Marquand, D. *Ramsay MacDonald* (London, 1977)

McCoy, D. R. *Calvin Coolidge. The Quiet President* (New York, London, 1967)

Middlemas, K. ed. *Thomas Jones: Whitehall Diary*. 2 vols. (London, 1969)

Middlemas, K. and Barnes, J. *Baldwin. A Biography* (London, 1969)

Miller, D. H. *Drafting the Covenant*. 2 vols. (New York, 1928)

Percy, E. 'Austen Chamberlain'. *Pub. Admin*. 15(1937), 125–7
Some Memories (London, 1958)

Petrie, C. *The Chamberlain Tradition* (London, 1938)

The Life and Letters of the Rt. Hon. Sir Austen Chamberlain. 2 vols. (London, 1939–1940)

A Historian Looks at His World (London, 1972)

Phillips, W. *Ventures in Diplomacy* (London, 1955)

Rose, N. *Vansittart. A Study of a Diplomat* (London, 1978)

Roskill, S. W. *Hankey Man of Secrets.* vol. II: *1919–1931* (London, 1972)

Swinton, Lord. *I Remember* (London, 1948)

Taylor, A. J. P. *Beaverbrook. A Biography* (New York, 1972)

ed. W. P. Crozier. *Off the Record* (London, 1973)

Thompson, G. H. *Front-Line Diplomat* (London, 1959)

Tilley, J. *London to Tokyo* (London, 1942)

Vansittart, Lord. *The Mist Procession* (London, 1958)

Wellesley, V. A. H. *Diplomacy in Fetters* (London, 1945)

Willert, A. *Washington and Other Memories* (Boston, 1971)

Wilson, T. ed. *The Political Diaries of C. P. Scott, 1911–1928* (London, 1970)

Winkler, J. K. *William Randolph Hearst. A New Appraisal* (New York, 1955)

Young, K. *Arthur James Balfour. The Happy Life of the Politician, Prime Minister, Statesman and Philosopher, 1848–1930* (London, 1963)

Contemporary Studies

Bell, A. C. *A History of the Blockade of Germany* (London, 1937)

Dennis, W. J. *Tacna-Arica; an account of the Chile–Peru boundary dispute and of the arbitration of the United States* (Hamden, Conn., 1967)

Gardener, A. J. *Portraits and Portents* (London, 1926)

Labour Research Department. *The Coal Shortage: why the Miners will win* (London, 1926)

Lippmann, W. *Men of Destiny* (New York, 1927)

Mowat, R. B. *The Diplomatic Relations of Great Britain and the United States* (London, 1925)

Noel-Baker, P. J. *Disarmament and the Coolidge Conference* (London, 1927)

Tilley, J.; and Gaselee, S. *The Foreign Office.* 2nd ed. (London, New York, 1933)

Toynbee, A. *et al. Survey of International Affairs 1924* (London, 1926); *1925.* 2 vols. (1927–1928); *1926* (London, 1928); *1927* (London, 1929); *1928* (London, 1929); *1929* (London, 1930)

Wheeler-Bennett, J. W. *Information on the Renunciation of War, 1927–8* (London, 1928)

Disarmament and Security Since Locarno, 1925–1931 (London, 1932)

Willert, A. *Aspects of British Foreign Policy* (New Haven, 1928)

The Road to Safety. A Study in Anglo-American Relations (London, 1952)

Williams, B. H. *The United States and Disarmament* [originally published in 1932] (Port Washington, New York, London, 1973)

Willson, B. *America's Ambassadors to England (1785–1928). A Narrative of Anglo-American Diplomatic Relations* (London, 1928)

Friendly Relations. A Narrative of Britain's Ministers and Ambassadors to America (1791–1930) (Boston, 1930)

Contemporary Articles

Anonymous. 'Comparative Tables of Armaments'. *FA*. 4(1925), 158–9
  'Comparative Naval Strengths'. *FA*. 5(1927), 425–6
  (P. Kerr), 'The Naval Conference'. *RT*. 68(September 1927), 659–83
  'Is there any maritime law?'. *New Republic*. LIII (December 1927)
Bailey, T. A. 'The Lodge Corollary to the Monroe Doctrine'. *PSQ*. 48(1933),
  220–39
Borah, W. E. 'One Great Treaty to Outlaw all Wars'. *NY Times*. (5 February
  1928)
Bridgeman, W. C. 'Naval Disarmament'. *JRIIA*. 6(1927), 335–49
Cecil of Chelwood, Viscount. 'American Responsibilities for Peace'. *FA*.
  6(1928), 357–8.
Chamberlain, A. 'Great Britain as a European Power', *JRIIA*. 9(1930), 180–8
Cushendun, Lord. 'Disarmament'. *FA*. 7(1928), 77–93
D'Abernon, Viscount. 'The Economic Mission to South America'. *JRIIA*.
  9(1930), 568–82
Dafoe, J. W. 'Canada and the United States'. *JRIIA*. 9(1930), 721–38
Dulles, A. 'Some Misconceptions About Disarmament'. *FA*. 5(1927), 413–24
Gerould, J. T. 'Great Britain's opposition to the freedom of the seas'. *Current
  History*. No. 27(October 1927), 112–15
Howard, E. 'British Policy and the Balance of Power'. *APSR*. 19(1925), 261–7
'J.G.M.' 'Naval Strategy'. *NB*. 6(November 1927), No. 52
  'Cecil vs. the Admirals'. *NB*. 7(November 1927), No. 3
Lippmann, W. 'Concerning Senator Borah'. *FA*. 4(1926), 211–22
MacDonald, J. R. 'War and America'. *The Nation*. (2 May 1928)
Spear, L. Y. 'Battleships or Submarines'. *FA*. 6(1927), 106–15

Historical Studies

Adamthwaite, A. P. *France and the Coming of the Second World War 1936–1939*
  (London, 1977)
Alford, B. W. E. *Depression and Recovery?* (London, 1972)
Allen, H. C. *Great Britain and the United States* (New York, 1955)
Alt, J.; and Herman, V. eds. *Cabinet Studies* (London, 1974)
Anonymous. *History of The Times*. vol. IV. Pt. 2 (London, 1954)
Arnot, R. P. *The Miners: Years of Struggle* (London, 1953)
Beloff, M. *Imperial Sunset*. vol. I (London, 1969)
Borg, D. *American Policy and the Chinese Revolution, 1925–1928* (New York, 1947)
Bourne, K. *The Foreign Policy of Victorian England 1830–1902* (Oxford, 1970)
Brandes, J. *Herbert Hoover and Economic Diplomacy; Department of Commerce
  Policy, 1921–1928* (Pittsburgh, 1962)
Briggs, A. *Victorian People. A Reassessment of Persons and Themes 1851–67*
  (Harmondsworth, 1955)
Buck, P. *Amateurs and Professionals in British Politics 1918–59* (Chicago, 1963)
Burns, D. R.; and Bennett, E. M. eds. *Diplomats in Crisis. United
  States–Chinese–Japanese Relations, 1919–1941* (Santa Barbara, Oxford,
  1974)

Butler, D.; and Sloman, S. *British Political Facts 1900–1975*. 4th ed. (London, 1975)

Canham, E. D. *Commitment to Freedom. The Story of 'The Christian Science Monitor'* (Cambridge, Mass., 1958)

Carlton, D. *MacDonald versus Henderson. The Foreign Policy of the Second Labour Government* (New York, 1970)

Clark, G. Kitson. *An Expanding Society, Britain 1830–1900* (Melbourne, 1967)

Connell, J. [pseudonym]. *The 'Office': A Study of British Foreign Policy and Its Makers, 1919–1951* (London, 1958)

Craig, G. A.; and Gilbert, F. eds. *The Diplomats 1919–1930*. vol. I: *The Twenties* (New York, 1963)

Davis, G. T. *A Navy Second to None* (New York, 1940).

Drummond, I. M. *British Economic Policy and the Empire, 1919–1939* (London, 1972)

Ellis, L. E. *Republican Foreign Policy, 1921–1933* (New Brunswick, New Jersey, 1968)

Ferrell, R. H. *Peace in Their Time. The Origins of the Kellogg–Briand Pact* (New Haven, 1952)

The American Secretaries of State and their Diplomacy. vol. xi: *Frank B. Kellogg – Henry L. Stimson* (New York, 1963)

Fry, M. G. *Illusions of Security. North Atlantic Diplomacy 1918–22* (Toronto, 1972)

Gibert, S. P. *Soviet Images of America* (New York, 1977)

Hardach, G. *The First World War 1914–1918* (London, 1977)

Hicks, J. D. *Republican Ascendancy 1921–1933* (New York, 1960)

Hinsley, F. H. *Command of the Sea. The Naval Side of British History from 1918 to the end of the Second World War* (London, Melbourne, Cape Town, Toronto, 1950)

ed. *British Foreign Policy Under Sir Edward Grey* (Cambridge, 1977)

Hogan, M. J. *Informal Entente: the private structure of cooperation in Anglo-American economic diplomacy 1918–1928* (Columbia, Missouri, 1977)

Humble, R. *Before the Dreadnought. The Royal Navy from Nelson to Fisher* (London, 1976)

Iriye, A. *From Nationalism to Internationalism. U.S. Foreign Policy to 1914* (London, Henley, Boston, 1977)

Jacobson, J. *Locarno Diplomacy. Germany and the West, 1925–1929* (Princeton, 1972)

James, R. Rhodes. *The British Revolution. British Politics 1880–1939* (London, 1978)

Kenney, M. D. *The Estrangement of Great Britain and Japan 1917–35* (Manchester, 1969)

Louis, W. R. *British Strategy in the Far East, 1919–39* (Oxford, 1971)

Lowe, C. J. *The Reluctant Imperialists*. 2 vols. (London, 1967)

and Dockrill, M. L. *The Mirage of Power*. 3 vols. (London, 1972)

and Marzari, F. *Italian Foreign Policy 1870–1940* (London, 1975)

Mackintosh, J. P. ed. *British Prime Ministers in the Twentieth Century*. vol. I: *Balfour to Chamberlain* (London, 1977)

Marder, A. J. *From Dreadnought to Scapa Flow*. vols. I & V (London, 1961, 1970)

Marks, S. *The Illusion of Peace* (London, 1976)

Mayer, A. J. *Politics and Diplomacy of Peacemaking. Containment and Counterrevolution at Versailles, 1918–1919* (New York, 1969)

McKercher, B. J. C.; and Moss, D. J. eds. *Shadow and Substance in British Foreign Policy, 1895–1939. Memorial Essays in Honour of the late Professor C. J. Lowe.* (University of Alberta Press, forthcoming)

Medlicott, W. N. *The Economic Blockade.* vol. I (London, 1952)
British Foreign Policy Since Versailles, 1919–1963. 2nd ed. (London, 1968)
Contemporary England 1914–1964 (London, 1976)

Merk, F. *The Monroe Doctrine and American Expansion* (New York, 1966)

Middleton, C. R. *The Administration of British Foreign Policy, 1782–1846* (Durham, N.C., 1977)

Moggeridge, D. E. *The Return to Gold, 1925* (Cambridge, 1969)

Morgan, K. O. *The Age of Lloyd George. The Liberal Party and British Politics, 1890–1929* (New York, London, 1971)

Neilson, Keith. *Strategy and Supply: the Anglo-Russian Alliance, 1914–1917* (London, forthcoming)

Néré, J. *The Foreign Policy of France from 1914 to 1945* (London, 1975)

Nicholas, H. G. *The United States and Britain* (Chicago, London, 1975)

Nish, I. H. *Japanese Foreign Policy, 1869–1942* (London, 1977)

Northedge, F. S. *The Troubled Giant. Britain Among the Great Powers, 1916–39* (London, 1966)

O'Connor, R. G. *Perilous Equilibrium: The United States and the London Naval Conference 1930* (Kansas, 1962)

Parrini, C. P. *Heir to Empire: United States Economic Diplomacy, 1916–1923* (Pittsburgh, 1969)

Perkins, D. *A History of the Monroe Doctrine.* rev. ed. (Boston, 1963)

Phillips, G. A. *The General Strike. The Politics of Industrial Conflict* (London, 1976)

Platt, D. C. M. *The Cinderella Service. British Consuls Since 1825* (London, 1971)

Pollard, J. E. *The Presidents and the Press* (New York, 1947)

Preston, R. A. *Canada and the Imperial Conference* (Durham, N.C. 1967)

Roskill, S. W. *Naval Policy Between the Wars.* 2 vols. (London, 1968, 1976)

Rowland, P. *Lloyd George* (London, 1975)

Siney, M. C. *The Allied Blockade of Germany* (Ann Arbor, 1955)

Singleton, M. K. *H. L. Mencken and the 'American Mercury' Adventure* (Durham, N.C., 1962)

Smith, D. M. *The Great Departure. The United States and World War I, 1914–1920* (New York, London, Sydney, 1965)

Sprout, H.; and Sprout, M. *Toward a New Order of Sea Power* (Princeton, 1946)

Stamworth, P.; and Giddens, A. eds. *Elites and Power in British Society* (Cambridge, 1974)

Steiner, Z. S. *The Foreign Office and Foreign Policy, 1898–1914* (Cambridge, 1969)

Stuart, G. H. *The Department of State. A History of Its Organisation, Procedure, and Personnel* (New York, 1949)

Taylor, A. J. P. *The Origins of the Second World War* (Harmondsworth, 1970)
English History 1914–1945 (Harmondsworth, 1970)

Taylor, P. M. *The Projection of Britain. British Overseas Publicity and Propaganda 1919–1939* (Cambridge, 1981)

Turner, J. *Lloyd George's Secretariat* (Cambridge, 1980)

Vinson, J. C. *The Parchment Peace: the United States and the Washington Conference 1921–1922* (Athens, Ga., 1955)

Waites, N. ed. *Troubled Neighbours. Franco-British Relations in the Twentieth Century* (London, 1971)

Walters, F. P. *A History of the League of Nations* (London, 1960)

Ward, A. J. *Ireland and Anglo-American Relations, 1899–1921* (London, 1965)

Watt, D. C. *Personalities and Policies. Studies in the formulation of British foreign policy in the twentieth century* (London, 1965)

Wilson, J. H. *American Business and Foreign Policy, 1920–1933* (Lexington, Ky., 1971)

Winkler, H. R. *The League of Nations Movement in Great Britain, 1914–1919* (New Brunswick, N.J., 1952)

Wrigley, P. G. *Canada and the Transition to Commonwealth. British–Canadian Relations 1917–1926* (Cambridge, New York, London, Melbourne, 1977)

Historical articles

Adamthwaite, A. P. 'Bonnet, Daladier and French Appeasement, April–September 1938'. *IR*. 3(1967), 222–41

Adler, S. 'The War Guilt Question and American Disillusionment 1918–1929'. *JMH*. 28(1956), 1–28

Birn, D. S. 'The League of Nations Union and Collective Security'. *JCH*. vol. IX, no. 3(1974), 131–59

Blair, J. L. 'I do not choose to run for President in Nineteen Twenty-Eight'. *Vermont History*. 30(1962)

Brebner, J. B. 'Canada, the Anglo-Japanese Alliance and the Washington Conference'. *PSQ*. 50(1935), 45–57

Burk, K. M. 'The Diplomacy of Finance: British Financial Missions to the United States, 1914–1918'. *HJ*. 22(1979), 351–72.

Burks, D. D. 'The United States and the Geneva Protocol of 1924: "A New Holy Alliance"?'. *AHR*. 64(1959), 891–905

Carlton, D. 'Great Britain and the League Council Crisis of 1926'. *HJ*. 11(1968), 354–64

  'Disarmament with Guarantees: Lord Cecil, 1922–1927'. *Disarmament and Arms Control*. vol. III. no. 2(1965)

  'Great Britain and the Coolidge Naval Conference of 1927'. *PSQ*. 83(1968), 573–98

  'The Anglo-French Compromise on Arms Limitation, 1928'. *JBS*. 8(1969), 141–62

Cecil, H. 'Lord Robert Cecil: A Nineteenth Century Upbringing'. *History Today*. 25(1975)

Costigliola, F. C. 'Anglo-American Financial Rivalry in the 1920s'. *JEH*. 37(1977), 911–34

Cross, J. A. 'Whitehall and the Commonwealth. The Development of British Departmental Organisation for Commonwealth Affairs'. *JCPS*. 2(1964), 187–206

Crowe, S. E. 'Sir Eyre Crowe and the Locarno Pact'. *EHR*. 87(1972), 49–74

Florry, H. 'The Arcos Raid and the Rupture of Anglo-Soviet Relations, 1927'. *JCH*. 12(1977), 707–23

Gibbs, N. 'The Naval Conferences of the Interwar Years: a study in Anglo-American Relations'. *Naval War College Review*. vol. 30. no. 1(1977–78), 50–63

Grün, G. A. 'Locarno: Idea and Reality'. *IA*. 31(1955), 477–85

Guttsman, W. L. 'Aristocracy and Middle Class in the British Political Elite, 1886–1916'. *BJS*. 5(1954), 12–32

Hall, H. D. 'The Genesis of the Balfour Declaration of 1926'. *JCPS*. 1(1963), 169–93

Hawley, E. W. 'Herbert Hoover, the Commerce Secretariat, and the Vision of an "Associated State", 1921–1928'. *JAH*. 61(1974–75), 116–40

Hillmer, N. 'A British High Commissioner for Canada'. *Journal of Imperial and Commonwealth History*. 1(1973), 339–56

Jacobson, J. 'The Conduct of Locarno Diplomacy'. *RP*. 34(1972), 67–81

Johnson, D. 'Austen Chamberlain and the Locarno Agreements'. *University of Birmingham Historical Journal*. 8(1961), 62–81

Kasurak, P. 'American foreign policy officials and Canada, 1917–1941: a look through bureaucratic glasses'. *International Journal*. 32(1977), 544–58

Leffler, M. P. 'Political Isolationism, Economic Expansion, or Diplomatic Realism: American Policy Toward Western Europe, 1921–1933'. *Perspectives in American History*. 8(1974), 413–61

Raffo, P. 'The Founding of the League of Nations Union'. *JCH*. 12(1977), 193–206

Sharp, A. J. 'The Foreign Office in Eclipse 1919–22'. *History*. 61(1976), 198–218

Stambrook, F. G. '"Das Kind" – Lord D'Abernon and the Origins of the Locarno Pact'. *Central European History*. 1(1968), 233–63

Steiner, Z. S.; and Dockrill, M. L. 'The Foreign Office Reforms'. *HJ*. 17(1974), 131–56

Warman, R. M. 'The Erosion of Foreign Office Influence in the Making of Foreign Policy, 1916–1918'. *HJ*. 15(1972), 133–59

Wells, Jr., S. F. 'British Strategic Withdrawal from the Western Hemisphere 1904–6'. *CHR*. 49(1968), 335–56

Wilkinson, R. 'Political Leadership and the late Victorian Public School'. *BJS*. 13(1962), 320–30

Unpublished dissertations and papers

Burk, K. M. 'British War Missions to the United States'. D.Phil. (Oxford, 1976)

Brode, M. J. 'Anglo-American Relations and the Geneva Naval Disarmament Conference of 1927'. Ph.D. (University of Alberta, 1972)

McKercher, B. J. C. 'The British foreign-policy-making élite and its attitudes towards the United States, November 1924–June 1929'. Ph.D. (University of London, 1979)

Nish, I. H. 'Anglo-Japanese Relations in the Shadow of the Washington Conference, 1922–29'. (paper for the Mt. Kisco Conference, 1974)

Pitt, M. R. 'Great Britain and Belligerent Maritime Rights from the Declaration of Paris, 1856, to the Declaration of London, 1909'. Ph.D. (University of London, 1964)

Rowe, E. A. 'The British General Election of 1919'. B.Litt. (Oxford, 1960)

Zuercher, R. L. 'Walter Lippmann and His Views of American Foreign Policy'. Ph.D. (Michigan State University, 1974)

INDEX